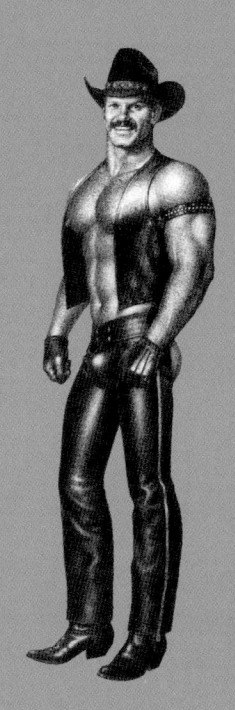

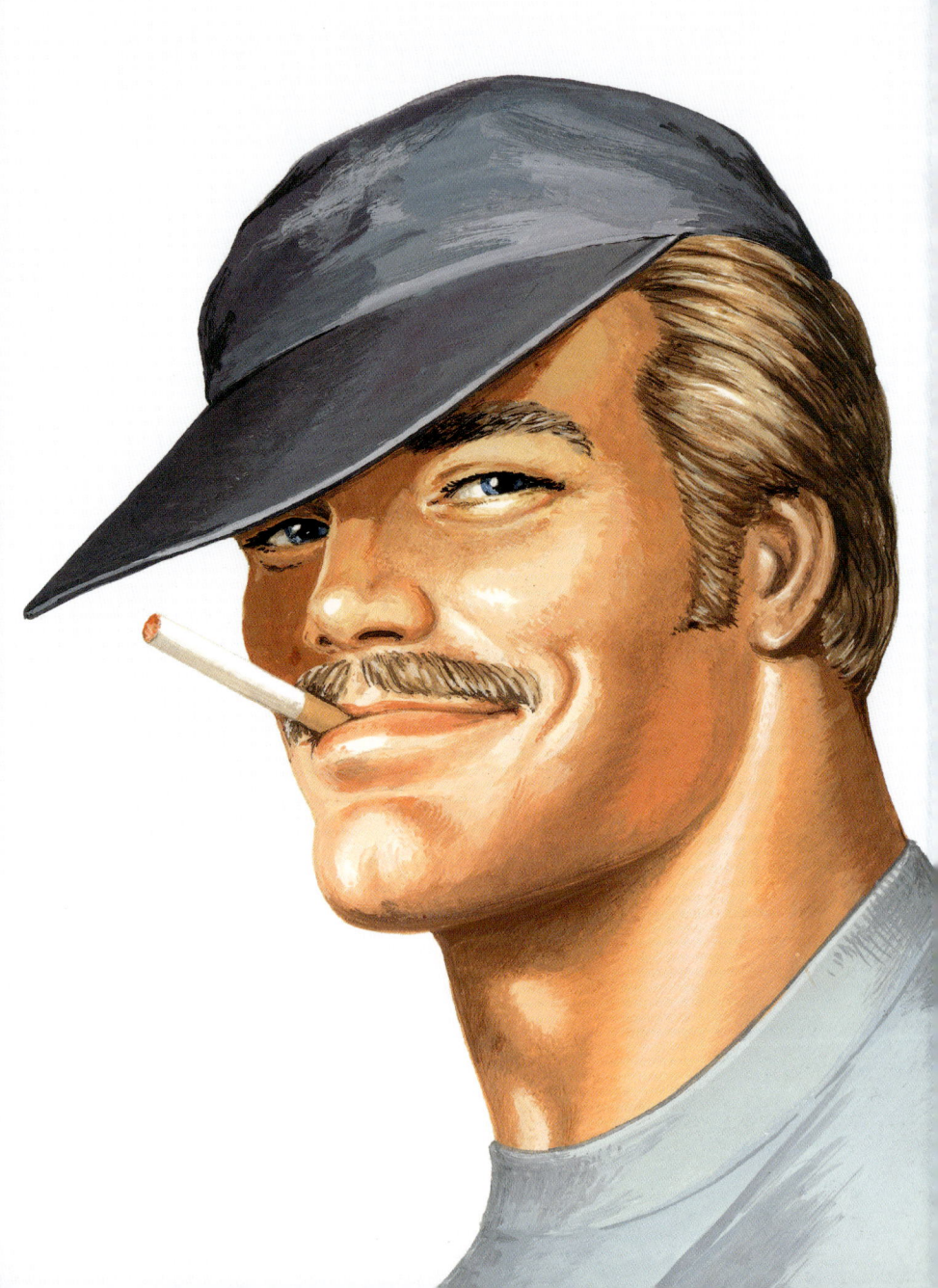

DIAN HANSON: THE LITTLE BOOK OF

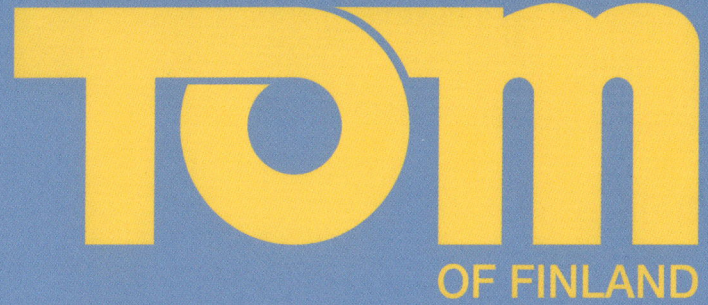

OF FINLAND

BLUE COLLAR

TASCHEN

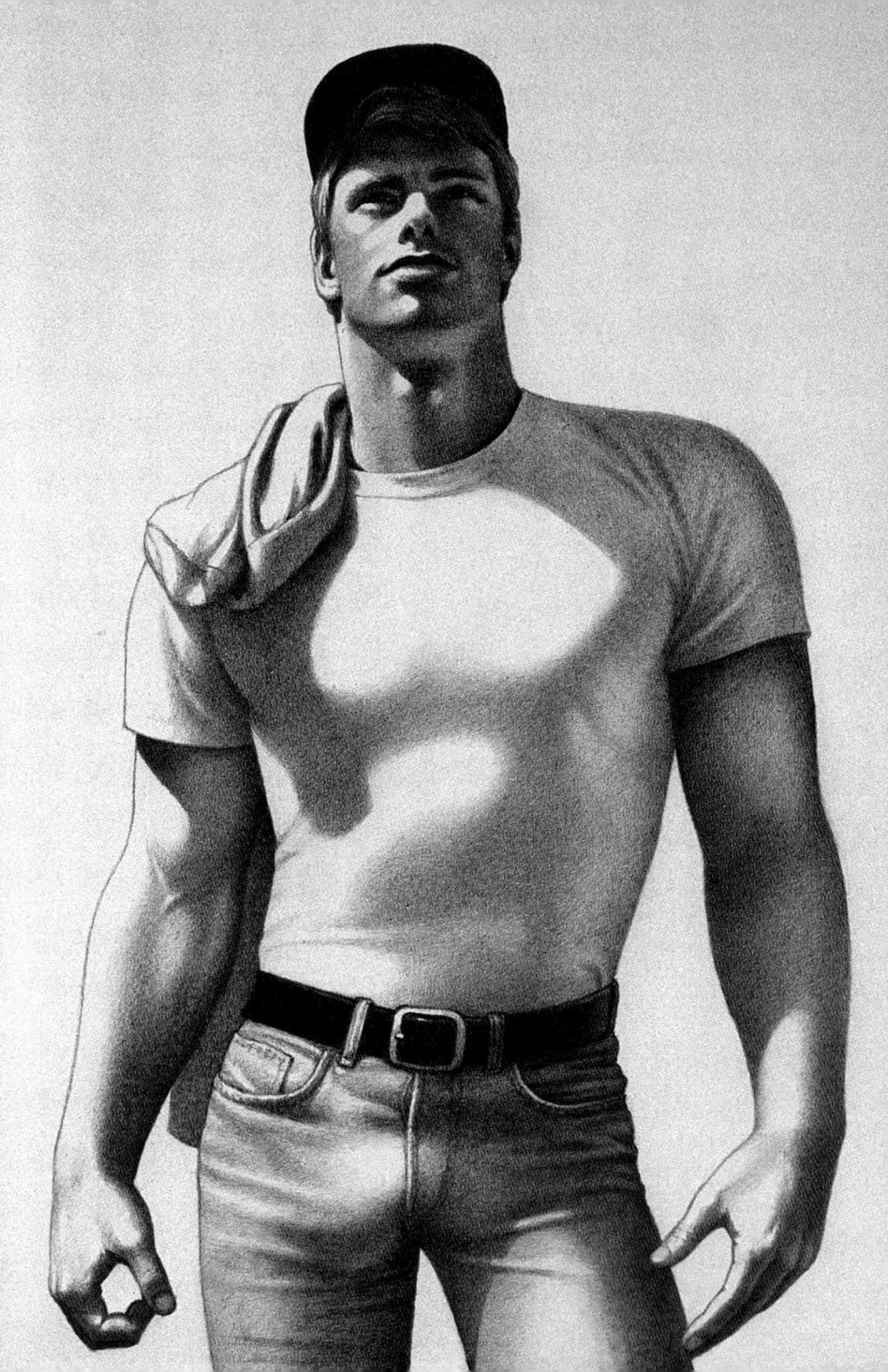

BLUE COLLAR MAN

By Dian Hanson

When Touko Laaksonen, the boy who would become Tom of Finland, was just 10 years old he drew his first sex comic. It wasn't about Felix the Cat or Mickey Mouse, but about two tough, blue collar men. In a lecture at the California Institute for the Arts in 1985 he said, "I had erotic fantasies very early. They were fantasies of grown-up men. I adored very much the handsome men in my neighborhood, and I had a strong fetish for leather and boots and for everything that went with a masculine image and profession."

Finland had, and has, no shortage of masculine professions. In 1930, when Tom was 10, the majority of Finns were farmers, who supplemented their income with logging. Loggers are a notoriously butch bunch, made more so in the far north by the high, heavy boots they wear for warmth and protection against rogue logs and errant saws. Tom was especially taken with the traditional beak-toed Lapp boots, featuring long, turned-back cuffs and heavy leather soles. In his drawings he paired them with tight jeans, impractical in the Finnish forests but far sexier than the shapeless trousers actually worn.

Blue collar men are a gay fantasy mainstay. Women prefer suits and ties and all the trappings of white collar success, but men understand that those who work with their hands—and arms, legs, chests and backs—develop better bodies and lusty appetites. Tom believed that to be a man interested in men is to fully embrace masculinity. He never understood the appeal of effeminacy, or why gay men couldn't be just as manly as loggers, fishermen, dockworkers and farm hands. In fact, there've always been entirely masculine gay men, including a fair share of loggers, fishermen, et al., but because homosexuality was universally illegal, punishable in Finland by a two-year prison sentence, any man who could stay closeted, did. That left only those constitutionally incapable of hiding to represent gay men to the world.

PAGE 4 1983, graphite on paper
BELOW Tom as Tom's Man, late 1960s
OPPOSITE *Man's Magazine*, December 1955, was a
classic American men's adventure title, catering to
blue collar fantasies of post-war male camaraderie

This skewed image of his fellow gays rankled Tom, so in his drawings he corrected what fear created, constructing a gay wonderland where intensely masculine men lived in open, affectionate camaraderie. As he described it, "I draw men who look healthy and masculine and relaxed, enjoying what they are doing. I show they can feel happy together, and they have a *right* to feel happy together." From the beginning, and always at the center of his fantasy world, were blue collar workers in the mold of his first youthful crush: a young farm worker, often redolent of fragrant sweat, who bundled hay in the fields surrounding his family's rural home. His portrayal of such men is credited as helping a wide demographic accept its true self. As Micha

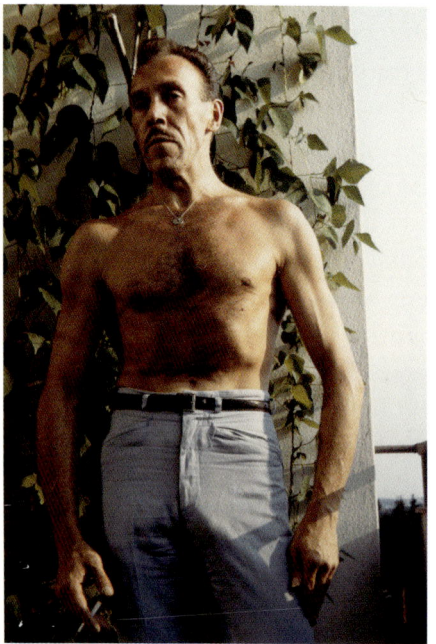

Ramakers quoted one working man in his book *Dirty Pictures: Tom of Finland, Masculinity and Homosexuality*, "Seeing two blue collar men enjoying each other made being gay more acceptable to me. I had all very negative associations with it. When I finally did come out, [Tom's art] made me feel more comfortable with the fact that I liked other men." At first Tom denied that he was, or wanted to be, an influence on gay culture, insisting he just made his drawings for self-stimulation. In 1988, again lecturing at Los Angeles' California Institute of

*"He corrected what fear created, constructing
a gay wonderland where intensely masculine
men lived in affectionate camaraderie."*

the Arts, he admitted, "I find out all these years I was lying to myself, that I wanted to change people's opinions; I want to make them understand things they didn't understand before, and even I wanted to influence the so-called straight people to understand and accept and see gayness in a positive way."

Touko took his first step towards reaching the world outside his pants in the mid '50s, when a friend returned from America with a copy of Bob Mizer's *Physique Pictorial*. He found inspiration in George Quaintance's paintings, particularly those of ranch hands in tight jeans and cowboy boots. Quaintance is credited with elevating blue jeans to fetish objects and Touko recognized George and Bob, who

often photographed boys in military and blue collar "uniforms," as kindred spirits. In 1956 he sent Mizer a selection of his own drawings and his first published work appeared on the cover of the Spring '57 issue, credited to "'Tom,' an artist who lives in Finland." Appropriately, the chosen image was a happy blond logger in high leather Lapp boots, at once exotic in attire and familiar in his grinning good looks. Mizer announced the two drawings in that issue as part of a series titled Men of the Forests of Finland, offering

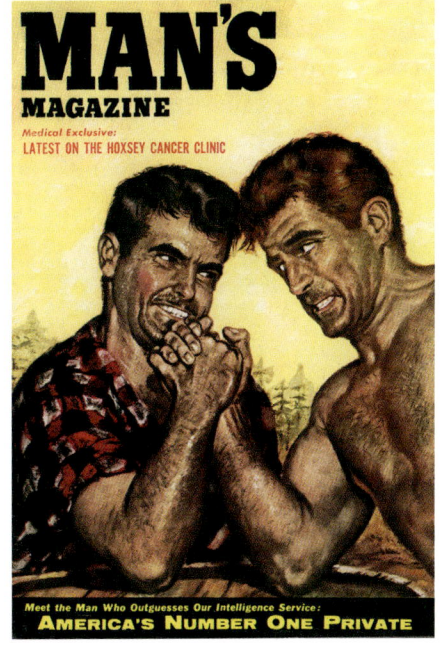

"By then men didn't need to exaggerate their masculinity to prove they were equal to any other."

prints for $1.50 each. The name "Tom of Finland" first appeared in the Winter 1957 issue, when Mizer published Touko's second set of drawings. George Quaintance's premature death was announced in that same issue, with Mizer noting that the artist "drove himself unmercifully…taking Benzedrine to stay awake." Despite frequent claims that *PP* readers instantly embraced Tom, artists Spartacus and Etienne dominated the pages until Tom began flattering Mizer by interpreting scenes from his films, starting in the Winter '58 issue. Several of Tom's stranger drawings came about this way, including renditions of *Boys in Prison, Revenge of the Triton* and *I Was a Teen-Age Bum.* The artistic sacrifice worked, however; in the 1960s Tom slowly edged out the other artists, until in the May 1963 issue Bob finally got it, writing, "The world of Tom is obviously a figment of his imagination because nowhere do such *magnificent* specimens exist—at least not in the quantity that Tom draws them. Yet his rugged youths have a believ-

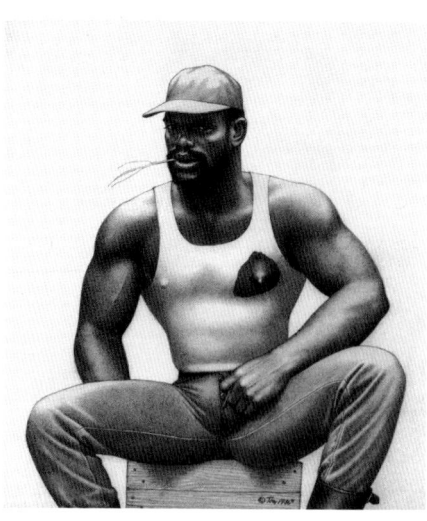

able quality, and they momentarily transport us from the real world filled with almost oppressive mediocrity to one peopled by the stalwart heroes we would all like to be. Of course, some people might prefer their make-believe world peopled with more sylvan creatures, lithe young things that flit about on tippy-toe, and fortunately there are artists who have also created such a world as this. We believe that most of our readers would prefer the more rugged approach." He then asked, "If we are wrong please let us know," and readers made it clear that Tom's blue collar heroes were exactly the men they wanted to be, and to have, launching Tom of Finland to international fame.

In 1988, 15 years after quitting his advertising job to draw full time, Tom reflected, "When I worked in advertising I had to wear a suit and tie every day and hated it. Then when I became freelance and I was in jeans and leather jacket and boots every day I began to be excited by this traditional uniform of business. That's when I came to understand each person's work clothes are just another kind of uniform, with their own fantasies." And by then men didn't need to exaggerate their masculinity to prove they were equal to any other.

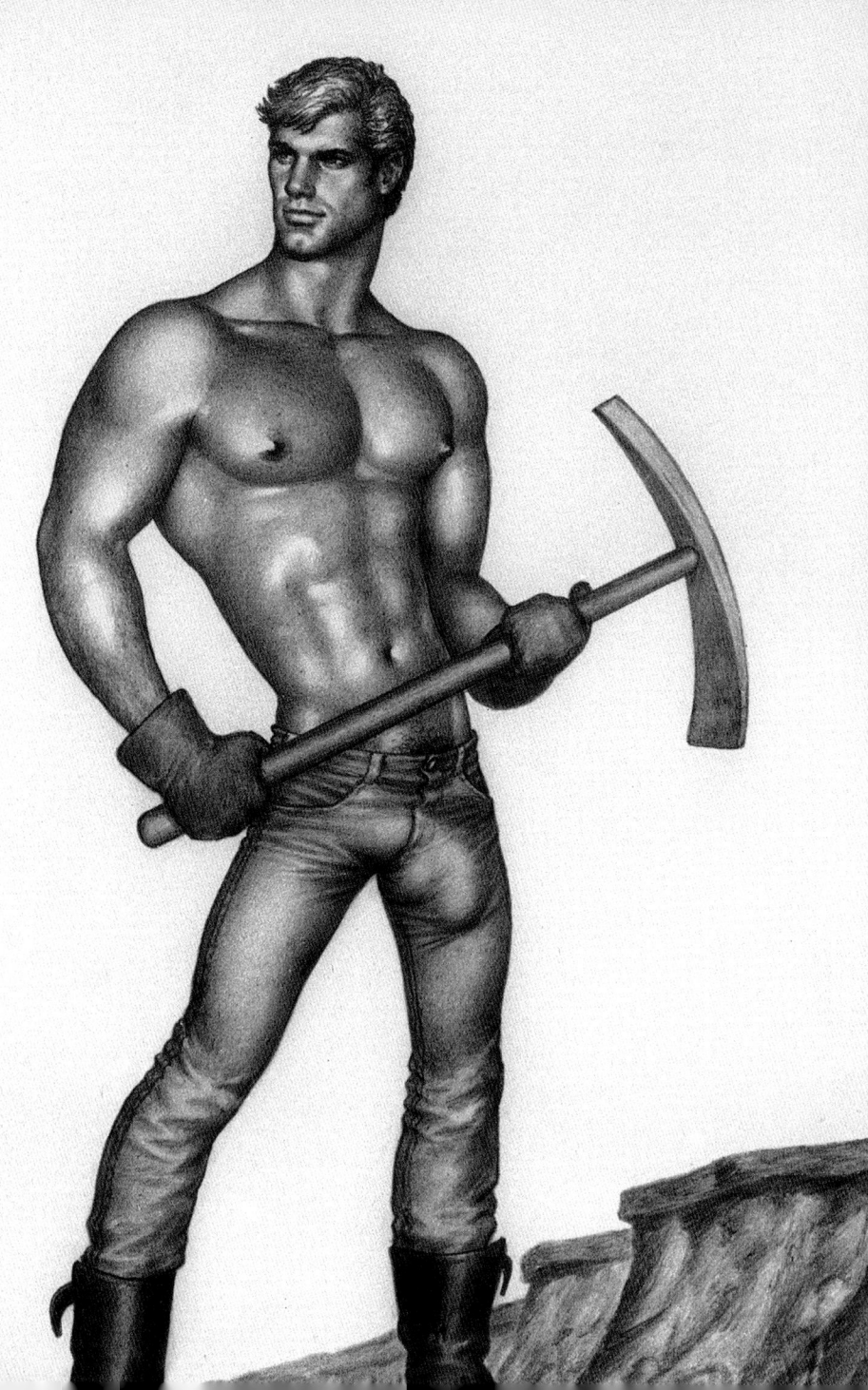

ARBEITER

Von Dian Hanson

Als Touko Laaksonen, der Junge, aus dem einmal Tom of Finland werden sollte, zehn Jahre alt war, zeichnete er schon seinen ersten Sex-Comic. Darin spielten weder Felix the Cat noch Mickey Mouse eine Rolle, sondern zwei robuste Arbeiter. Bei einem Vortrag, den er 1985 am California Institute for the Arts hielt, sagte er: „Erotische Phantasien hatte ich bereits sehr früh. Das waren Phantasien, die sich um erwachsene Männer drehten. Die stattlichen Männer aus meiner Nachbarschaft bewunderte ich sehr. Ich fuhr total auf Leder und Stiefel ab, fetischisierte alles, was mit einer bestimmten Vorstellung von Männlichkeit und Berufen für harte Kerle zu tun hatte."

In Finnland gab es – und gibt es noch immer – keinen Mangel an Berufen, für die es echte Männer braucht. 1930, als Tom 10 war, waren die meisten Finnen Bauern, die sich mit Holzfällen ein zusätzliches Einkommen sicherten. Holzfäller sind bekanntermaßen raue Burschen, erst recht ganz oben im Norden, wo sie schwere Stiefel tragen, um sich die Füße warm zu halten und gegen gefährliche Baumstümpfe und abrutschende Sägen geschützt zu sein. Tom hatte ein besonderes Faible für die traditionellen, spitz zulaufenden Stiefel der Lappen mit ihren langen, gewendeten Stulpen und schweren Ledersohlen. In seinen Zeichnungen kombinierte er sie mit engen Jeans, die für die finnischen Wälder zwar ungeeignet waren, aber entschieden sexier wirkten als die schlabbrigen Hosen, die tatsächlich getragen wurden.

Arbeiter gehören zum wichtigsten Personal schwuler Phantasien. Frauen stehen eher auf Anzüge, Krawatten und das ganze Drum und Dran, das wirtschaftlichen Erfolg signalisiert; Männern hingegen ist klar, dass jene, die mit bloßen Händen arbeiten – und dazu auch Arme, Beine, Brust und Rücken einsetzen müssen – straffere Körper und herzhaftere Gelüste entwickeln. Tom war davon überzeugt, dass man als Mann, der auf Männer scharf ist, Männlichkeit

in ihrer ganzen Pracht wahrnehmen sollte; er begriff nie, was an Wei-
bisch-Weichlichem so anziehend sein soll. Von Kopf bis Fuß masku-
line schwule Männer gab es in der Tat schon immer, darunter auch
so manche Holzfäller oder Fischer, doch weil Homosexualität über-
all illegal war – und in Finnland mit zwei Jahren Gefängnis bestraft
wurde – hielt das jeder, so gut er konnte, geheim. So repräsentier-
ten also nur jene ihre Homosexualität in aller Öffentlichkeit, die ihre
schwulen Neigungen nicht verbergen konnten. Tom wurmte dieses
verzerrte Bild, das von schwulen Männern existierte. So korrigierte
er in seinen Zeichnungen das, was aus bloßer Angst entstanden war,
und schuf sich ein schwules Wunderland, in dem ungemein masku-
line Kerle eine offene Kameradschaft voller Zuneigung auslebten. Er
selbst beschrieb einmal: „Ich zeichne Männer, die gesund, maskulin
und entspannt aussehen und Freude an dem haben, was sie tun. Ich
zeige, dass sie gemeinsam ihr Glück genießen können und auch *das
Recht* dazu haben". Arbeiter gehörten von Anfang an zu den Grundfi-
guren seiner jugendlichen Schwärmereien und standen auch stets im
Mittelpunkt seiner Phantasiewelt: ein junger, oft verführerisch nach
Schweiß riechender junger Landarbeiter, der Heu auf den Feldern, die
das ländliche Heim seiner Familie umgaben, bündelte. Seine Darstel-
lung solcher Männer soll einer großen Zahl von Menschen geholfen
haben, ihr wahres Ich zu akzeptieren. In seinem Buch *Dirty Pictures:
Tom of Finland, Masculinity and Homosexuality* zitiert Micha Ramakers einen Arbeiter: „Zu sehen, wie zwei Arbeiter Spaß miteinan-
der hatten, machte es mir leichter, mein Schwulsein zu akzeptieren.
Bis dahin waren meine Neigungen für mich nur mit negativen Asso-
ziationen verbunden. Als ich mich schließlich outete, sorgte Toms
Kunst dafür, dass ich mit der Tatsache, andere Männer zu mögen, bes-
ser leben konnte." Tom stritt zunächst ab, dass er einen Einfluss auf

> *„So korrigierte er in seinen Zeichnungen das, was aus*
> *bloßer Angst entstanden war, und schuf sich ein schwules*
> *Wunderland, in dem ungemein maskuline Kerle eine*
> *offene Kameradschaft voller Zuneigung auslebten."*

die Schwulenkultur hatte oder haben wollte, und behauptete, er habe seine Zeichnungen nur zur Selbststimulierung angefertigt. In einem späteren Vortrag, den er 1988 am California Institute of the Arts in Los Angeles hielt, gestand er dann ein: „Ich stellte fest, dass ich mich all die Jahre selbst belogen habe, dass ich die Ansichten der Leute sehr wohl ändern wollte; ich will, dass sie Dinge verstehen, die sie vorher nicht verstanden haben, und ich wollte sogar die sogenannten Heterosexuellen beeinflussen, damit sie Schwulsein verstehen und akzeptieren und insgesamt positiv beurteilen."

Mitte der 1955er-Jahre, als ein Freund mit einem Exemplar von Bob Mizers *Physique Pictorial* aus Amerika zurückkam, unternahm Touko seinen ersten Schritt, die Welt außerhalb seines Umfelds zu errei-

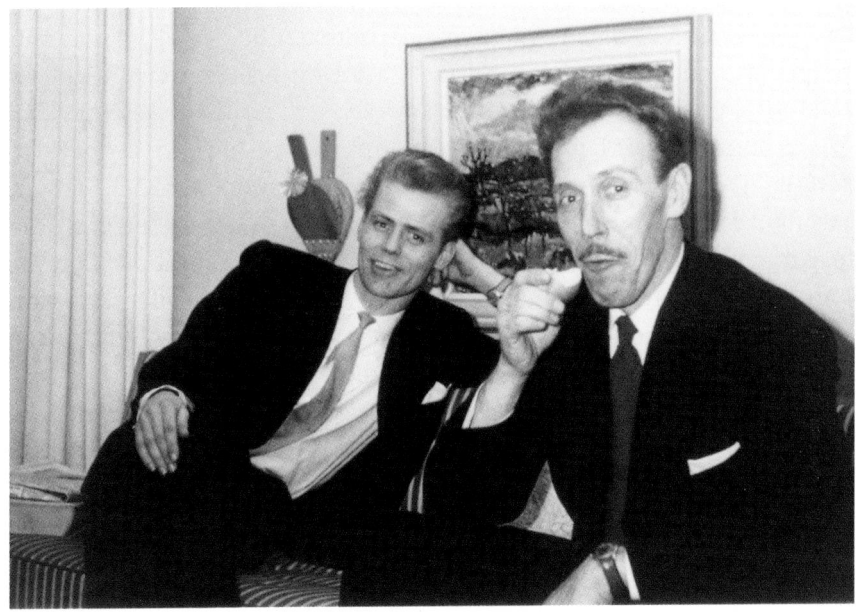

„Von nun an mussten Männer ihre Maskulinität nicht mehr herausstellen, um zu beweisen, dass sie jedem anderen ebenbürtig sind."

chen. George Quaintances Malereien, vor allem die von Rancharbeitern in engen Jeans und Cowboystiefeln, inspirierten ihn. Quaintance wird zugeschrieben, Blue Jeans zu Fetischobjekten erhoben zu haben, und Touko erkannte in George und Bob, die häufig Jungs in Militär- und Arbeiter-„Uniformen" fotografierten, Seelenverwandte. 1956 schickte er Mizer eine Auswahl seiner eigenen Zeichnungen, woraufhin auf dem Cover der *Physique Pictorial*-Ausgabe vom Frühjahr 1957 eine dieser Zeichnungen mit dem Verweis „Tom, ein Künstler, der in Finnland lebt" als sein erstes veröffentlichtes Werk erschien. Passenderweise stellte das Bild einen gut gelaunten blonden Holzfäller in Lappen-Lederstiefeln dar, der zum einen, im Hinblick auf seine Kleidung, exotisch, zum anderen, in Bezug auf sein blendendes Aussehen und sein fröhliches Grinsen, ganz vertraut wirkte. Mizer vermeldete zu den in dieser Ausgabe abgebildeten beiden Zeichnungen, sie gehörten zu einer Serie mit dem Titel *Männer aus den Wäldern Finnlands* und bot Drucke zum Preis von $ 1,50 pro Exemplar an. Der Name „Tom of Finland" tauchte zum ersten Mal in der Ausgabe vom Winter 1957 auf, als Mizer Toms zweite Auswahl von Zeichnungen veröffentlichte. In der gleichen Ausgabe wurde George Quaintances früher Tod bekanntgegeben, eine Meldung, die Mizer mit der Bemerkung versah, der Künstler habe „sich rücksichtslos verausgabt... und Benzedrin genommen, um wach zu bleiben". Ungeachtet häufig wiederholter Behauptungen, die *PP*-Leser hätten Tom sofort akzeptiert, dominierten zunächst die Künstler Spartacus und Etienne die Seiten, bis Tom Mizer umschmeichelte, indem er Szenen von dessen Filmen in Zeichnungen interpretierte, die erstmals in der Ausgabe vom Winter 1958 veröffentlicht wurden. Etliche von Toms seltsameren Zeichnungen, darunter die Bilder zu *Boys in Prison*, *Revenge of the Triton* und *I Was a Teenage-Bum*, kamen auf diese Weise zustande. Das künstlerische Opfer lohnte sich allerdings; im Laufe der 1960er-Jahre stach Tom die anderen Künstler nach und nach aus. In der Ausgabe vom Mai 1963 wurde schließlich deutlich, dass Bob begriffen hatte. Er schrieb: „Toms Welt ist offensichtlich ein Produkt seiner Phantasie, denn so prächtige Typen gibt es nirgendwo. Trotzdem haben seine wilden, jungen Kerle durchaus glaubwürdige Eigenschaften, und sie versetzen uns vorübergehend aus einer realen Welt voller beklemmenden Mittelmaßes in ein Universum, das von jenen unerschütterlichen Helden bevölkert ist, die wir alle sein wollen. Klar, manche mögen ihre eigene Traumwelt mit Waldgeistern bevorzugen, ranken und schlanken kleinen Kerlen, die auf Zehenspitzen herumhuschen, und glücklicherweise gibt es Künstler, die auch solche Welten geschaffen haben. Wir glauben allerdings, dass die meisten unserer Leser eher auf die wilden Kerle stehen." Abschließend bat er, „sollten wir uns irren, lasst es uns bitte wissen", und die Leser gaben zu verstehen, dass Toms Arbeiterhelden genau den Typ Mann darstellten, den sie selbst verkörpern und den sie haben wollten. Damit beförderten sie Tom of Finland zu internationalem Ruhm.

1988, fünfzehn Jahre nachdem er seinen Job in der Werbebranche zugunsten einer hauptberuflichen Arbeit als Zeichner aufgegeben hatte, bemerkte Tom nachdenklich: „Als ich in der Werbung arbeitete, musste ich jeden Tag Anzug und Krawatte tragen, und ich hasste das. Als ich dann ein Freischaffender wurde und tagtäglich in Jeans, Lederjacke und Stiefeln herumlief, fing jene traditionelle Geschäftsuniform an, mich zu reizen. Mit einem Mal begriff ich, dass die Arbeitskleidung eines jeden nur die Variante einer Uniform ist, die ihre eigenen Phantasien erweckt." Von nun an mussten Männer ihre Maskulinität nicht mehr herausstellen, um zu beweisen, dass sie jedem anderen ebenbürtig sind.

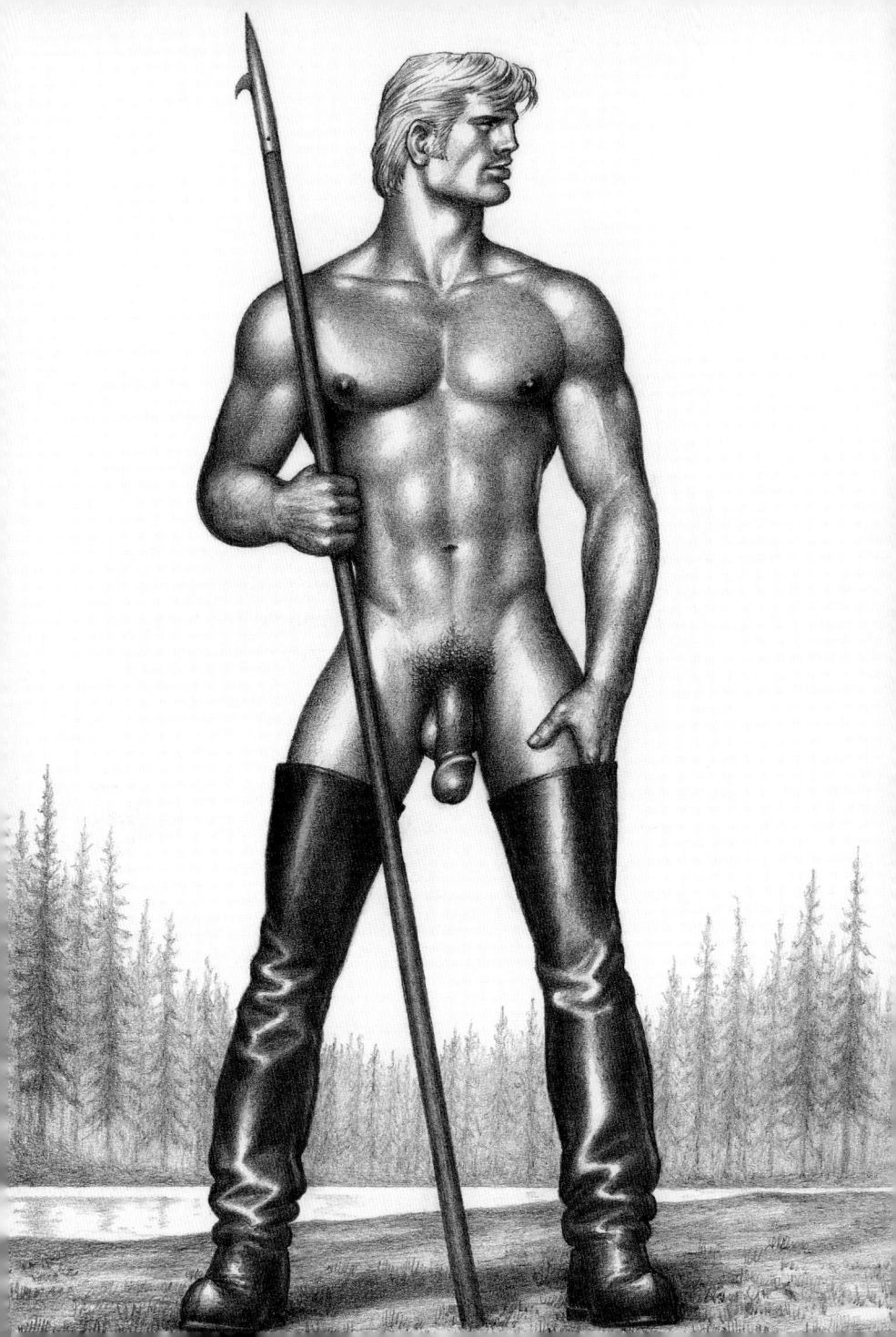

LES PROLÉTAIRES

Par Dian Hanson

A dix ans, Touko Laaksonen, l'enfant qui deviendrait Tom of Finland, dessina sa première bande dessinée. Il ne s'agissait pas de Félix le chat ni de Mickey Mouse, mais de deux robustes ouvriers. Lors d'une conférence à la California Institute of the Arts en 1985, il déclara : « J'ai développé des fantasmes érotiques très tôt. Je fantasmais sur des hommes adultes. J'adorais les beaux mâles de mon quartier et je fétichisais le cuir, les bottes, tout ce qui correspondait à une image ou une profession virile. »

La Finlande n'a jamais manqué de professions viriles. En 1930, quand Tom avait dix ans, la majorité des Finlandais étaient des agriculteurs qui augmentaient leurs revenus avec l'abattage du bois. Les bûcherons sont connus pour leur allure virile, surtout dans le Nord avec les lourdes bottes hautes qu'ils portent pour se protéger du froid, des troncs rebelles et des scies baladeuses. Tom était particulièrement séduit par les bottes traditionnelles lapones avec leur pointe recourbée vers le ciel, leur partie supérieure pouvant se rabattre et leurs épaisses semelles en cuir. Dans ses dessins, il les associait à des jeans, peu pratiques dans les forêts finlandaises mais infiniment plus sexy que les pantalons sans forme qui étaient portés en réalité.

Les ouvriers font fantasmer beaucoup d'homosexuels. Les femmes préfèrent les costards cravates et tous les attributs de la réussite en col blanc, mais les hommes savent que ceux qui travaillent avec leurs mains (et bras, jambes, torse, dos) développent de plus beaux corps et un plus grand appétit sexuel. Pour Tom, être un homme intéressé par les hommes revenait à accepter pleinement sa masculinité. Il ne comprit jamais l'attrait de l'homme efféminé, ni pourquoi les gays ne pouvaient être aussi virils que les bûcherons, les pêcheurs, les dockers et les ouvriers journaliers. De fait, il y eut toujours des homosexuels très masculins, parmi lesquels de nombreux bûcherons,

PAGE 16 1969, graphite on paper
BELOW 1984, graphite on paper, collection of Volker Morlock

pêcheurs, etc., mais l'homosexualité étant alors universellement réprouvée, passible en Finlande de deux ans de prison, les hommes qui le pouvaient restaient dans le placard. Par conséquent, l'homosexualité n'était affichée aux yeux de tous que par ceux qui, par nature, ne pouvaient se cacher. Cette image biaisée des gays dérangeait Tom, si bien qu'il corrigeait dans ses dessins ce que la peur avait engendré, construisant un monde gay merveilleux où des hommes très masculins vivaient une camaraderie ouverte et affectueuse. Il déclara : « Je dessine des hommes sains, virils, à l'aise dans leur corps et prenant du plaisir à ce qu'ils font. Je montre qu'ils peuvent être heureux entre eux et ont le droit d'être heureux entre eux. » Dès le début, les prolétaires occupèrent une place centrale dans son monde

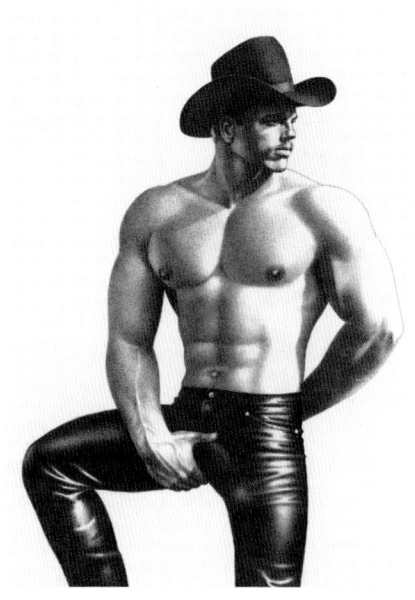

imaginaire, inspirés par son premier béguin d'adolescent : un jeune ouvrier agricole, qui fleurait bon la sueur et bottelait la paille dans les champs autour de la maison des parents de Tom à la campagne. Ses dessins semblent en avoir aidé beaucoup à accepter leur vraie nature. Dans son livre *Dirty Pictures: Tom of Finland, Masculinity and Homosexuality*, Micha Ramakers cite un ouvrier déclarant : « De voir deux ouvriers se donner du plaisir l'un à l'autre m'a rendu l'homosexualité plus acceptable.

« Il corrigeait dans ses dessins ce que la peur avait engendré, construisant un monde gay merveilleux où des hommes très masculins vivaient une camaraderie ouverte et affectueuse. »

Quand je suis enfin sorti du placard, l'art de Tom m'a fait me sentir plus à l'aise avec le fait d'aimer d'autres hommes. » Les premiers temps, Tom nia exercer ou vouloir exercer une influence sur la culture gay, affirmant qu'il ne dessinait que pour se stimuler lui-même. Toutefois, en 1988, lors d'une autre conférence à la California Insitute of the Arts, il reconnut : « Je me suis menti durant toutes ces années. En fait, je voulais changer l'opinion des gens, leur faire comprendre ce qu'ils refusaient de voir et même influencer les "hétéros" pour qu'ils acceptent l'homosexualité et la voient sous un jour positif. »

Touko sortit enfin la main de son slip pour s'intéresser au monde extérieur, lorsqu'un ami revint des Etats-Unis avec un numéro du magazine de Bob Mizer, *Physique Pictorial*. Il y vit les œuvres de George Quaintance, notamment celles montrant de jeunes ouvriers agricoles portant des jeans moulants et des bottes de cow-boy. Quaintance est l'un des premiers à avoir fétichisé le blue-jean. Touko reconnut en lui et en Bob (qui photographiait souvent de jeunes hommes en « uniformes » de militaires ou d'ouvriers) deux âmes sœurs. En 1956, il envoya à Mizer une sélection de ses dessins. Sa première œuvre publiée parut en couverture de *PP* au printemps 1957, attribuée à « Tom, un artiste vivant en Finlande ». L'image choisie représentait un beau bûcheron portant de hautes bottes lapones, à la fois exotique par sa tenue et familier par sa blondeur et ses traits enjoués. Mizer annonça que les dessins inclus dans le numéro faisaient partie d'une série intitulée « Les hommes des forêts de Finlande » et proposait des reproductions à 1,50$ pièce. Le nom « Tom of Finland » apparut dans le numéro de l'hiver 1957, lorsque Mizer publia une seconde série de dessins. La mort prématurée de Quaintance fut annoncée dans le même numéro, Mizer déclarant que l'artiste s'était « tué à la tâche... prenant de la benzédrine pour rester éveillé ». Bien que l'on affirme

*« **A cette époque, les hommes n'avaient plus
besoin d'exagérer leur masculinité pour
prouver qu'ils valaient autant que les autres.** »*

souvent à tort que les lecteurs de *PP* s'entichèrent immédiatement de Tom, les illustrateurs Spartacus et Etienne continuèrent à dominer le magazine jusqu'à ce que Tom entreprenne de flatter Mizer en représentant des scènes de ses films à partir du numéro de l'hiver 1958. Cela donna quelques-uns de ses dessins les plus étranges, notamment des interprétations de *Boys of Prison*, *Revenge of the Triton* et *I Was a Teen-Age Bum*. Ce sacrifice artistique paya. Dans les années 1960, Tom éclipsa progressivement ses deux confrères. Dans le numéro de mai 1963, Bob comprit enfin et écrivit : « Le monde de Tom est une invention de son imagination, car il n'existe nulle part des spécimens aussi magnifiques, du moins pas en abondance comme dans ses dessins. Pourtant, ses rudes gaillards ont une qualité cré-

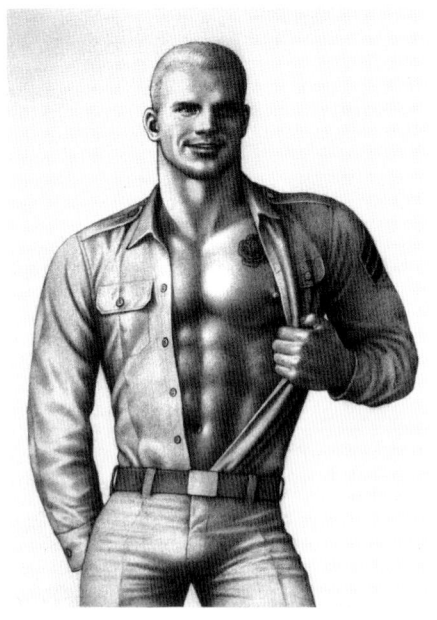

dible et ils nous transportent momentanément d'un monde réel, rempli d'une médiocrité presque oppressante, dans un autre peuplé par les vaillants héros que nous aimerions être. Naturellement, certains préfèrent sans doute que leur monde imaginaire soit peuplé de créatures plus sylvestres, de jeunes éphèbes élancés qui folâtrent sur la pointe des pieds et, heureusement, il existe des artistes qui ont aussi créé ce genre d'univers.. Nous pensons que la plupart de nos lecteurs préfèrent une vision plus virile. Si nous nous trompons, faites-le nous savoir.» Les lecteurs lui firent rapidement savoir que les héros prolétaires de Tom étaient exactement le genre d'hommes qu'ils voulaient être et voulaient avoir, lançant ainsi la célébrité internationale de Tom.

En 1988, quinze ans après avoir quitté son travail dans la publicité pour dessiner à plein temps, Tom observa : « Quand je travaillais dans la publicité, je devais porter un costume et une cravate tous les jours. Je détestais ça. Devenu freelance, j'ai porté des jeans, un blouson en cuir et des bottes tous les jours. C'était aussi une tenue de travail, mais cela m'excitait. J'ai alors compris que ce que nous portons pour travailler n'est jamais qu'un uniforme, dans lequel chacun de nous investit ses propres fantasmes.» Il faut dire aussi qu'à cette époque les hommes n'avaient plus besoin d'exagérer leur masculinité pour prouver qu'ils valaient autant que les autres.

OPPOSITE 1988, graphite on paper, collection of Volker Morlock

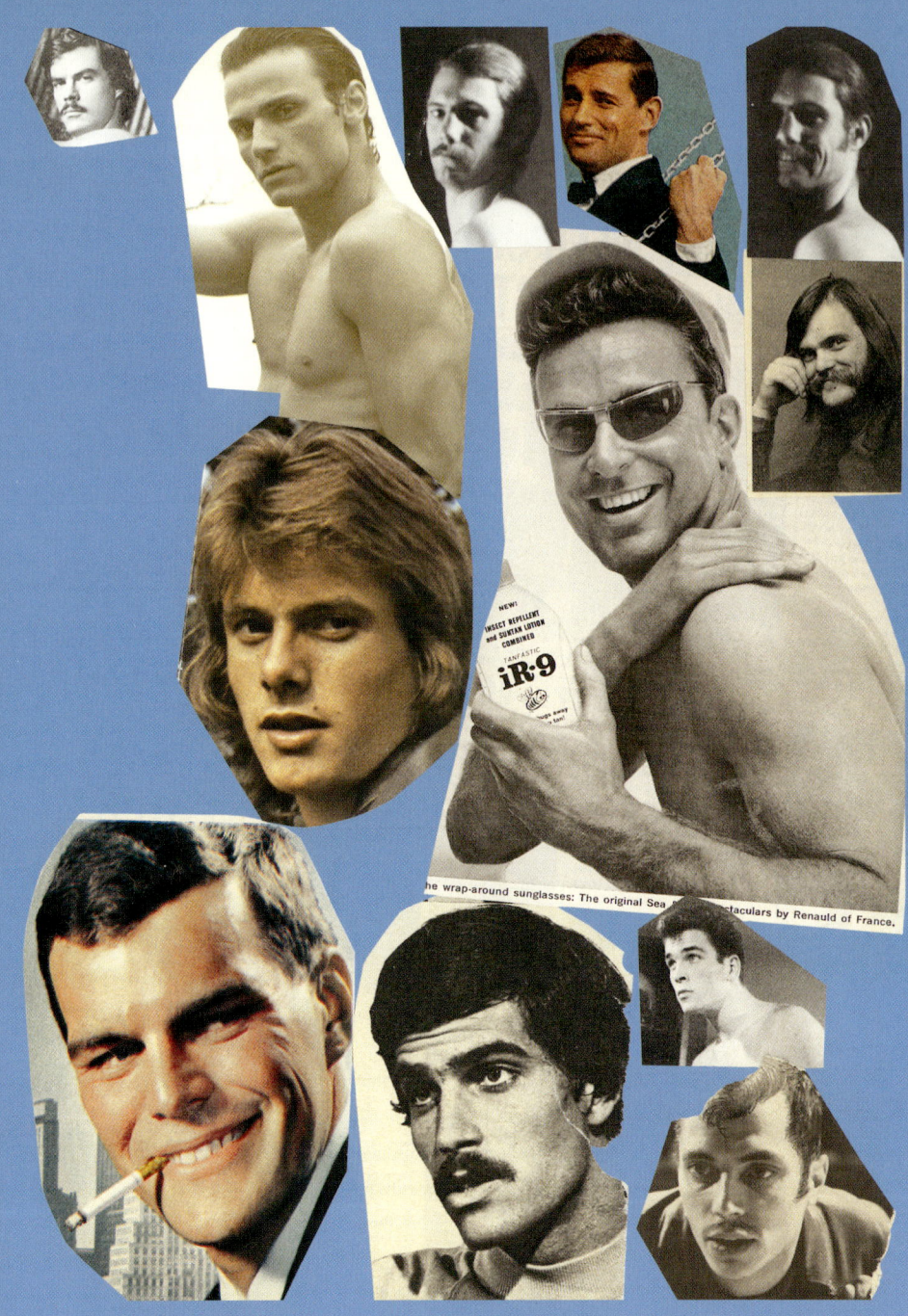

the wrap-around sunglasses: The original Sea ... ...ctaculars by Renauld of France.

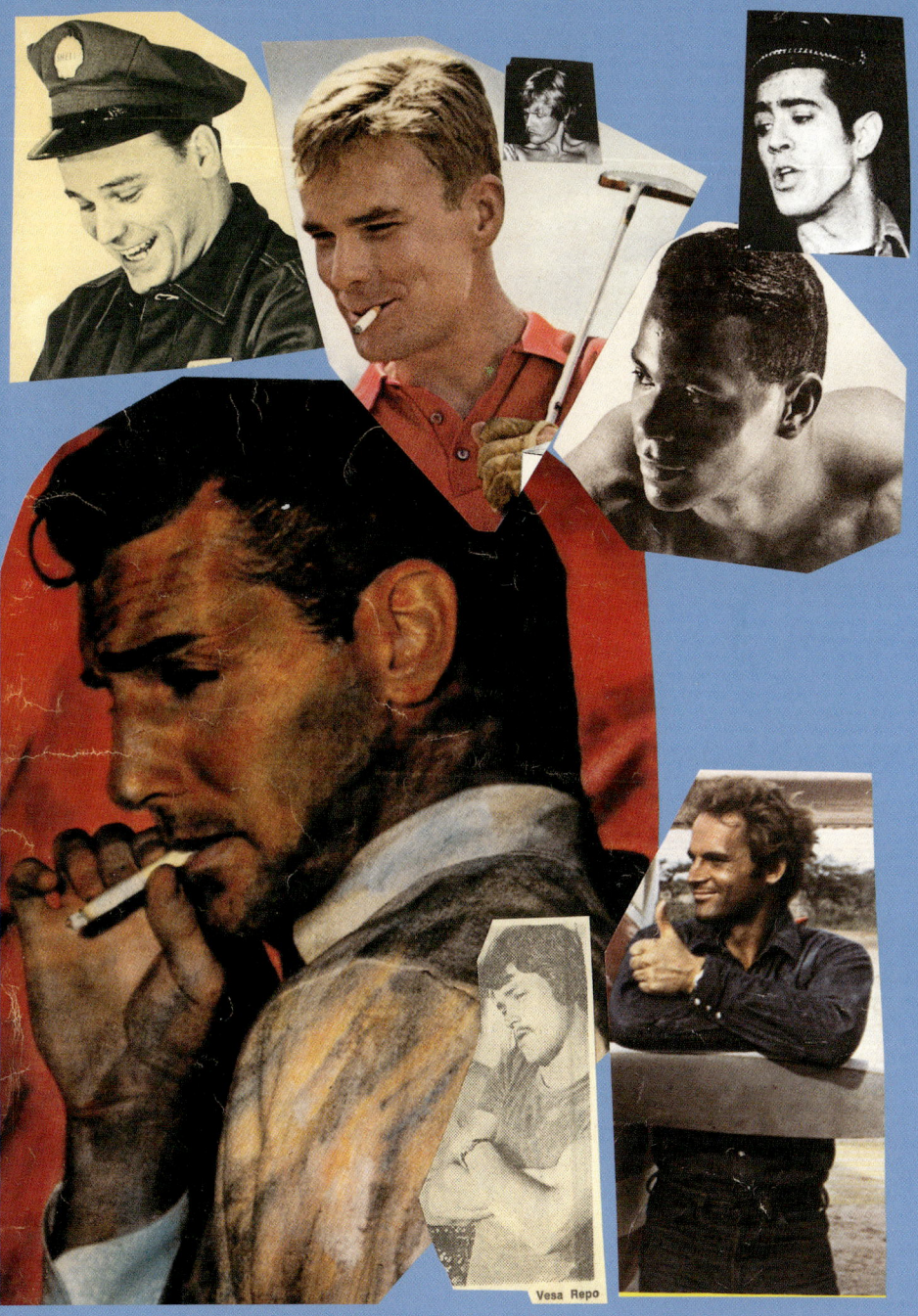

OPPOSITE AND ABOVE Two collages of handsome manly faces from Tom's reference files   **23**

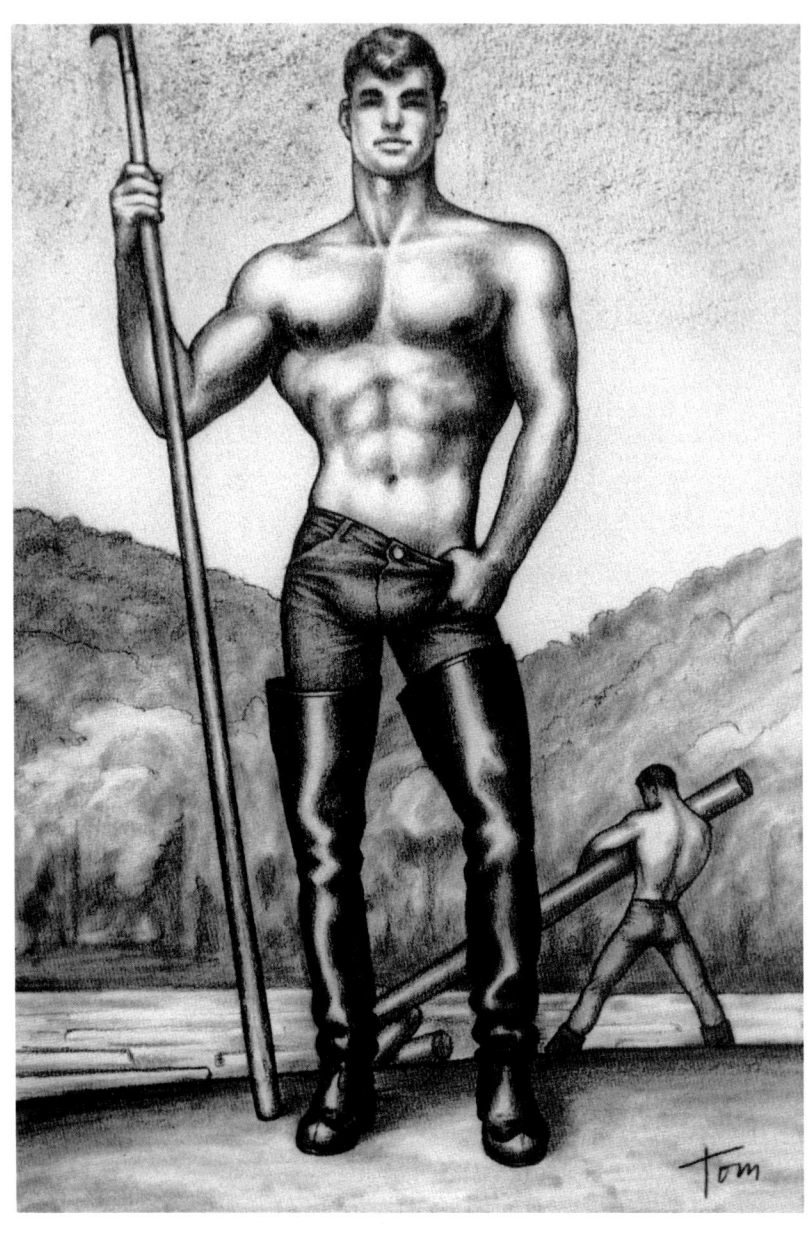

ABOVE 1957, graphite on paper
OPPOSITE 1956, graphite on paper

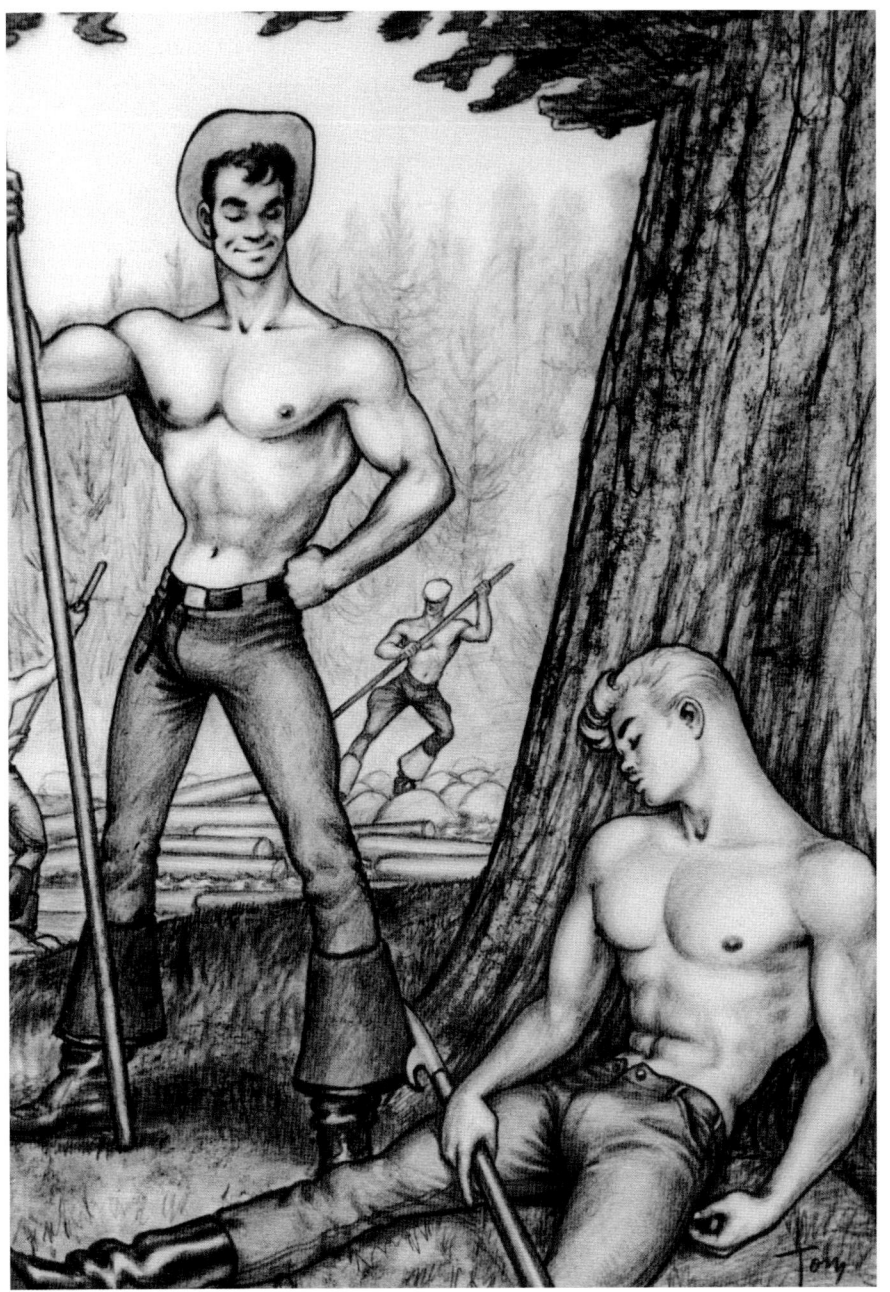

"Tom himself said his characters were prototypes, his own idealized version of how a gay man should look and act."
—SALON

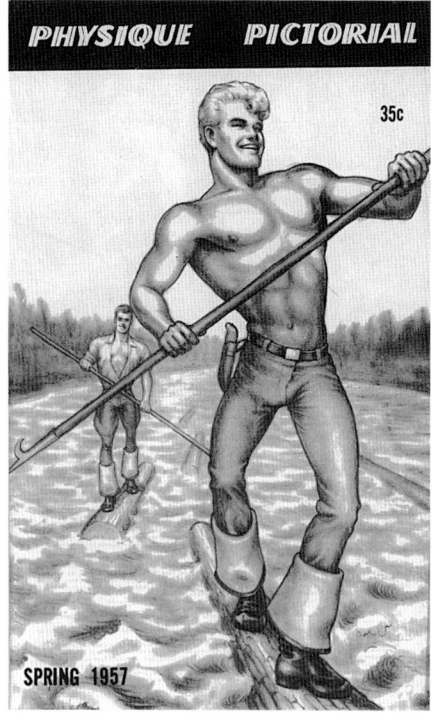

LEFT Tom's first cover of *Physique Pictorial*, Spring 1957
OPPOSITE 1957, graphite on paper

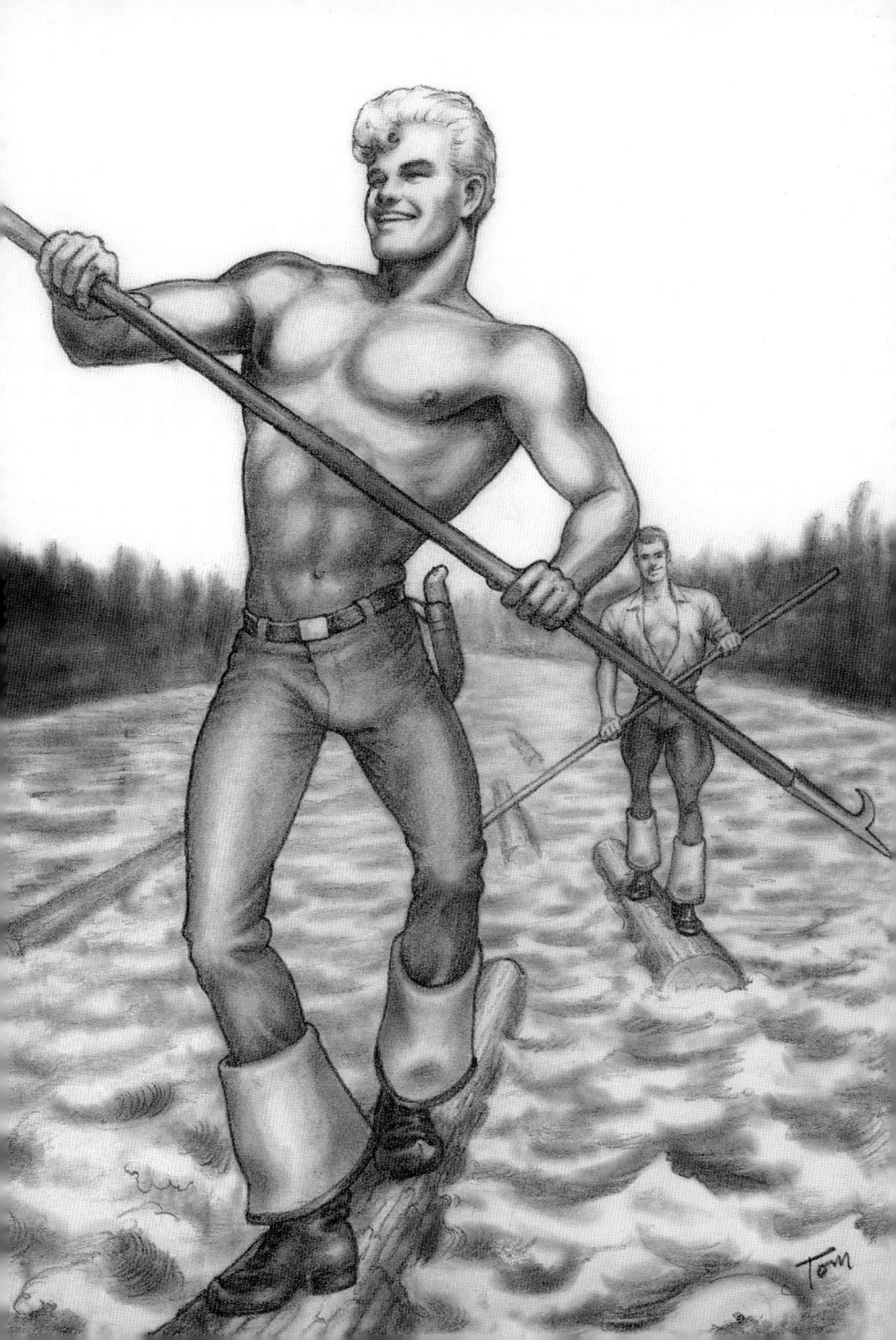

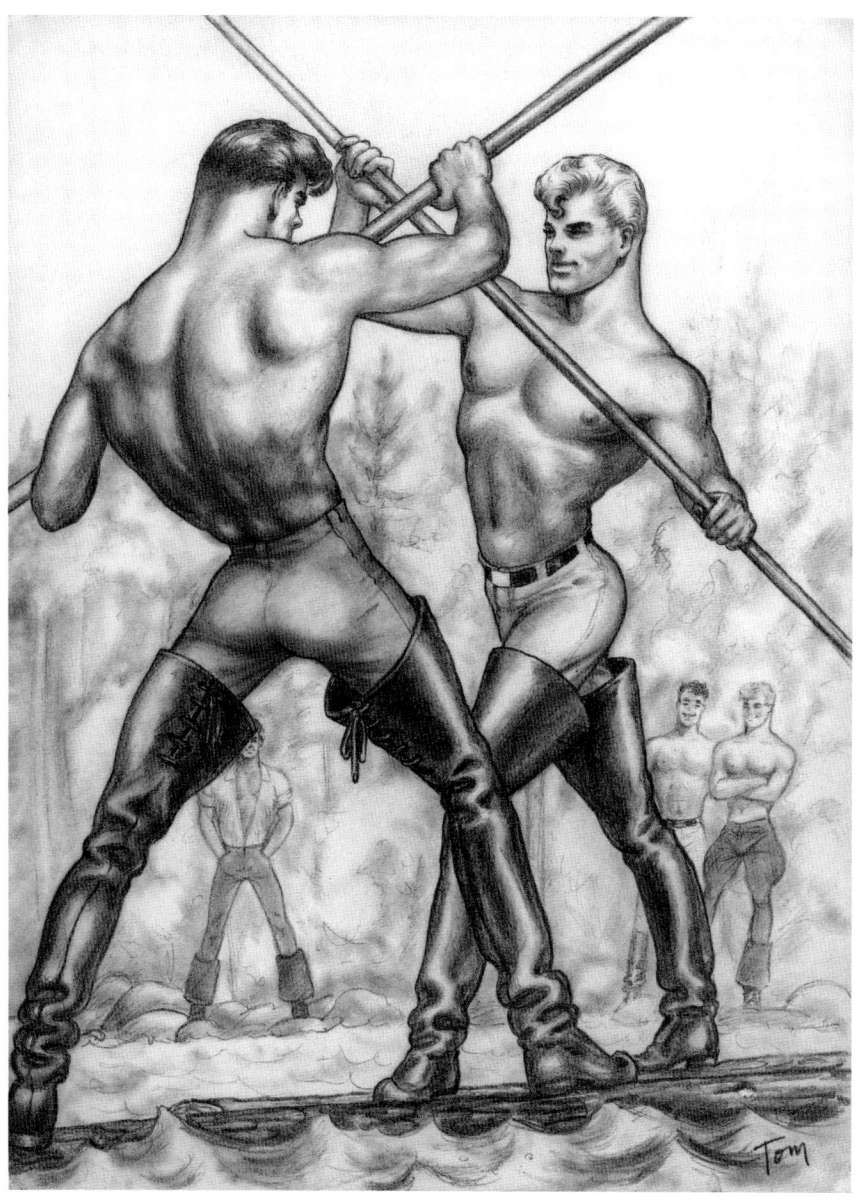

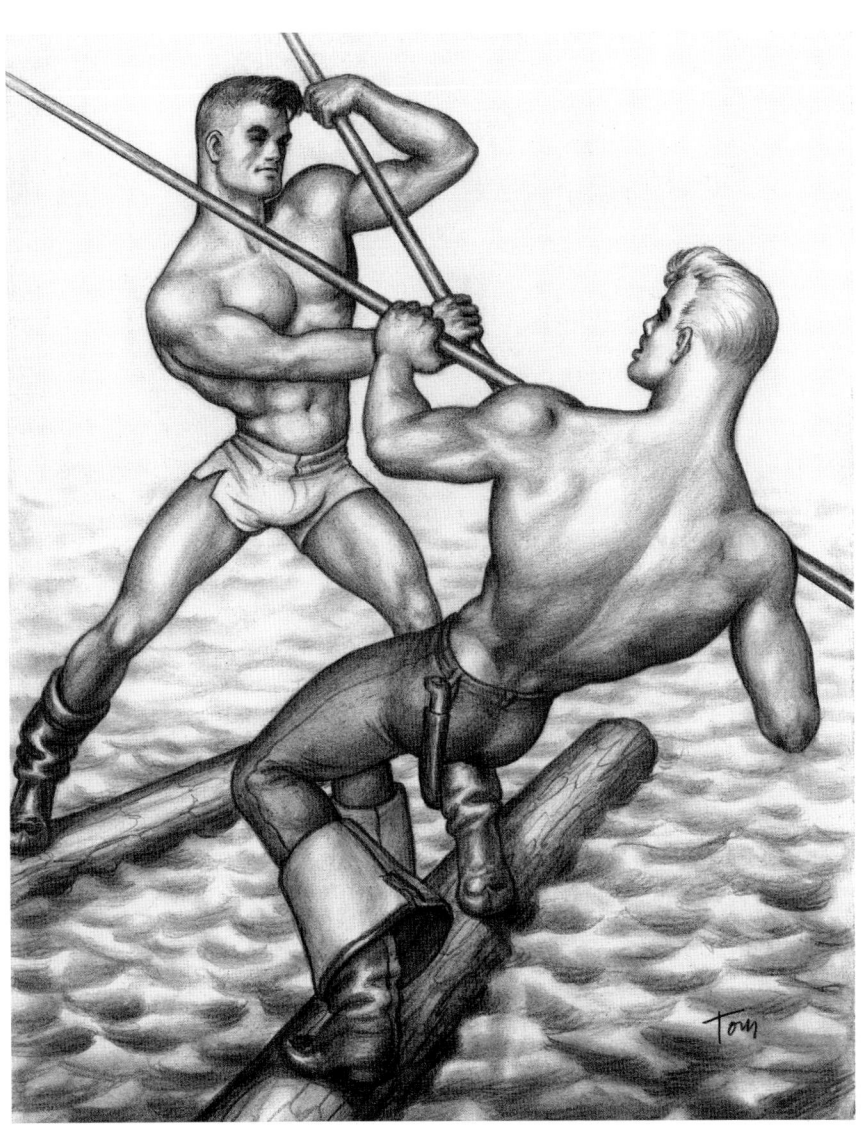

OPPOSITE AND ABOVE 1957, graphite on paper

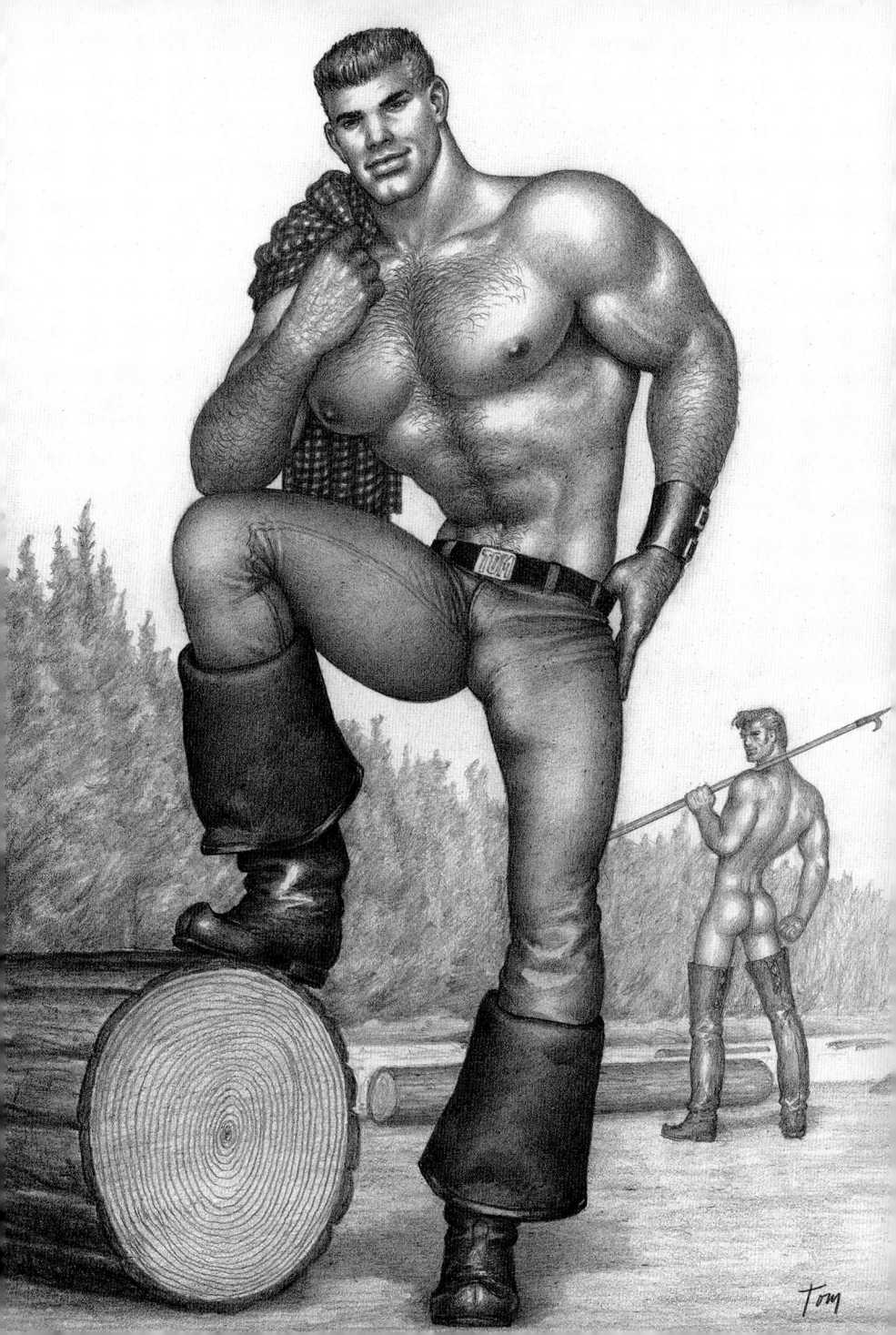

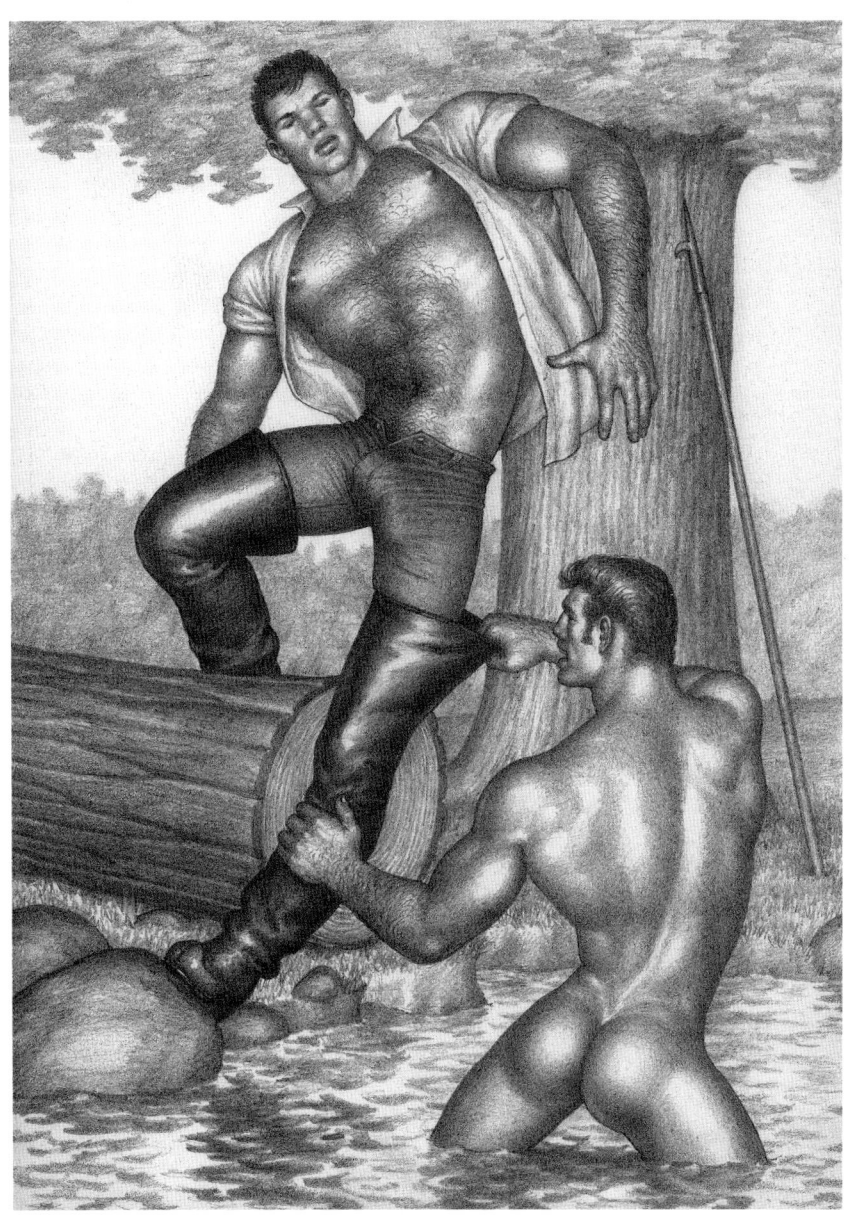

OPPOSITE 1966, graphite on paper, collection of Volker Morlock
ABOVE 1966, graphite on paper

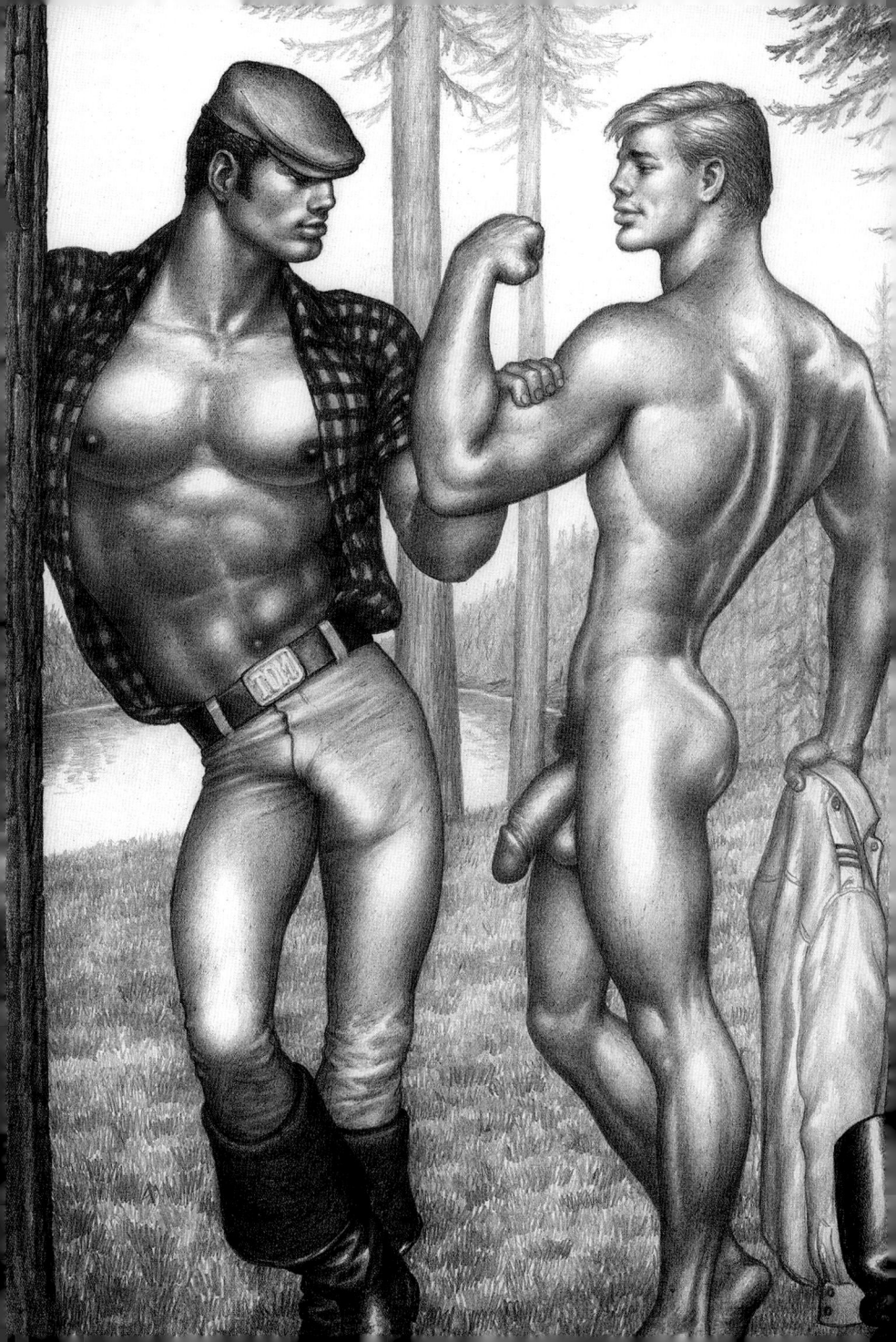

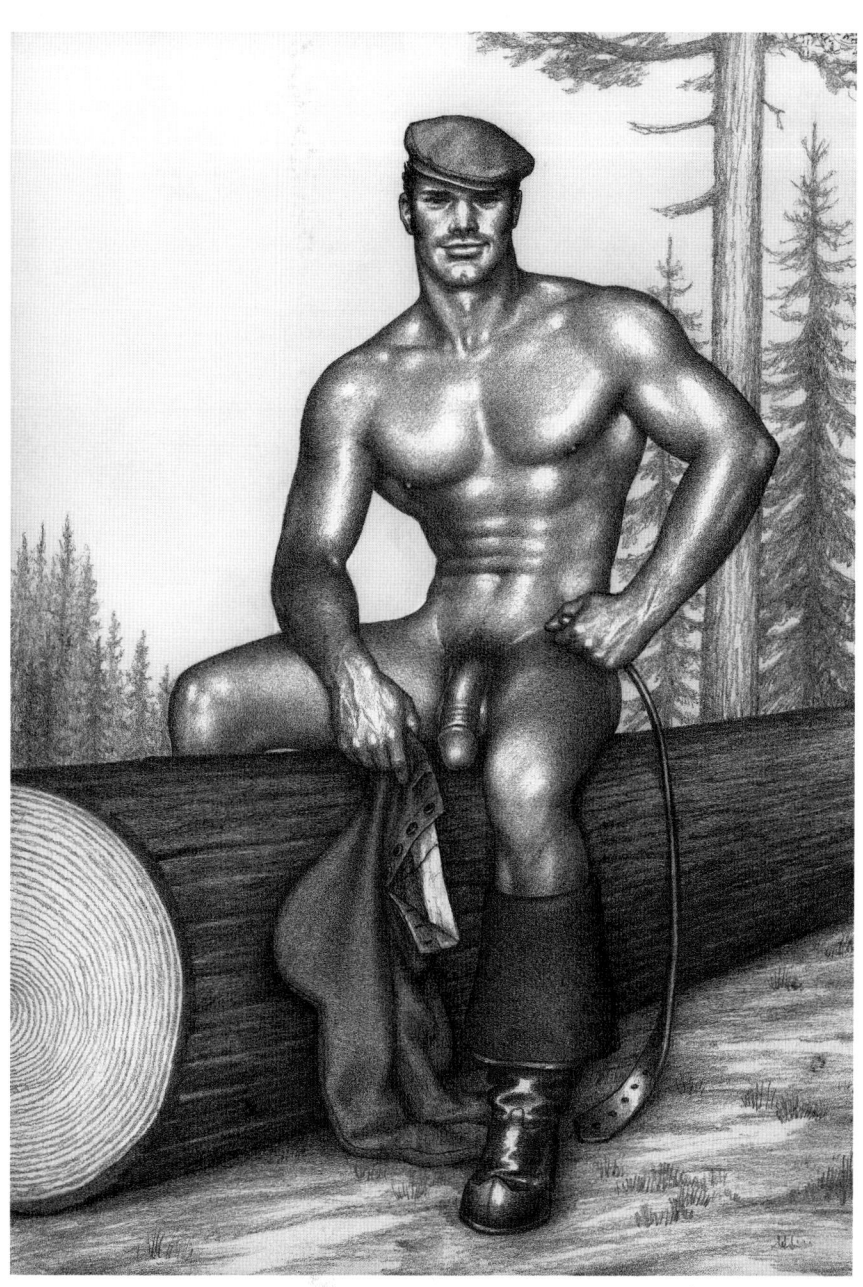

OPPOSITE 1968, graphite on paper
ABOVE 1974, graphite on paper

"*For the members of society struggling with the image of gay people previously perpetuated by the media, Tom opened a bold, shiny new door into the 'club' of traditional masculinity.*"
—LUCY FREELAND, THE CULTURE TRIP

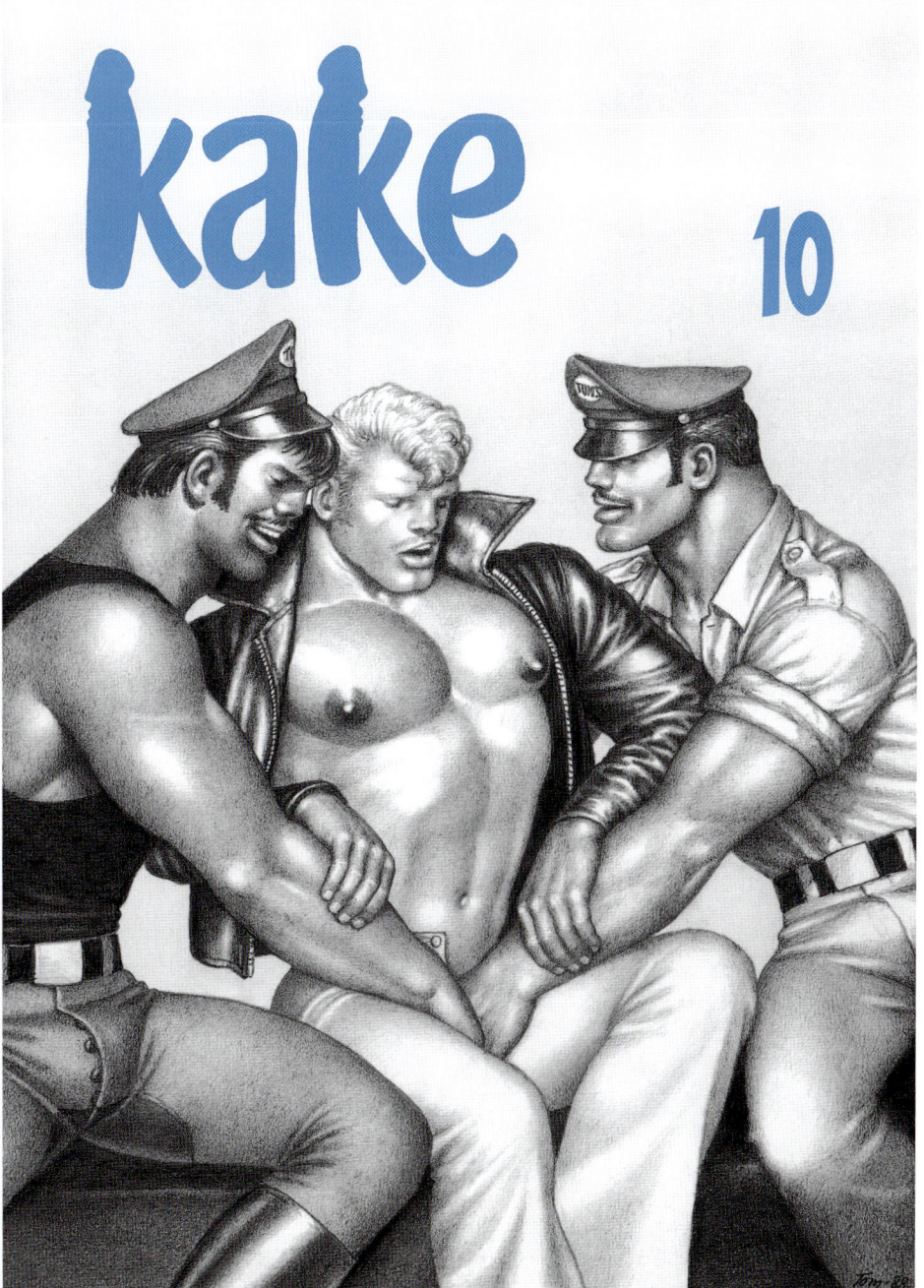

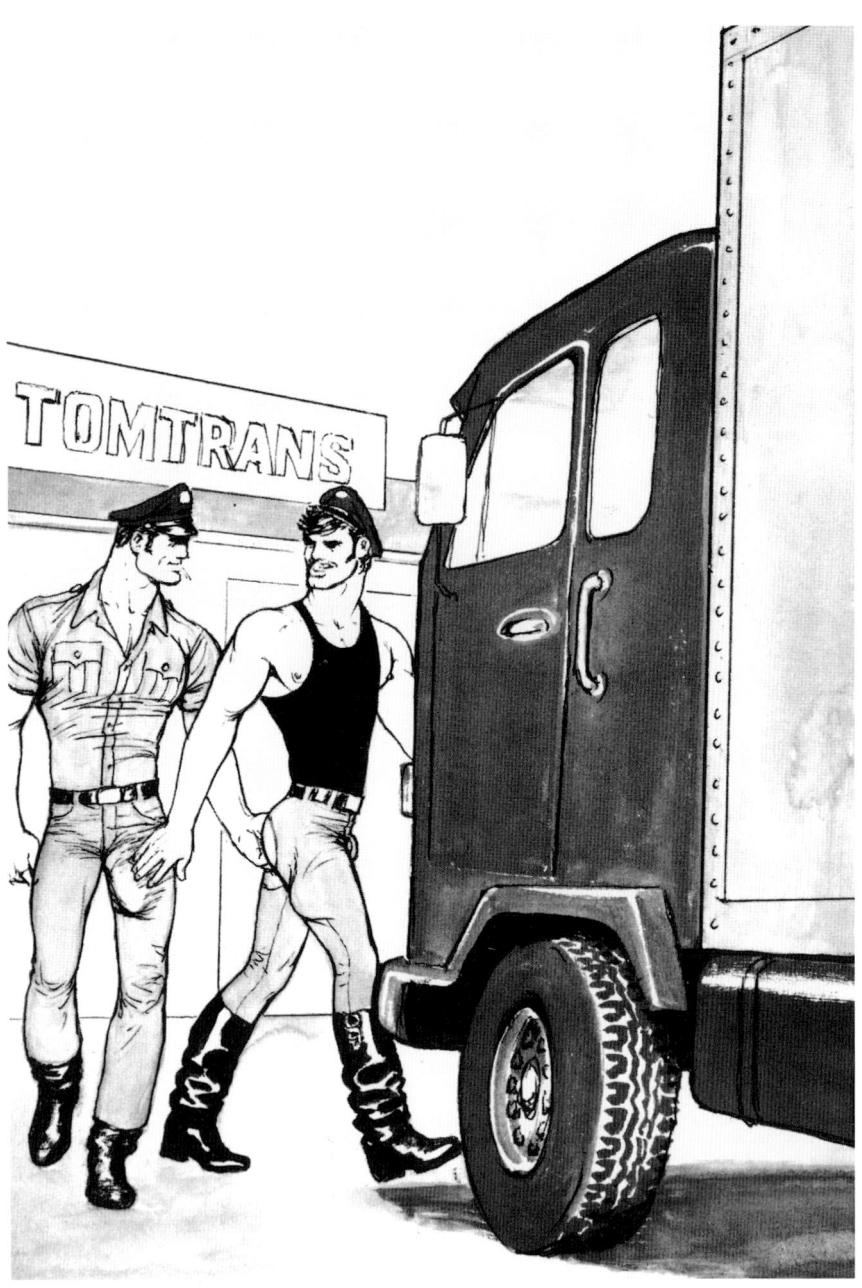

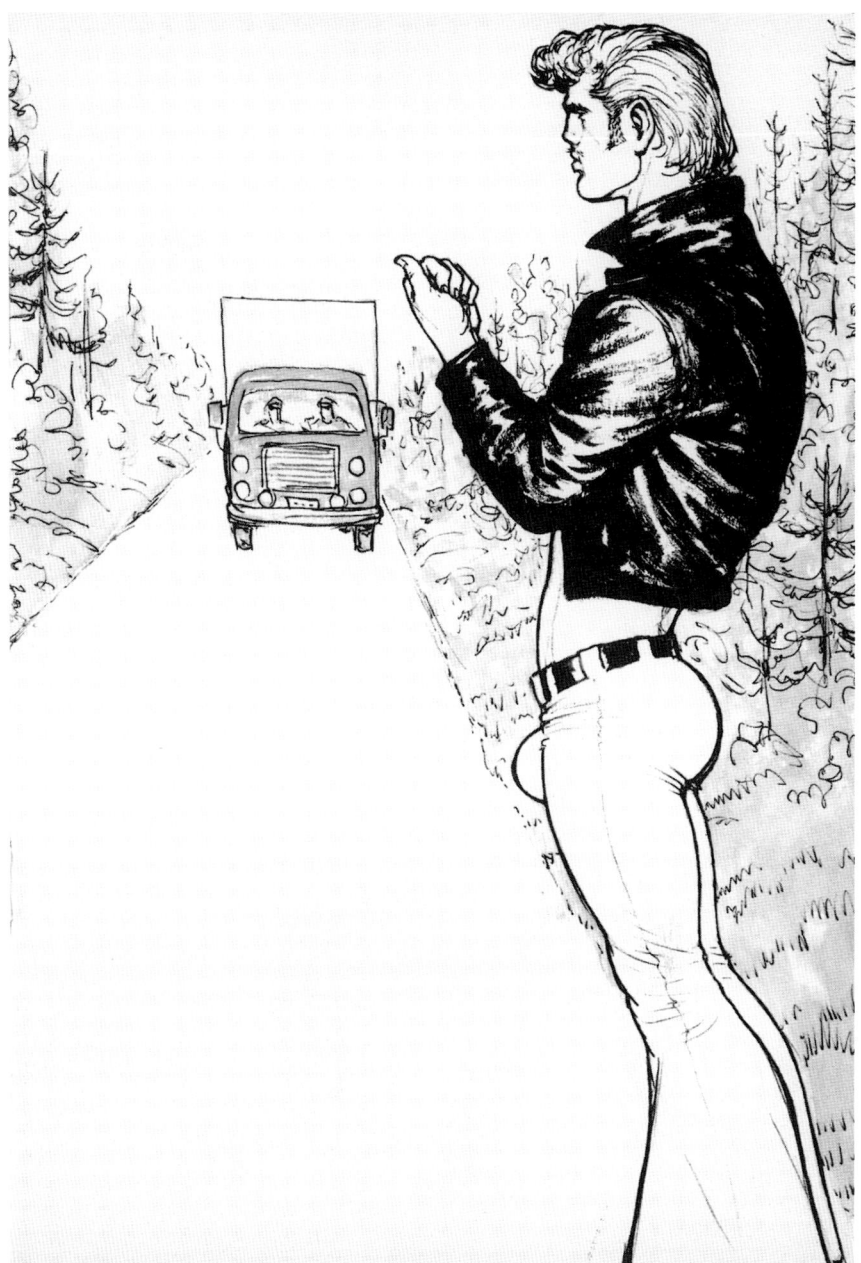

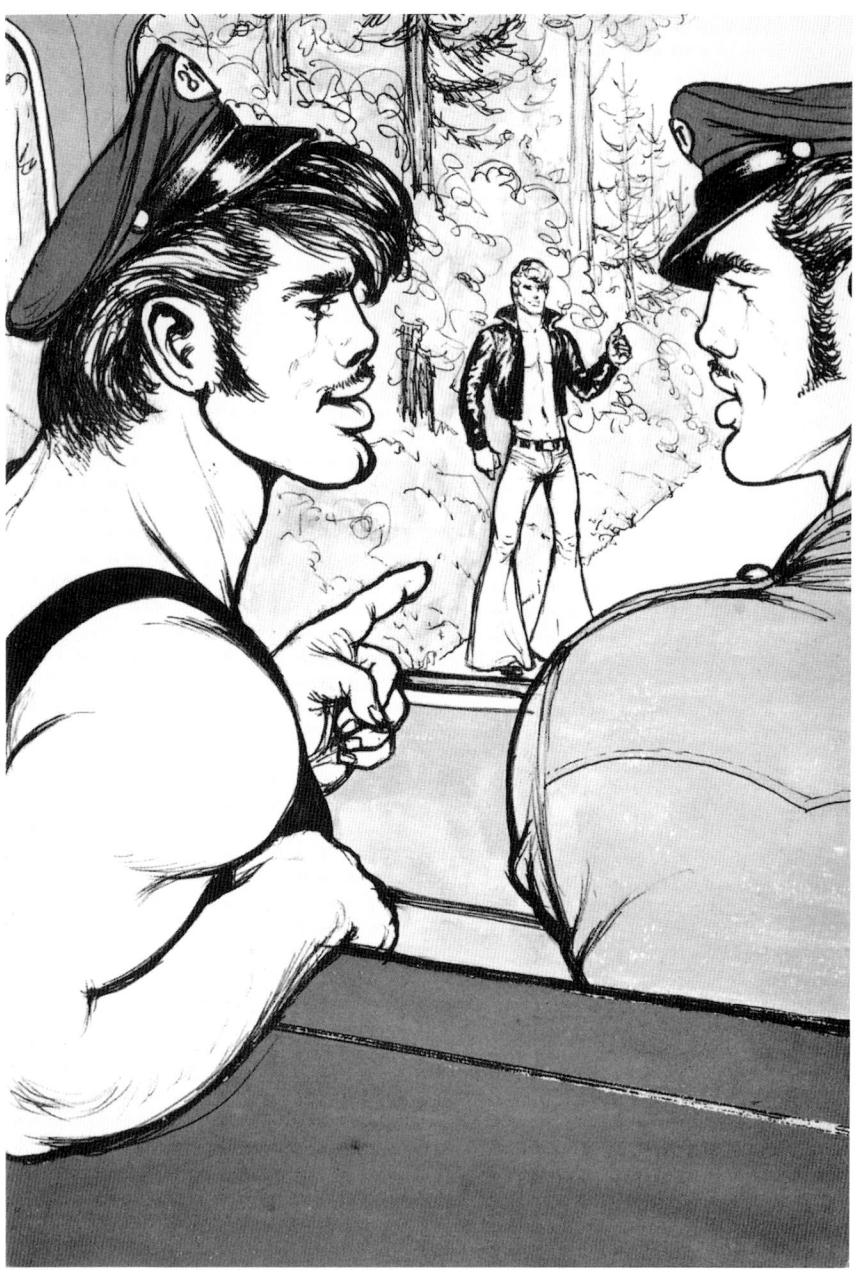

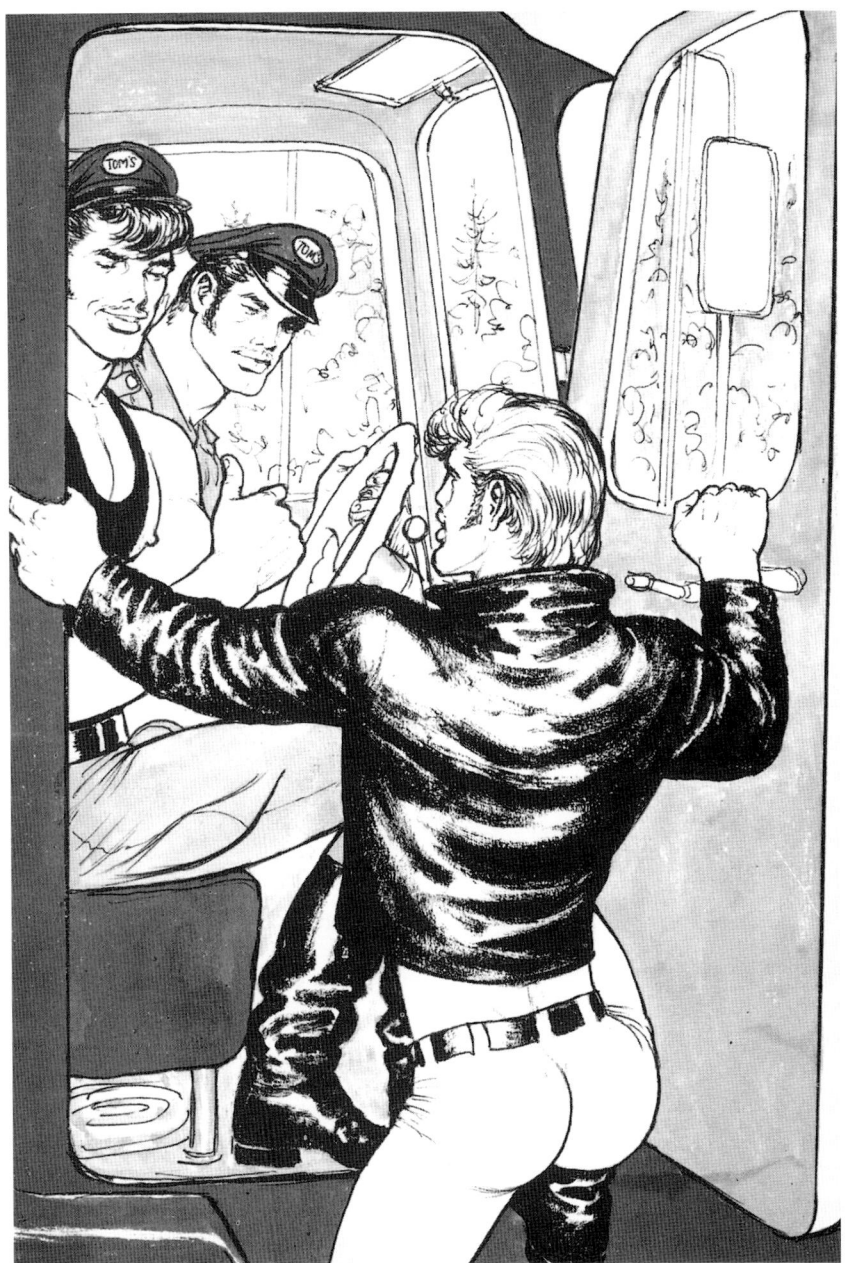

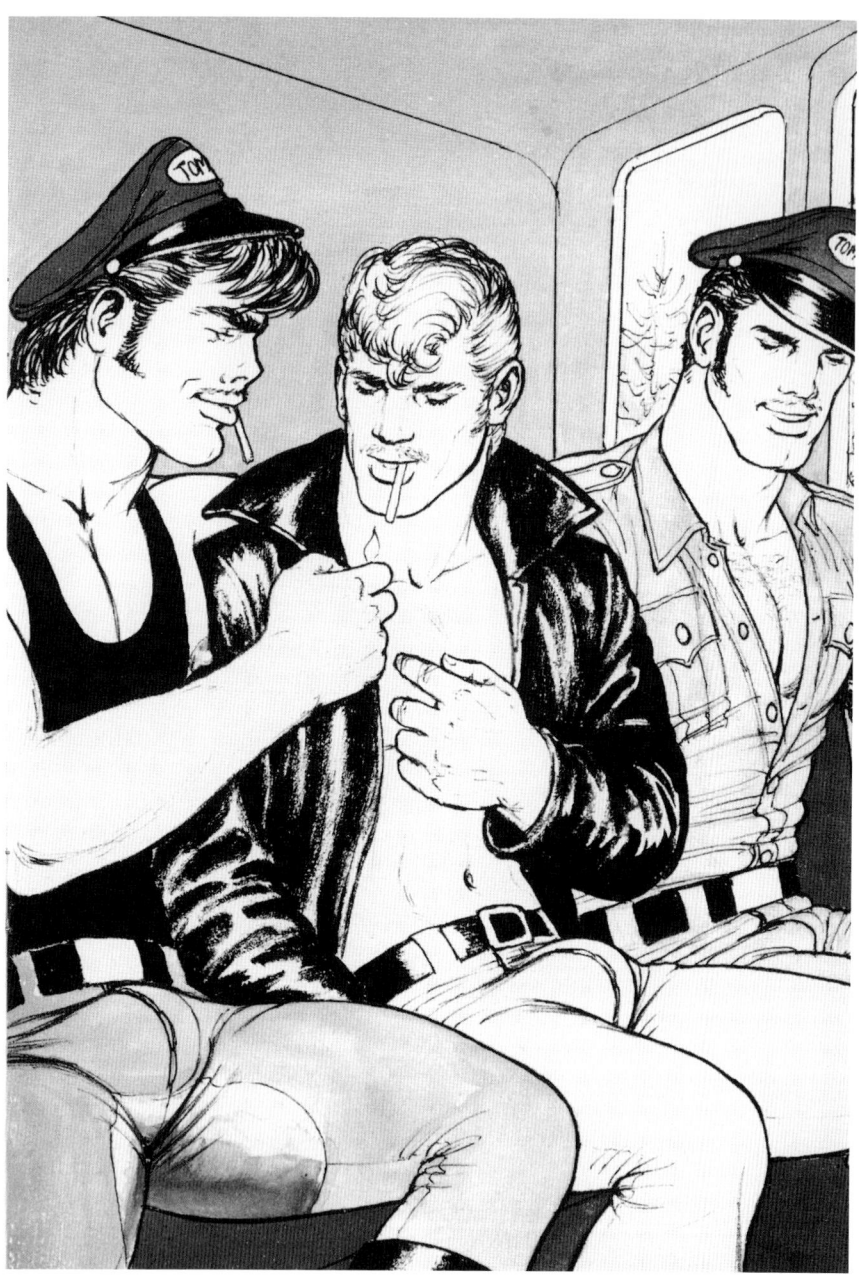

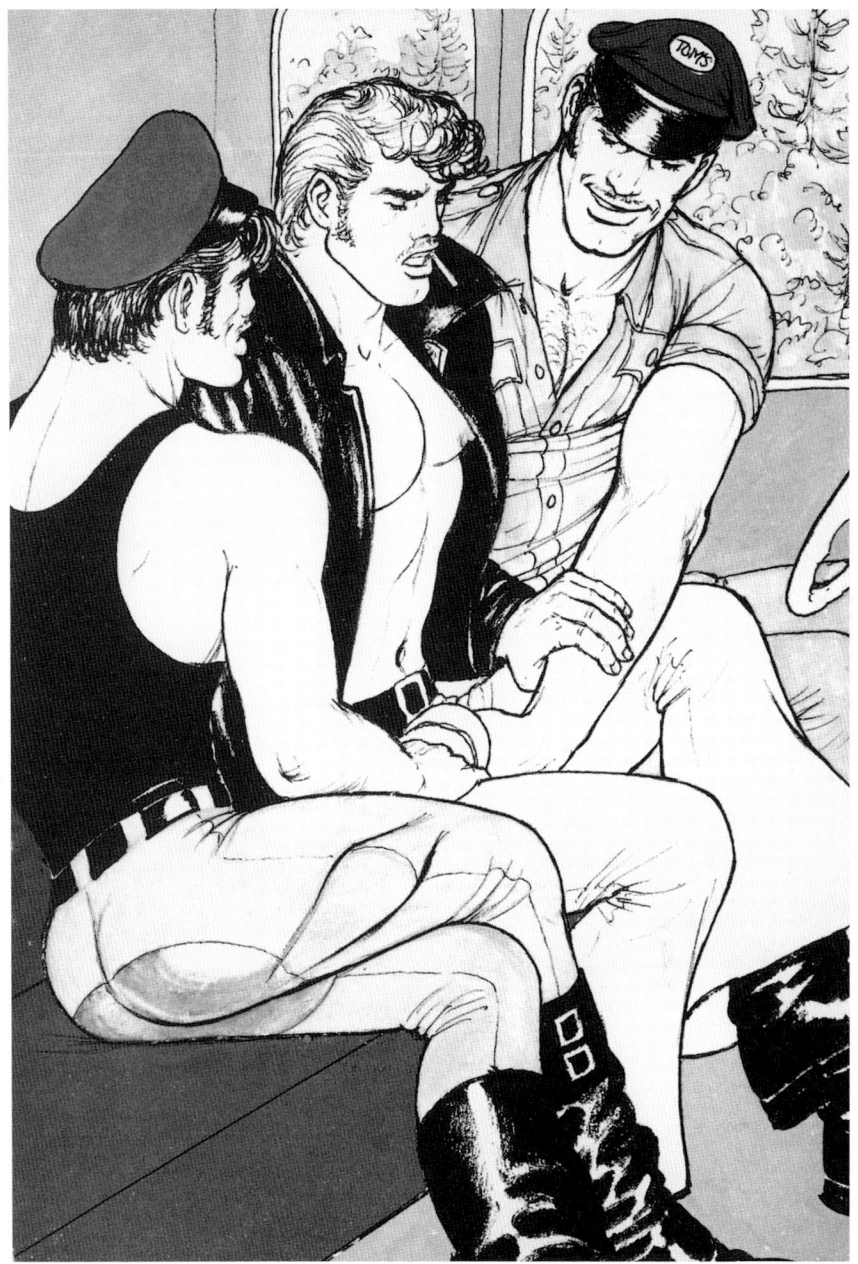

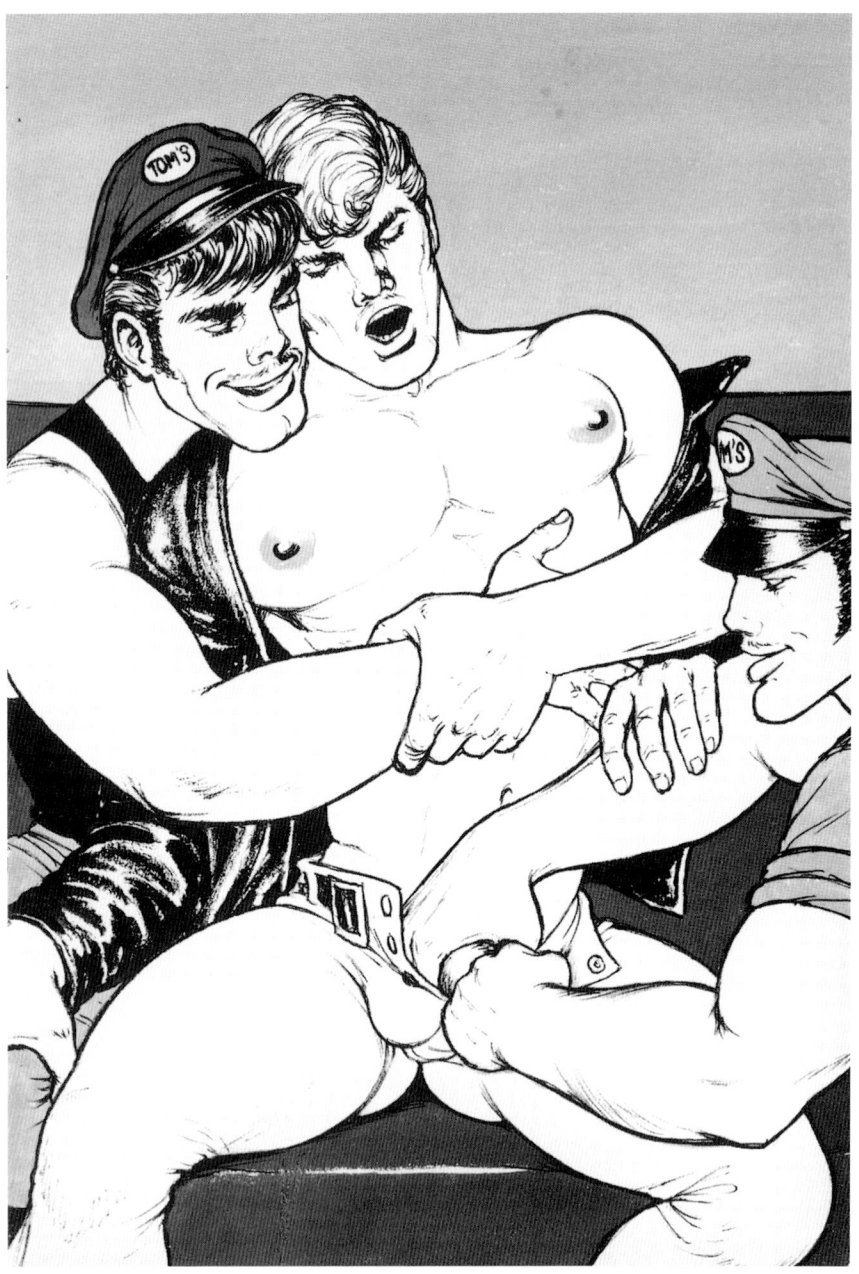

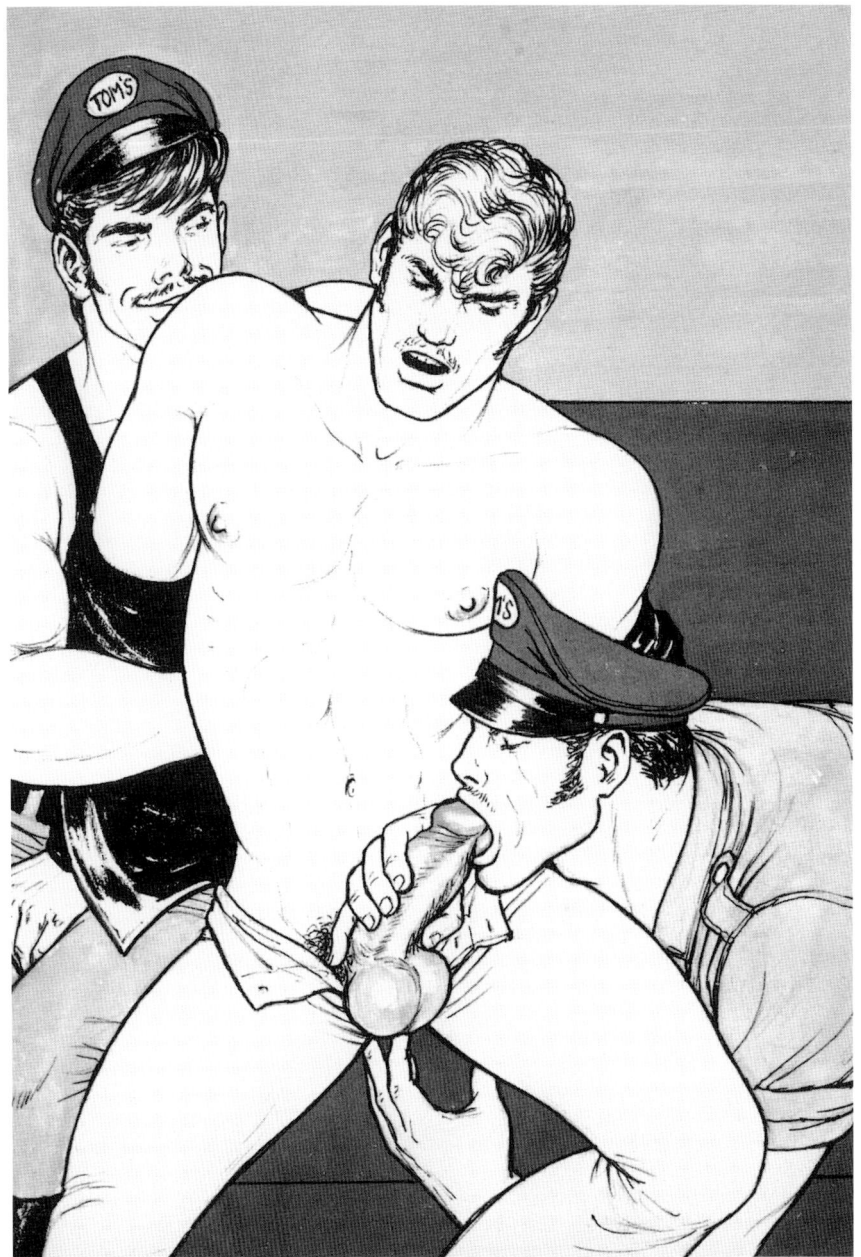

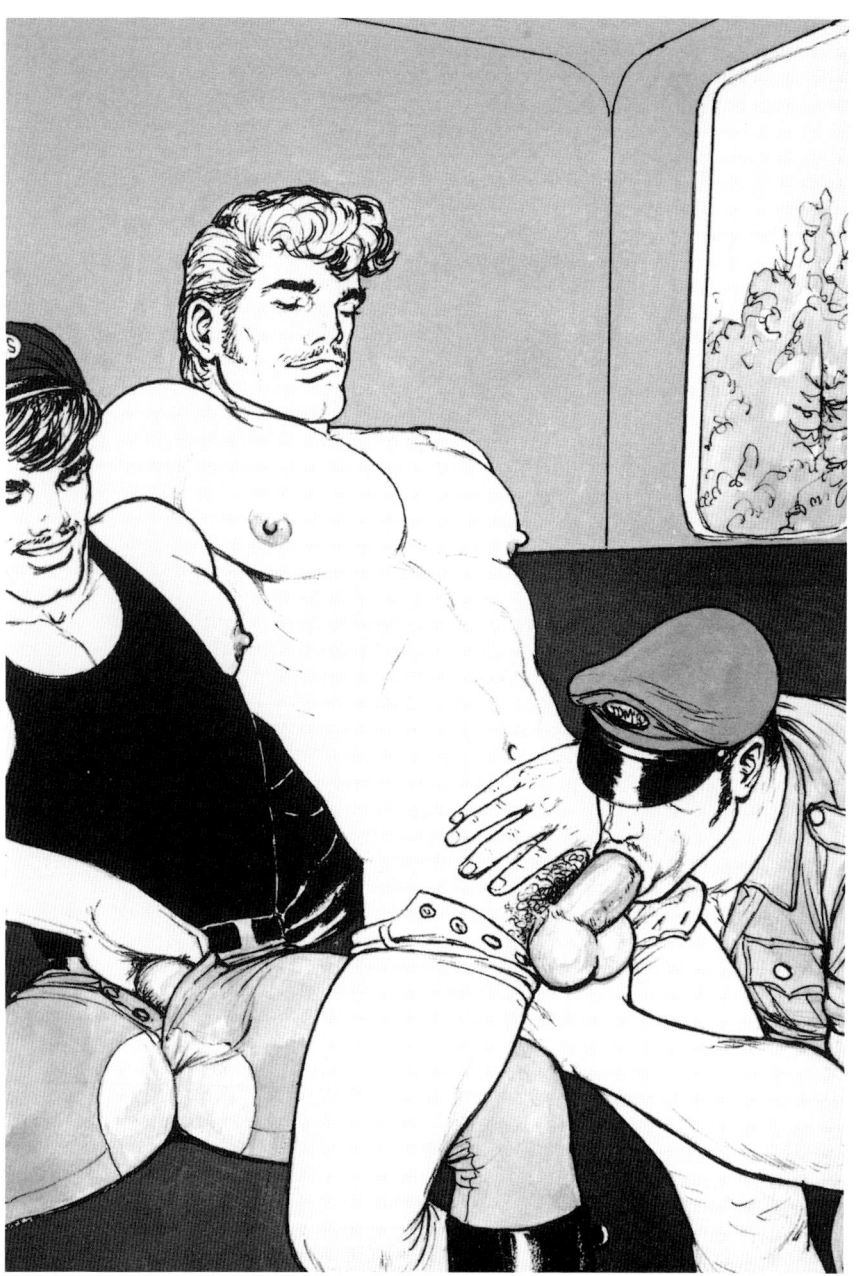

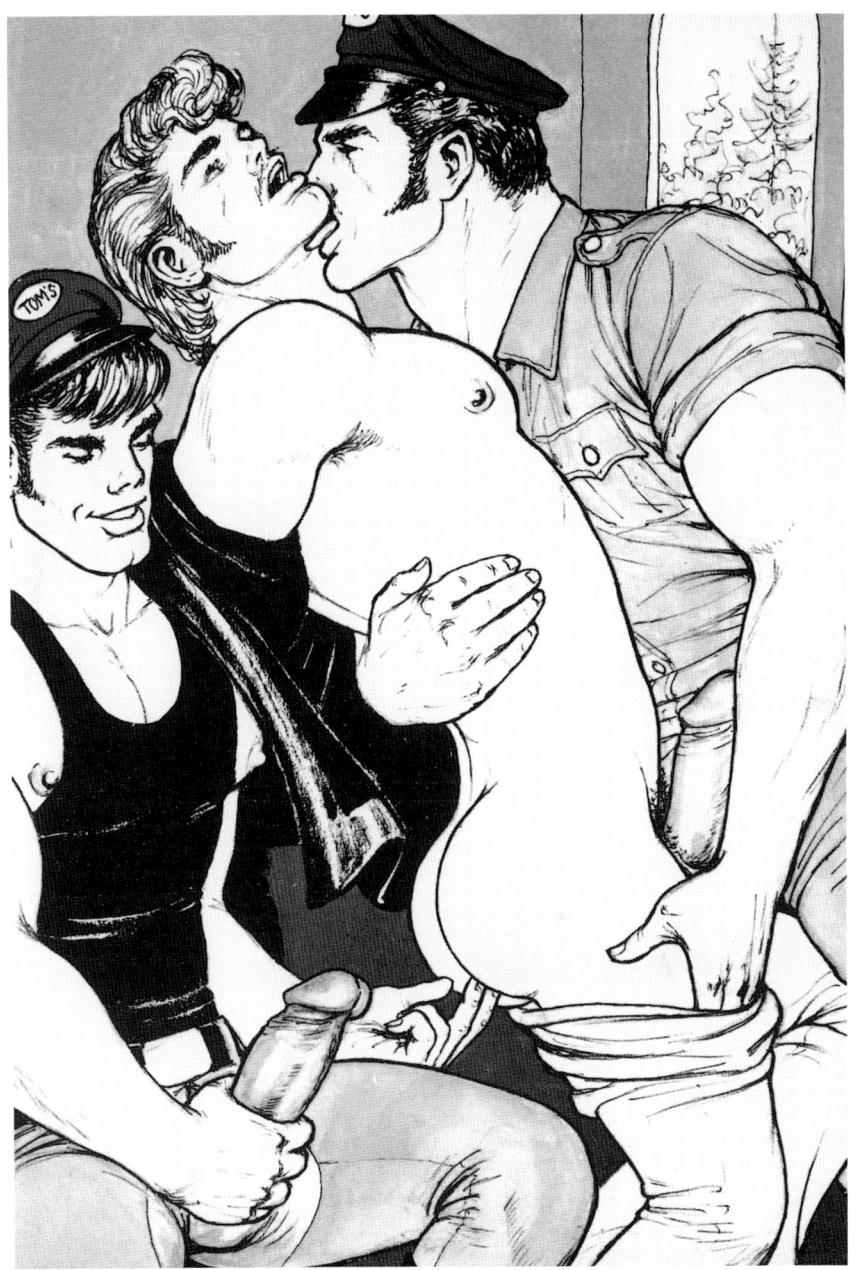

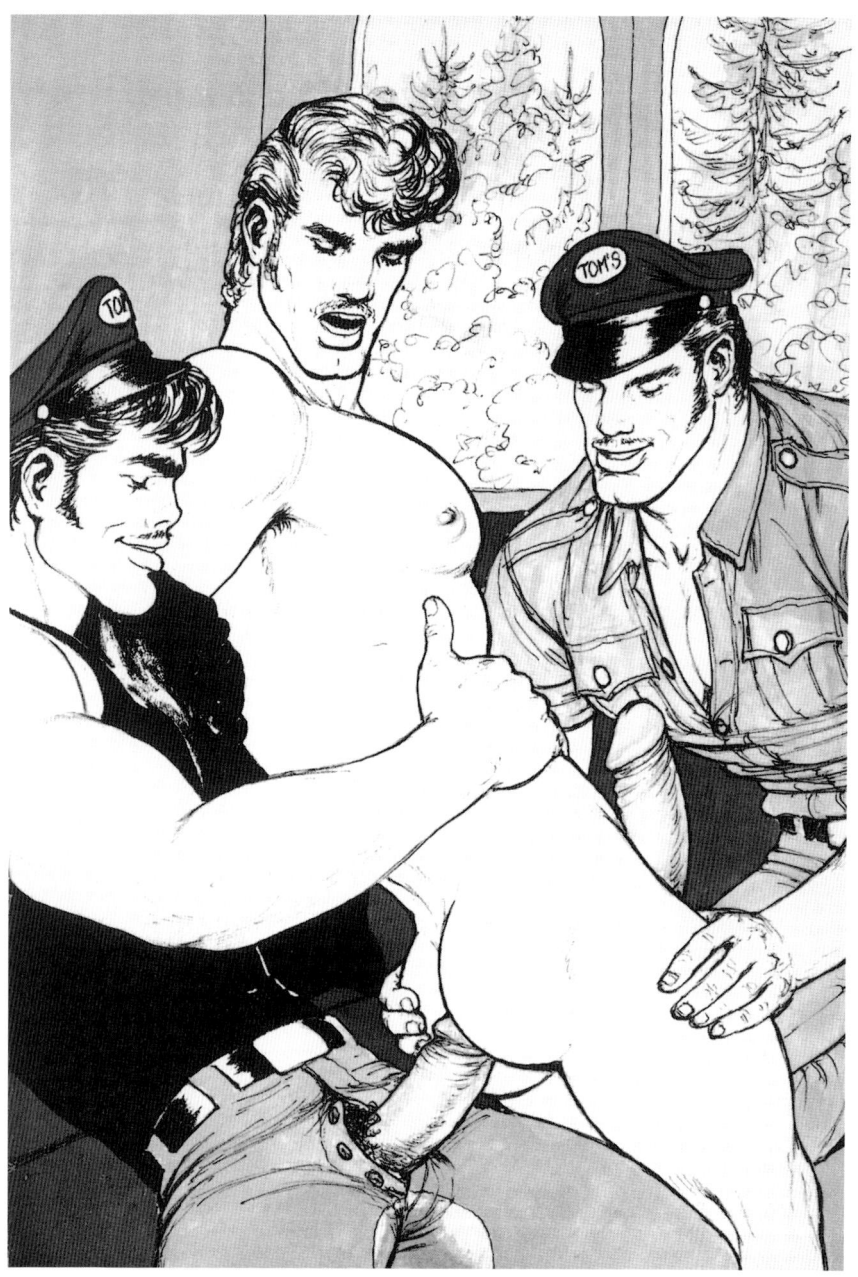

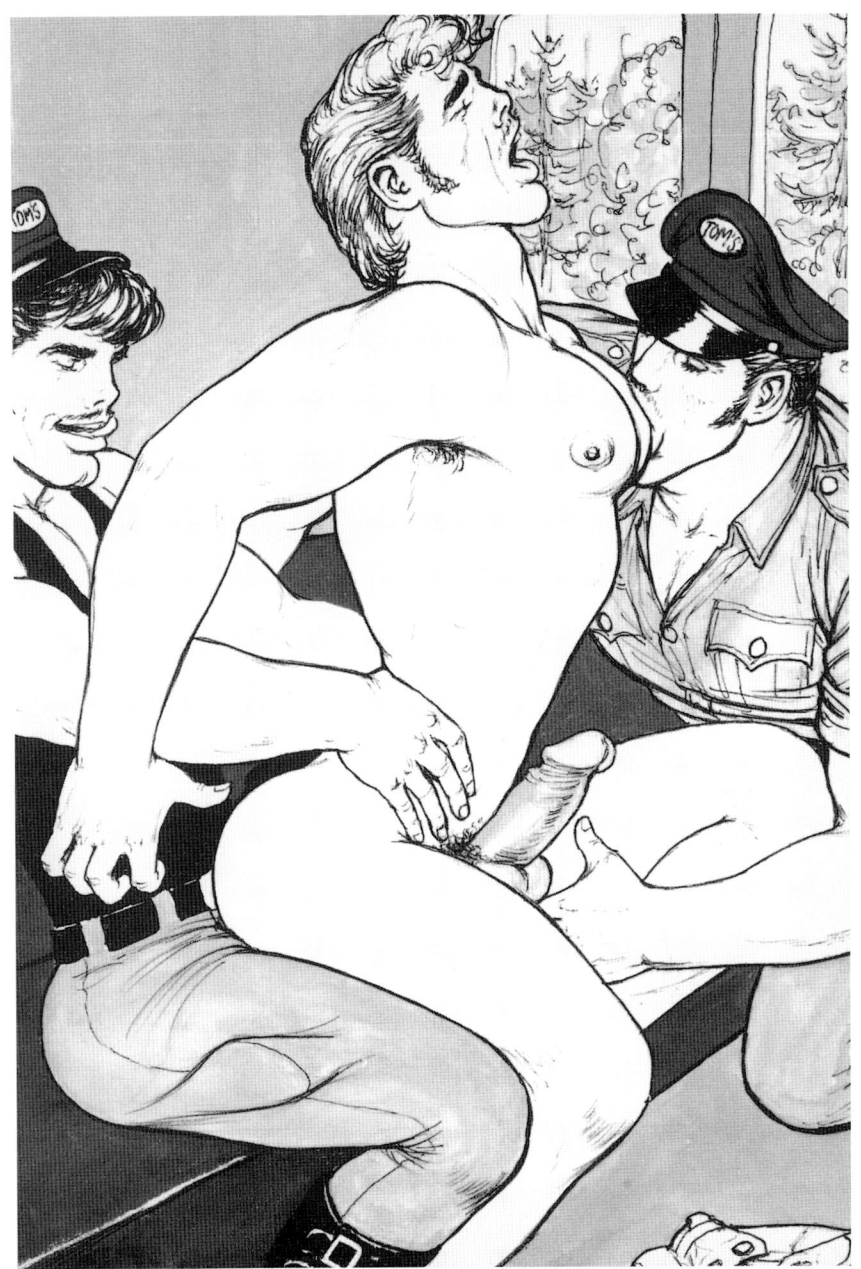

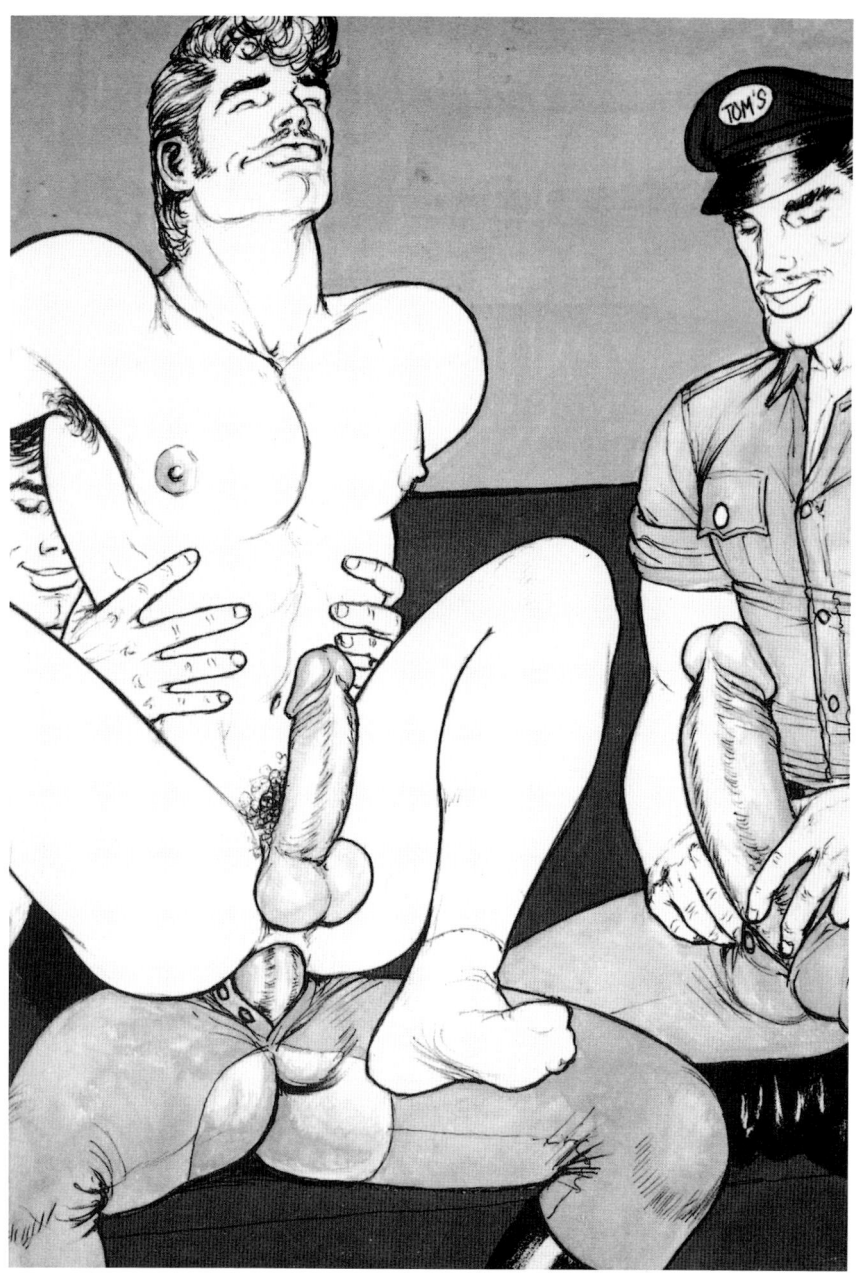

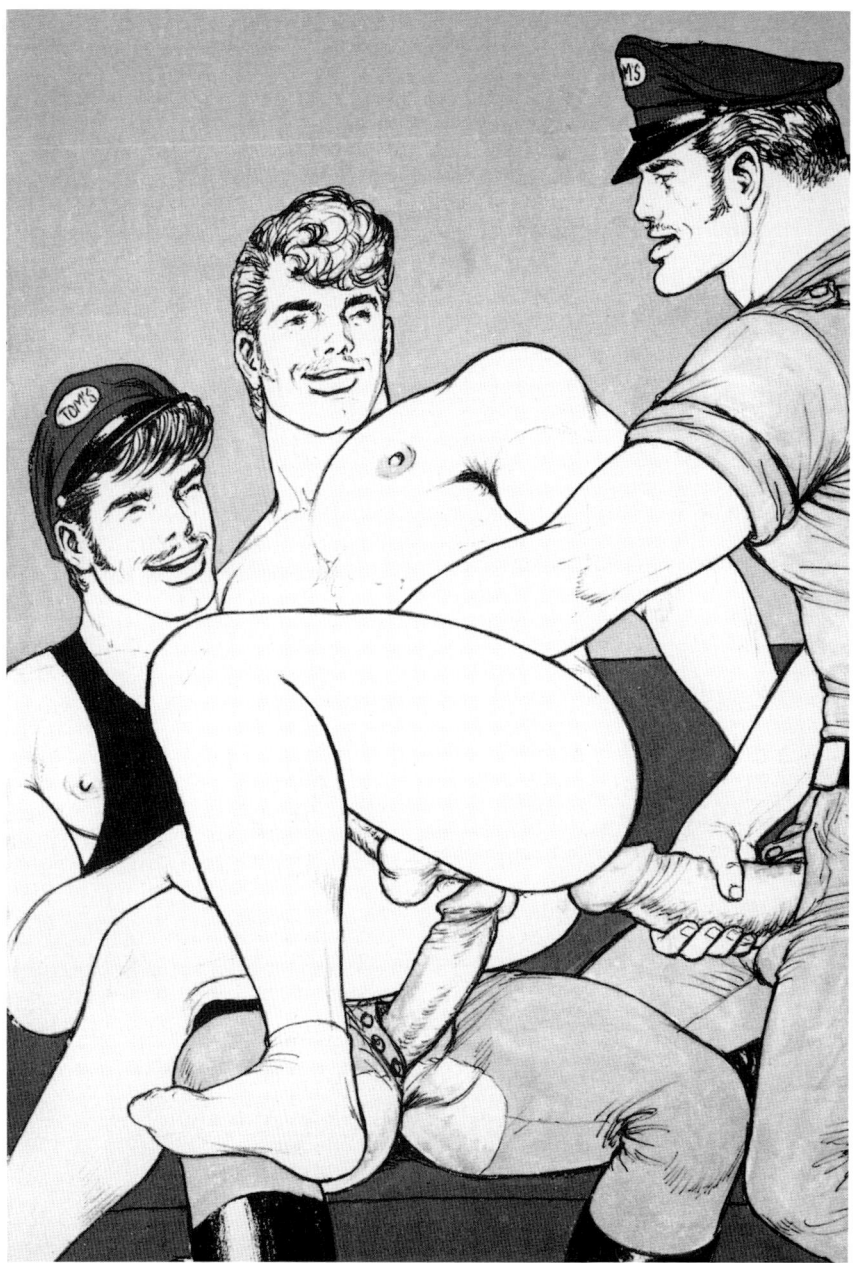

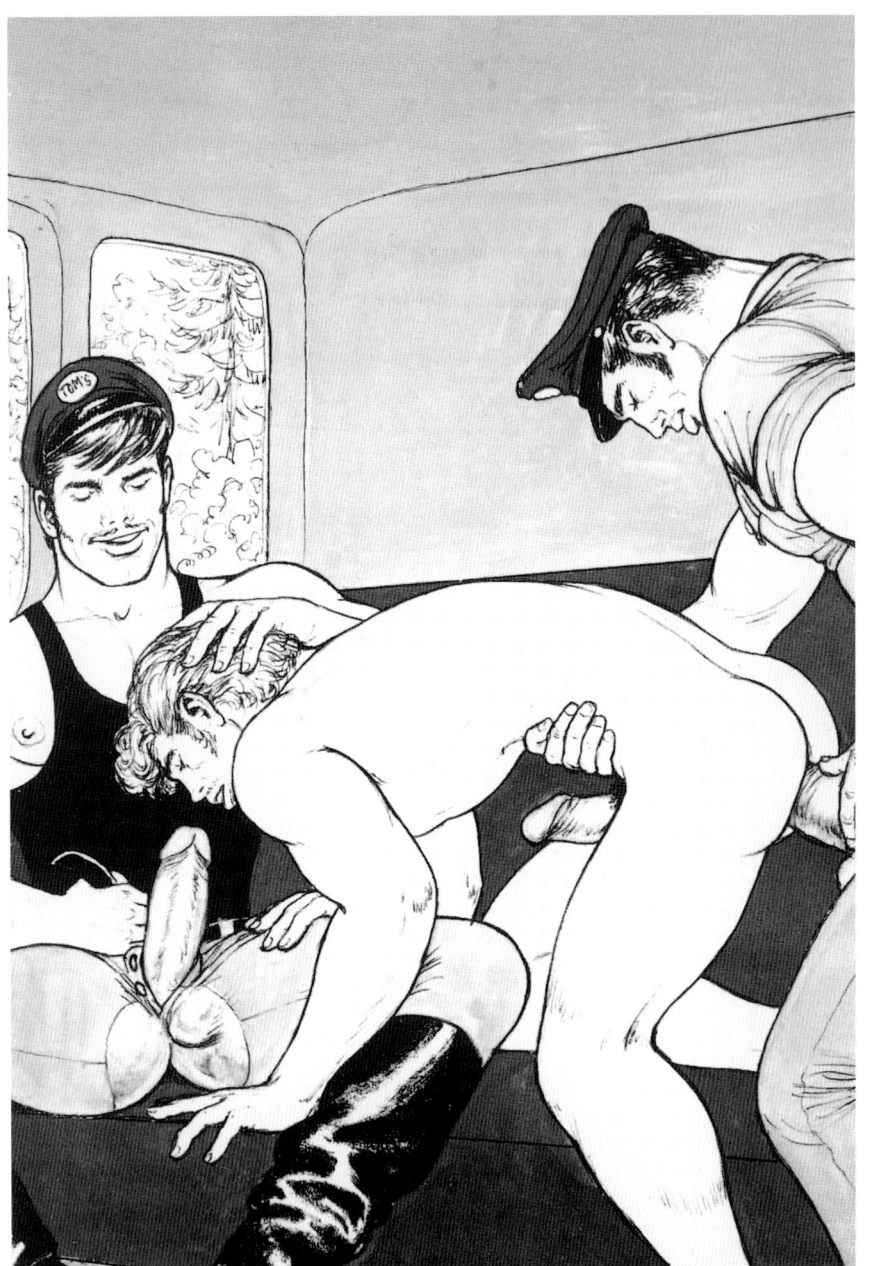

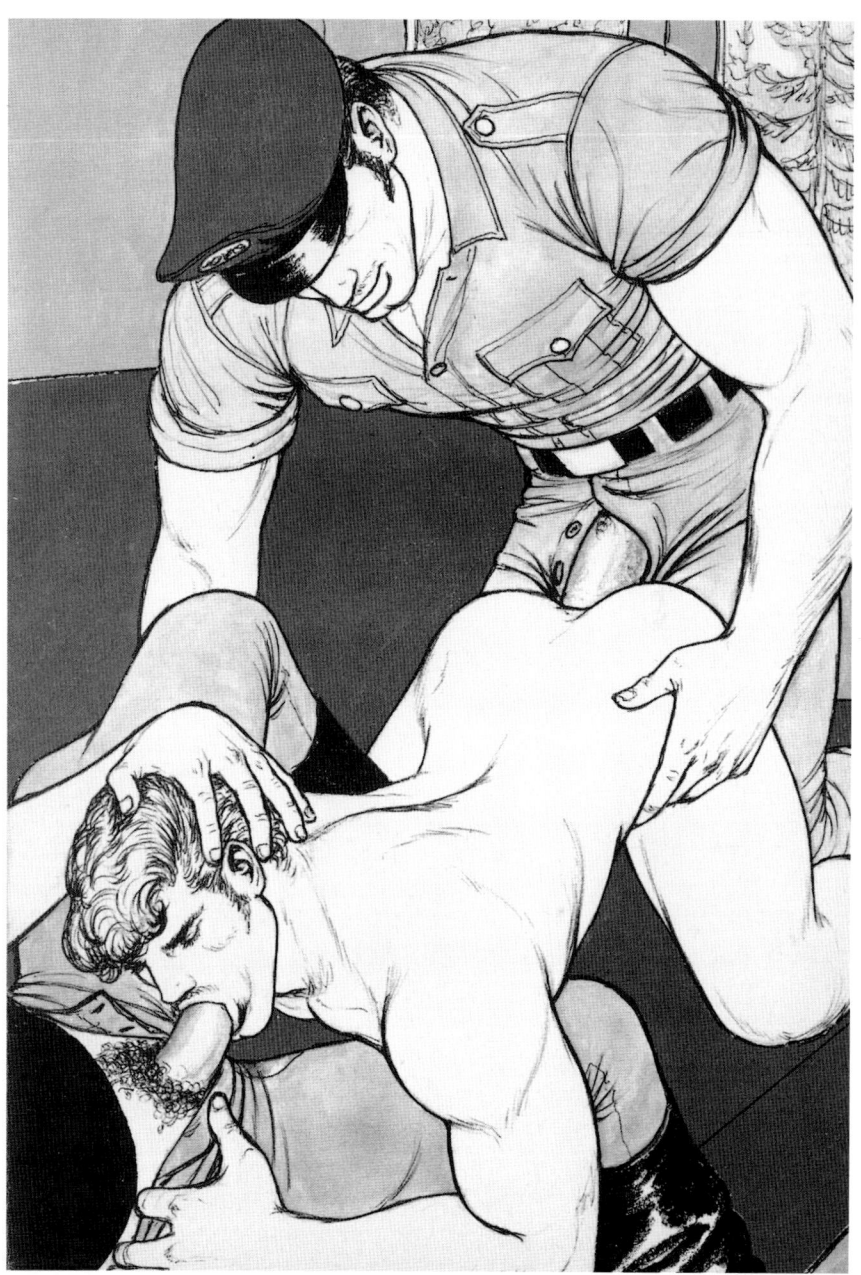

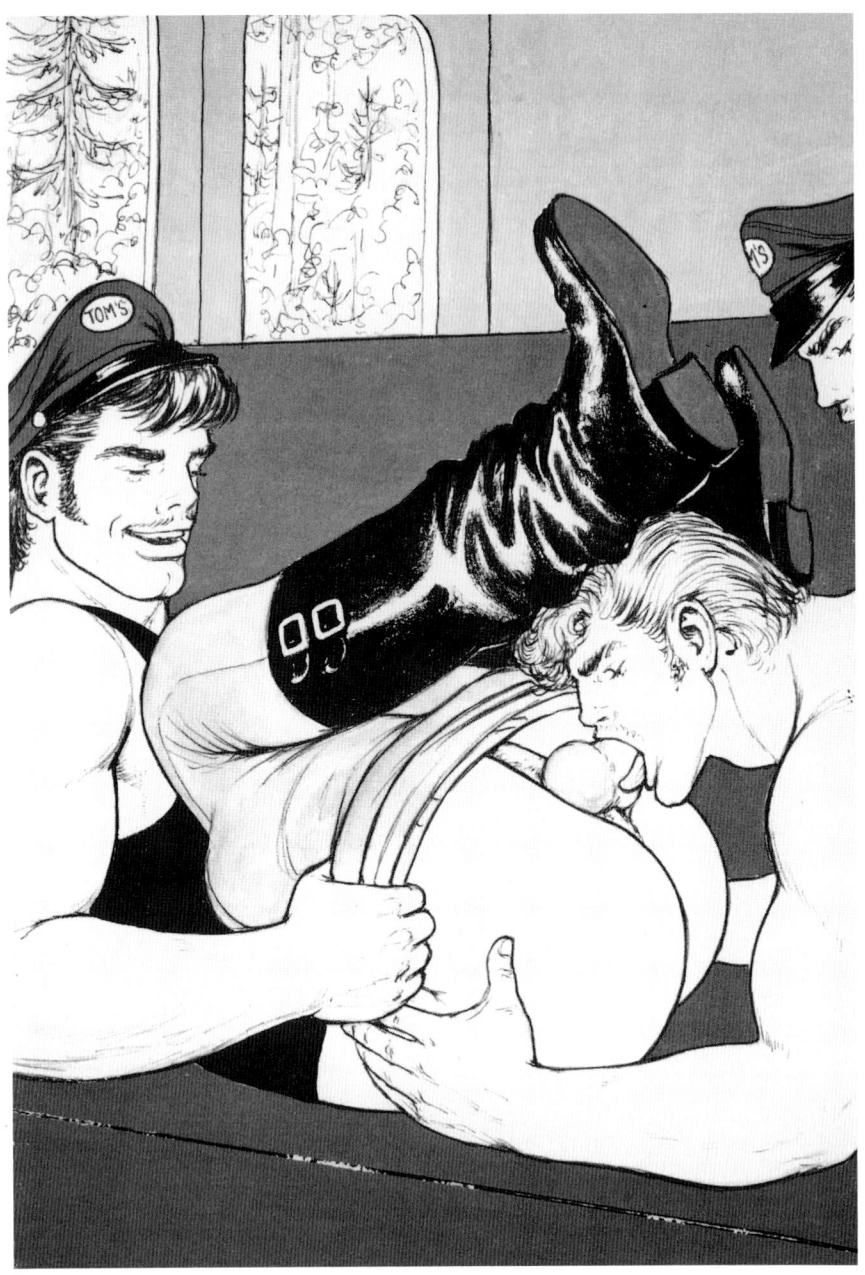

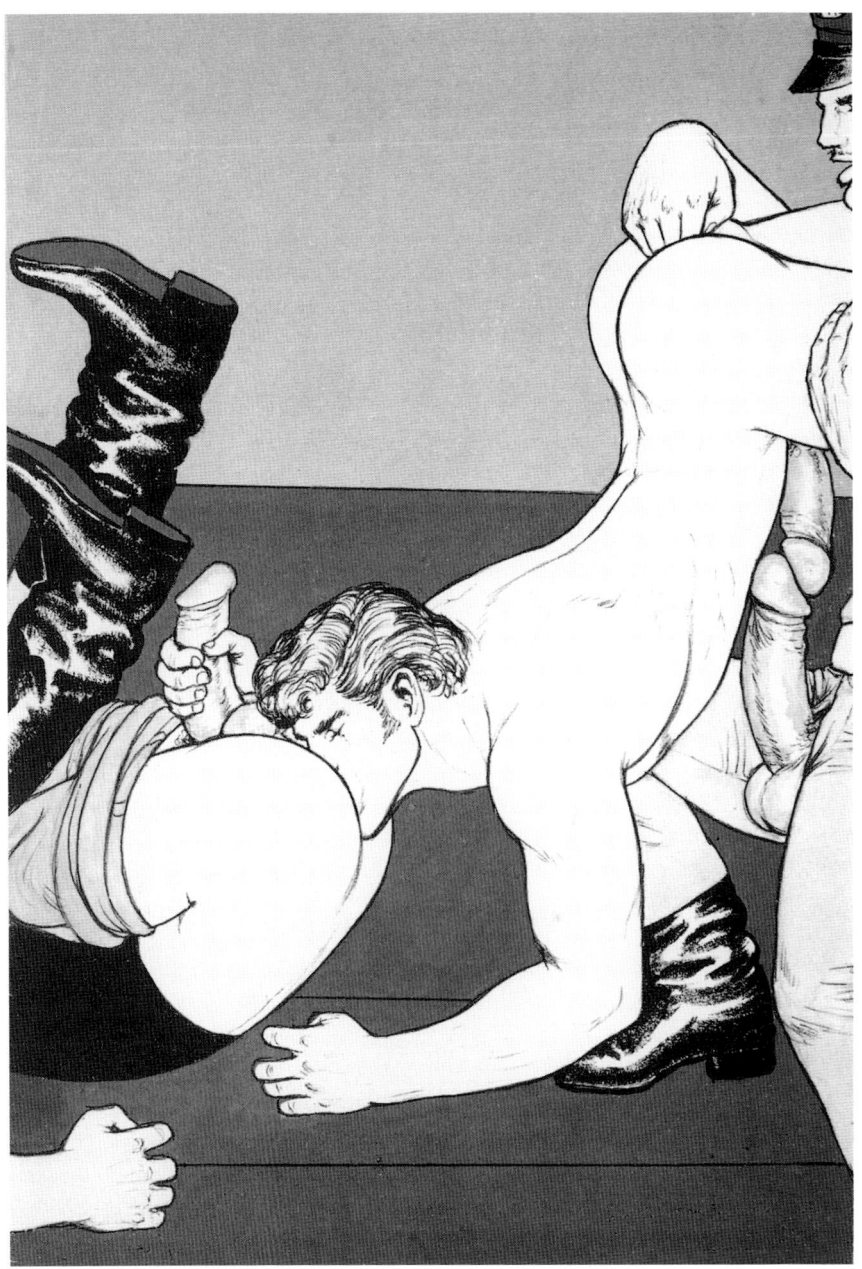

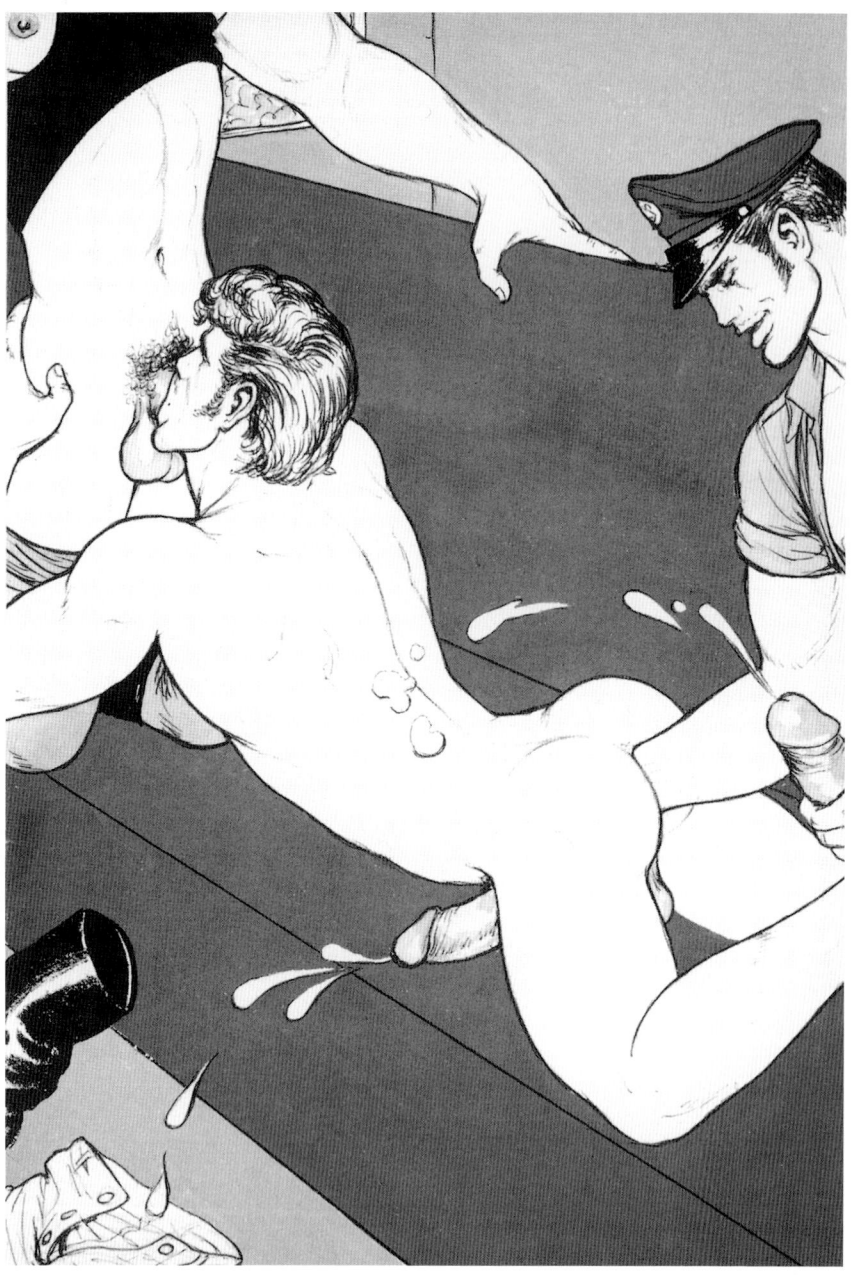

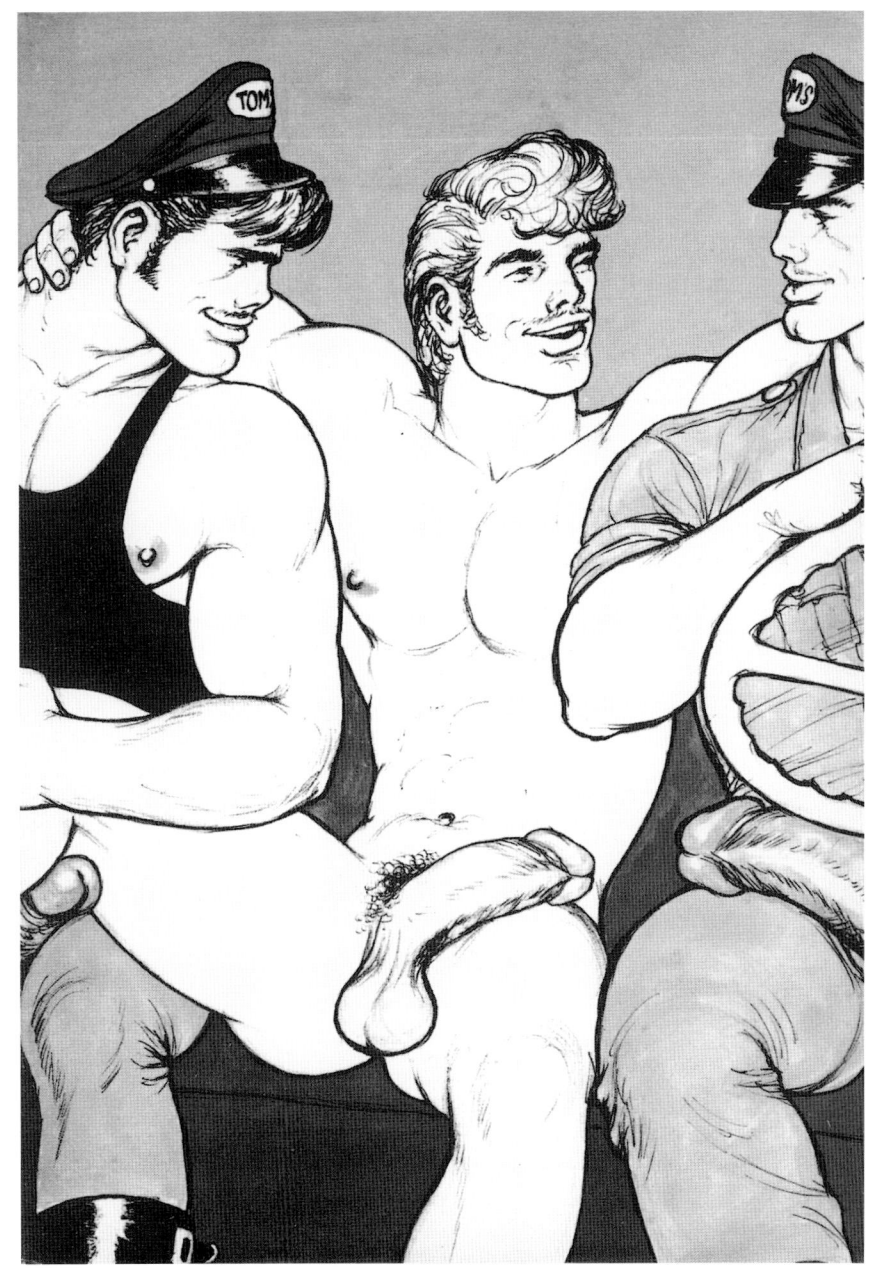

"Tom's sculptured physiques descend, via modern muscle magazines, from Michelangelo's homoerotic dreams, where the male chest and biceps are extravagantly enlarged and complicated."
—CAMILLE PAGLIA

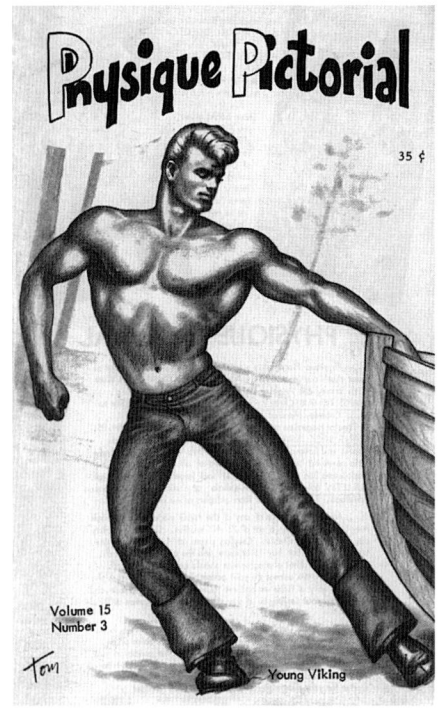

LEFT Cover of *Physique Pictorial*, Vol. 15, No. 3, 1966
OPPOSITE 1957, graphite on paper

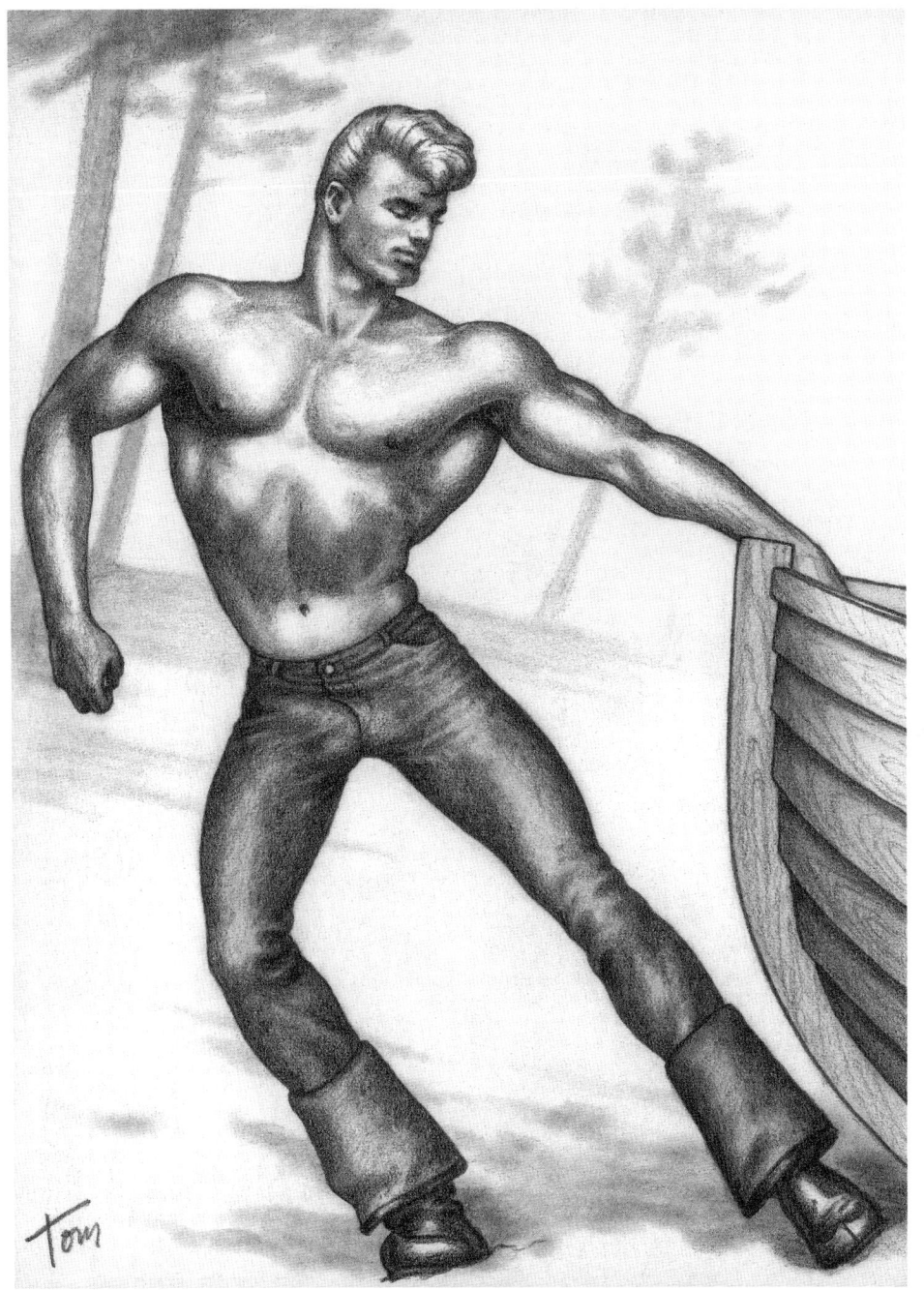

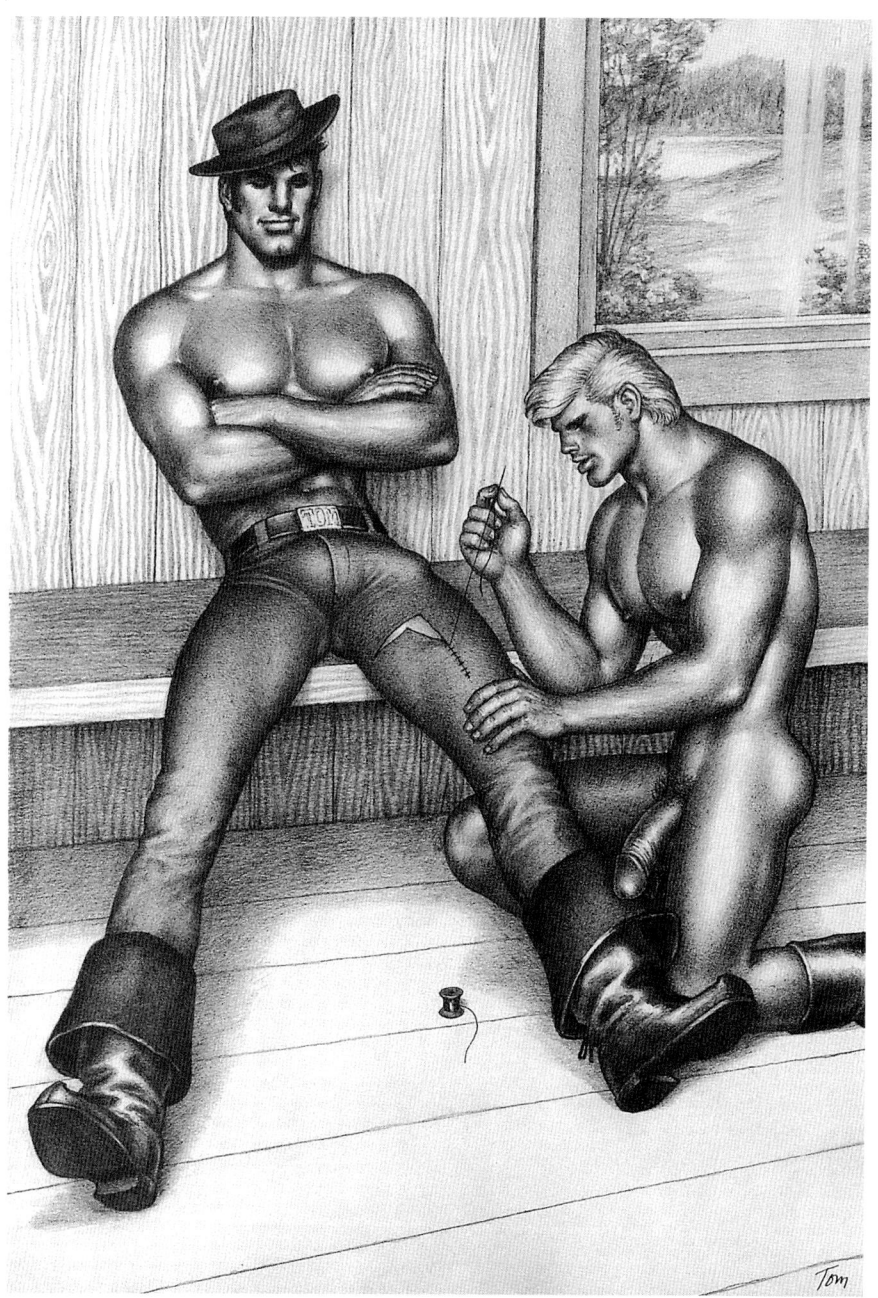

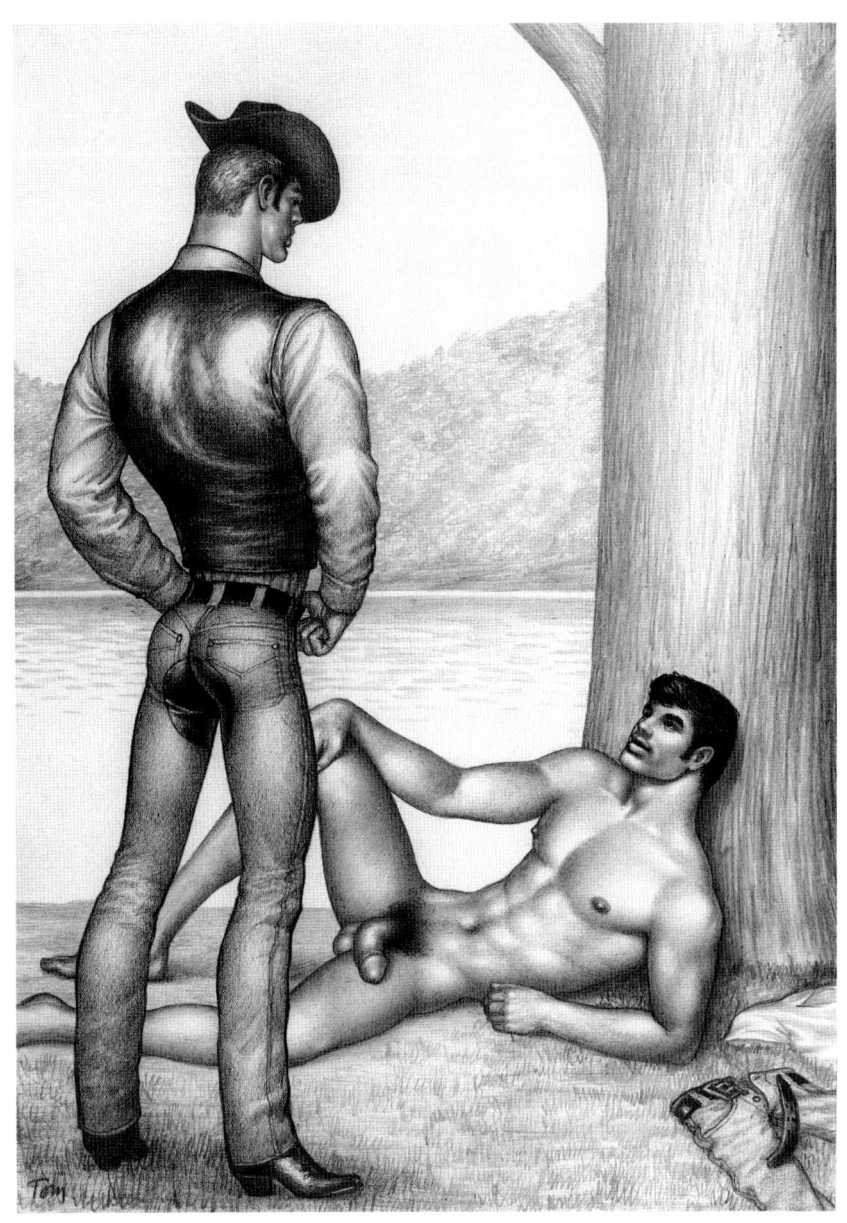

OPPOSITE 1974, graphite on paper
ABOVE 1965, graphite on paper

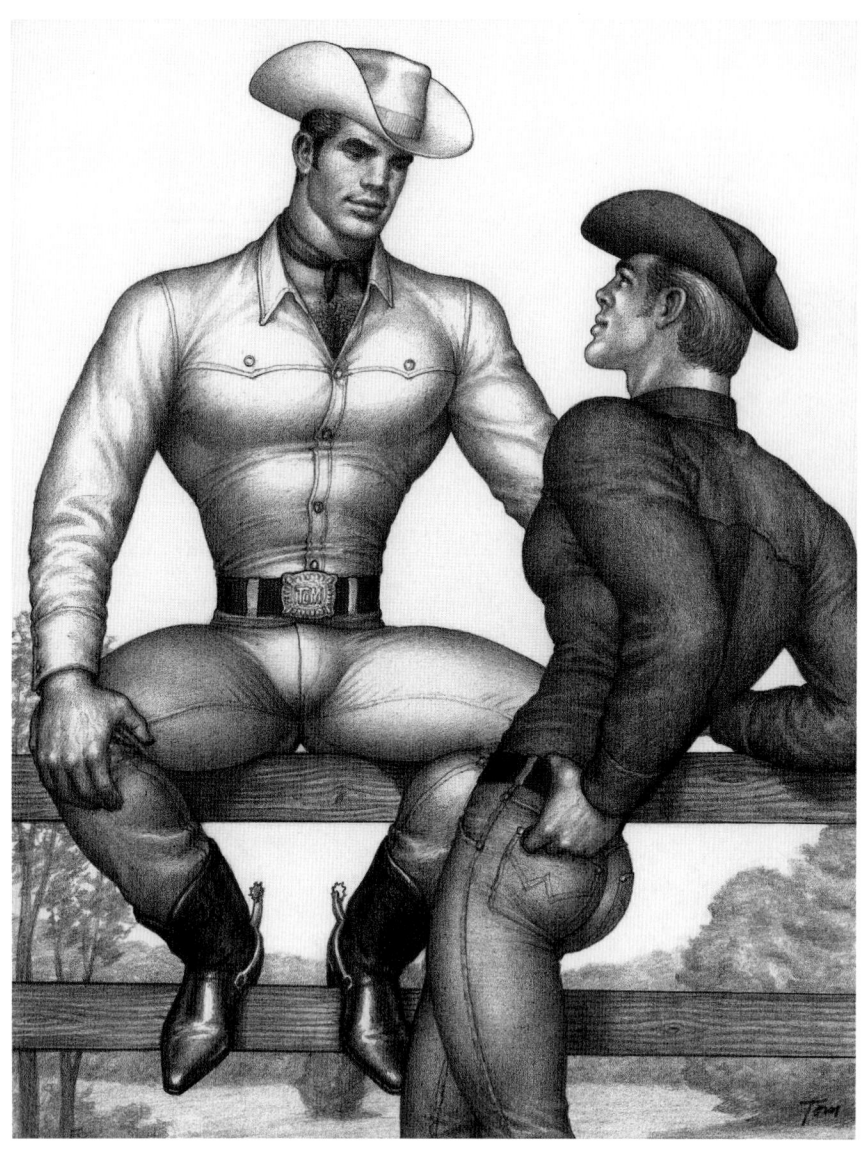

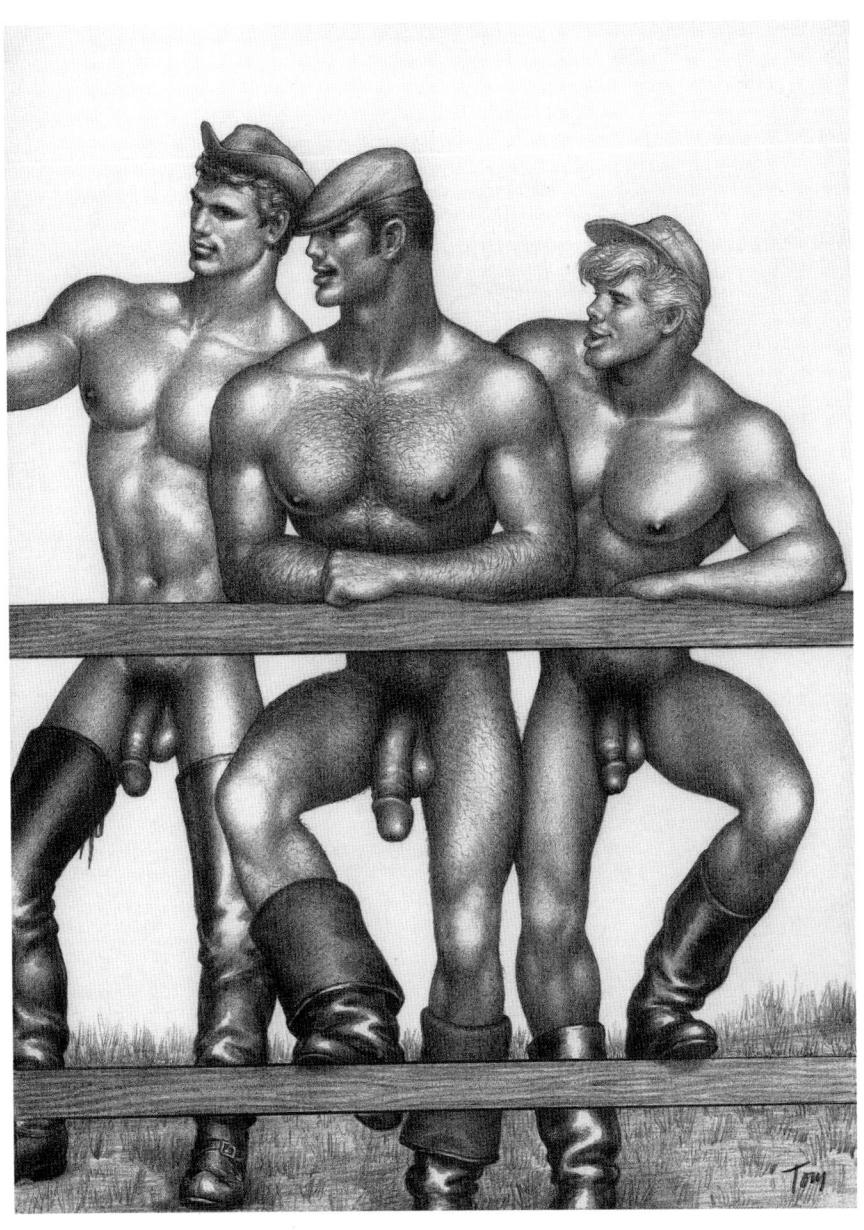

OPPOSITE AND ABOVE 1964, graphite on paper

"*I believe there is a lot to the world that can't be seen or touched, and if you turn away from that you are avoiding an important part of life, maybe the very heart of it.*"

—TOM OF FINLAND

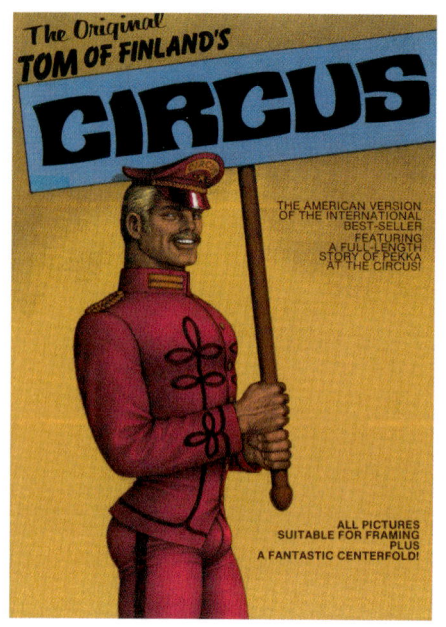

LEFT Cover of *The Original Tom of Finland's Circus,* 1975
OPPOSITE 1975, graphite on paper

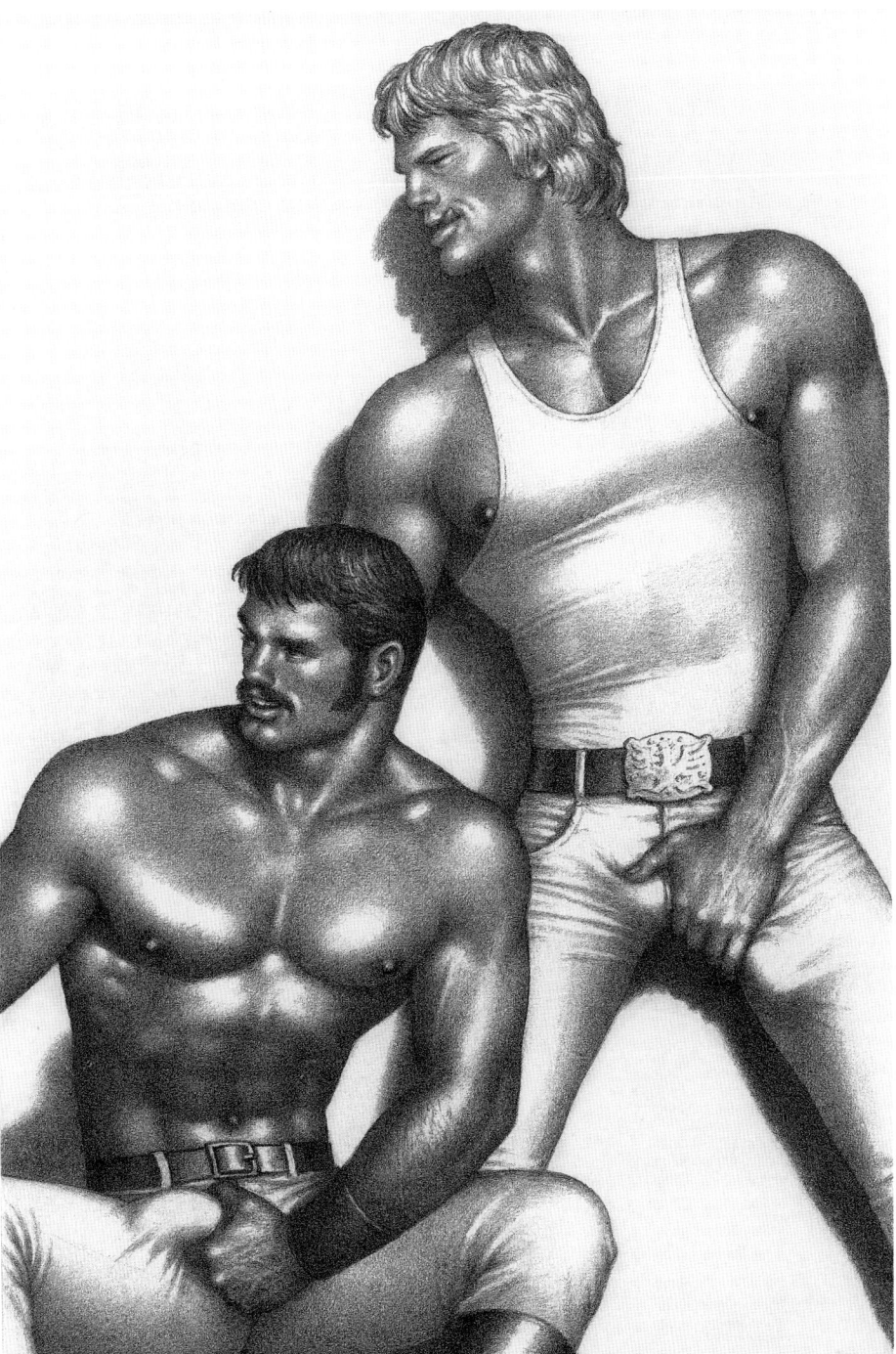

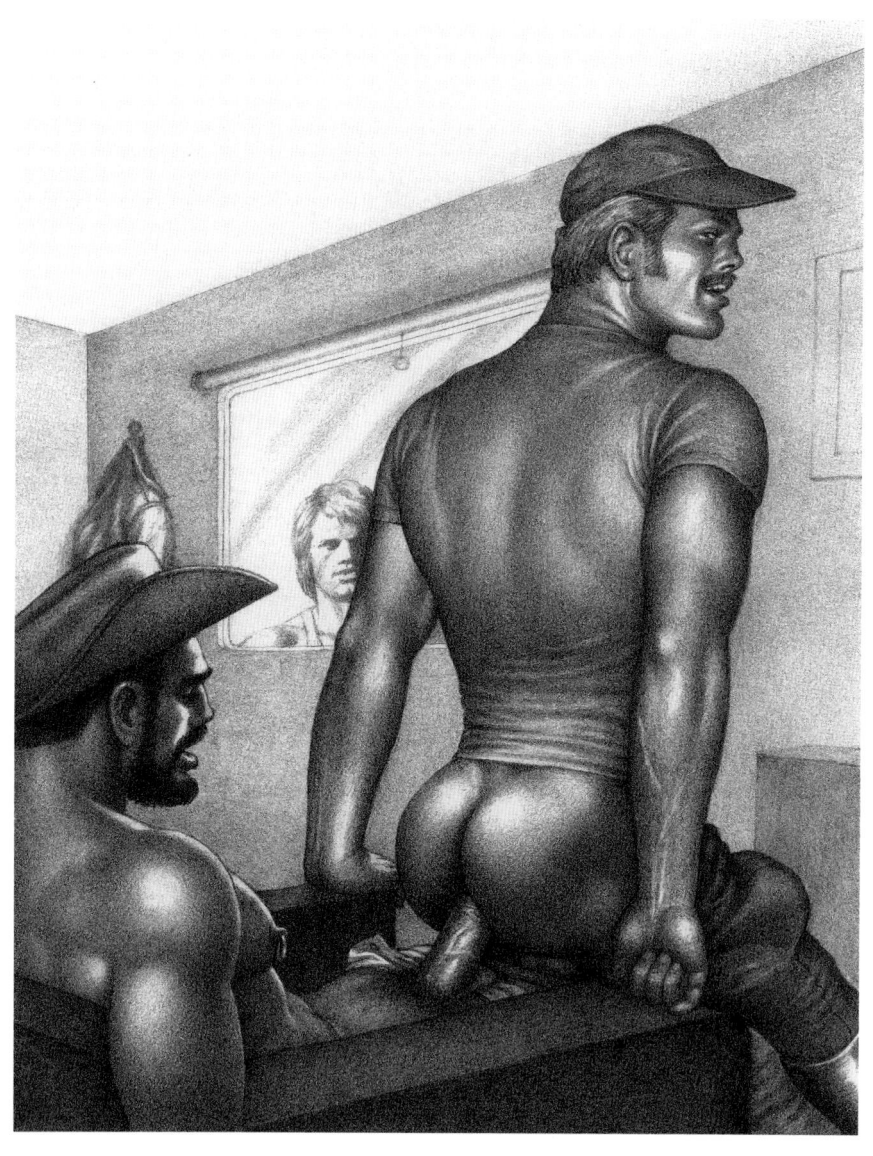

ABOVE AND OPPOSITE 1975, graphite on paper

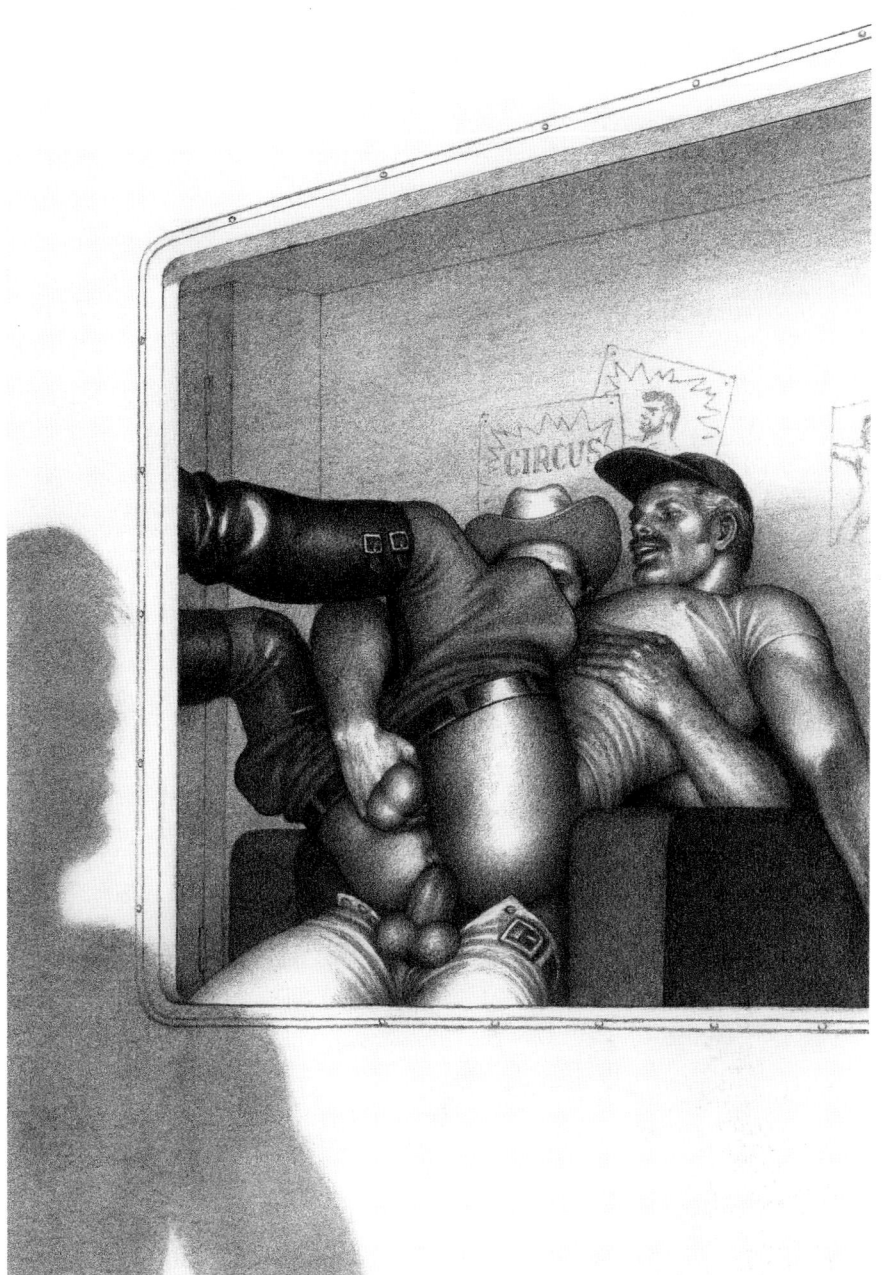

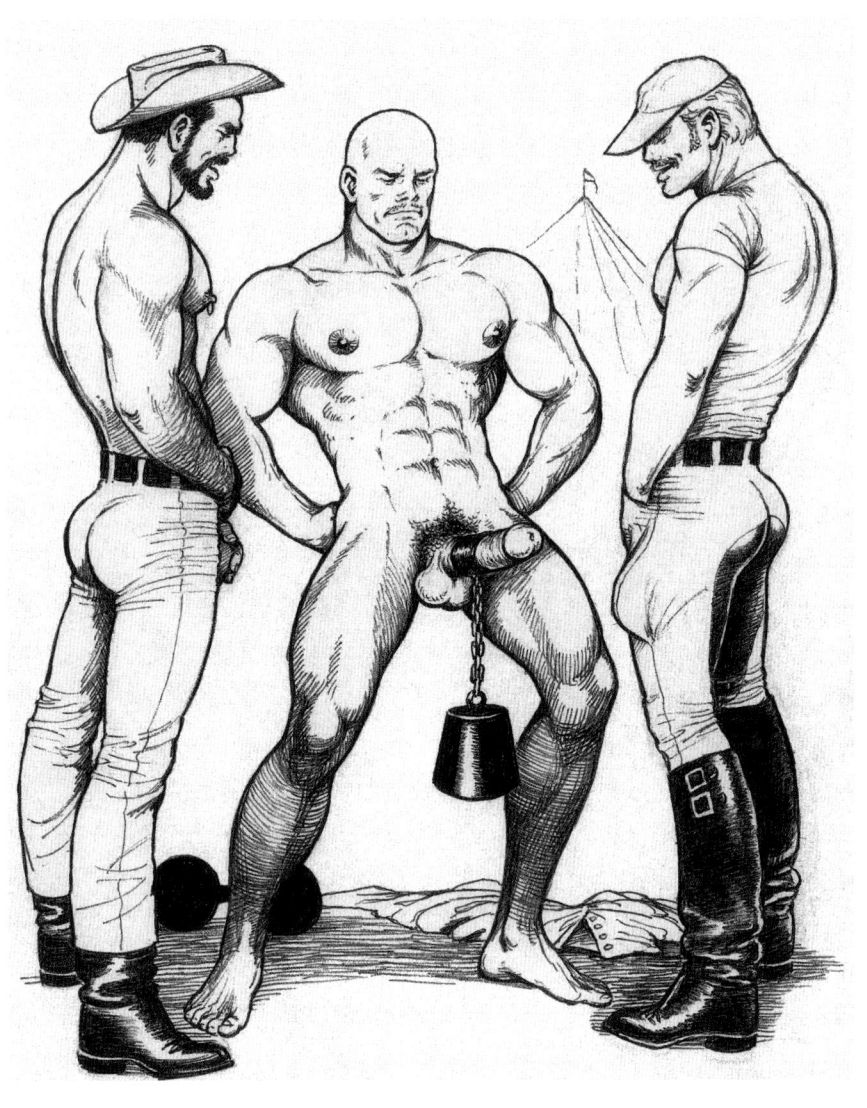

ABOVE 1975, pen and ink on paper
OPPOSITE 1975, graphite on paper

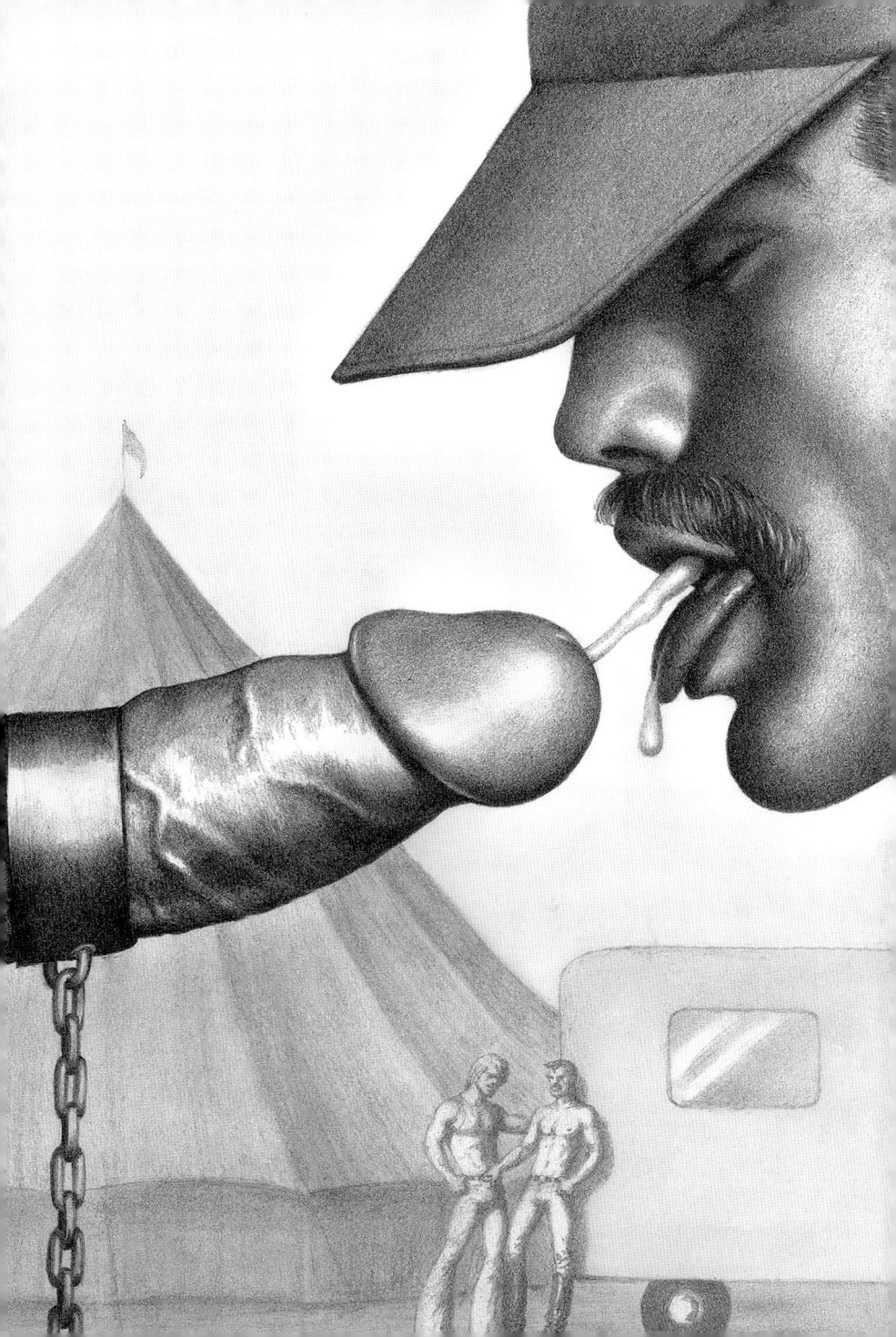

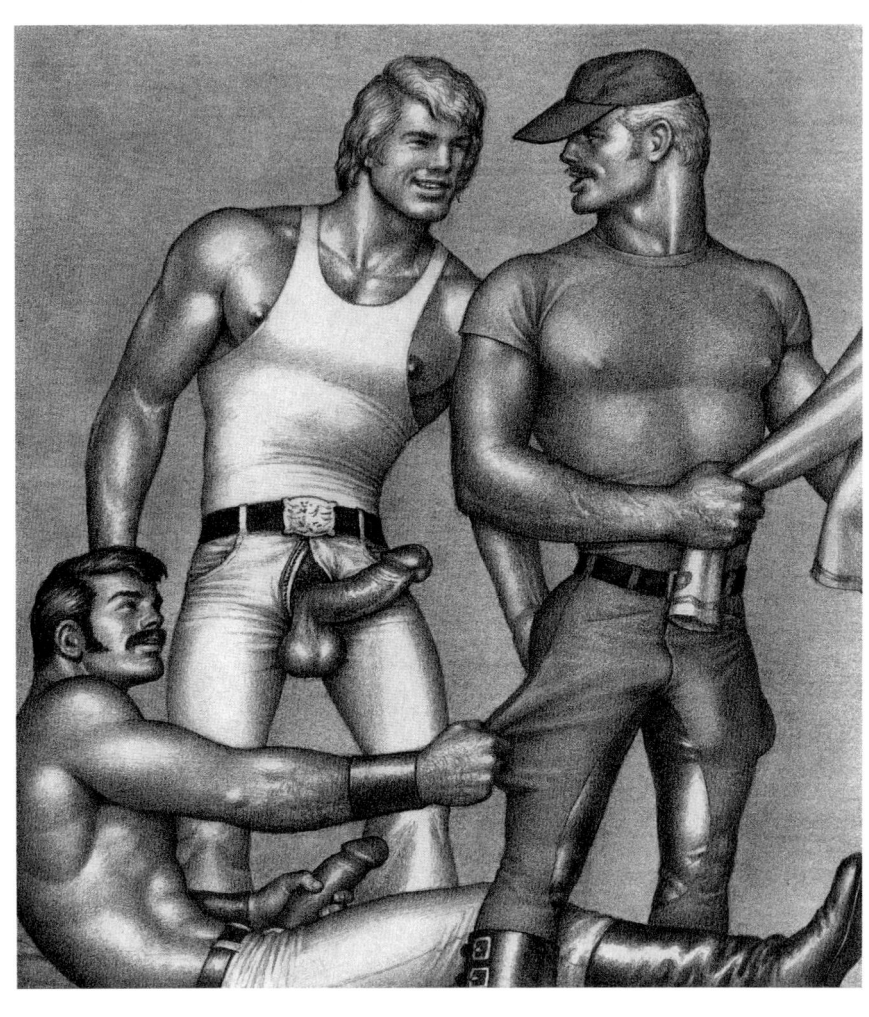

ABOVE 1975, graphite on paper
OPPOSITE 1975, pen and ink on paper

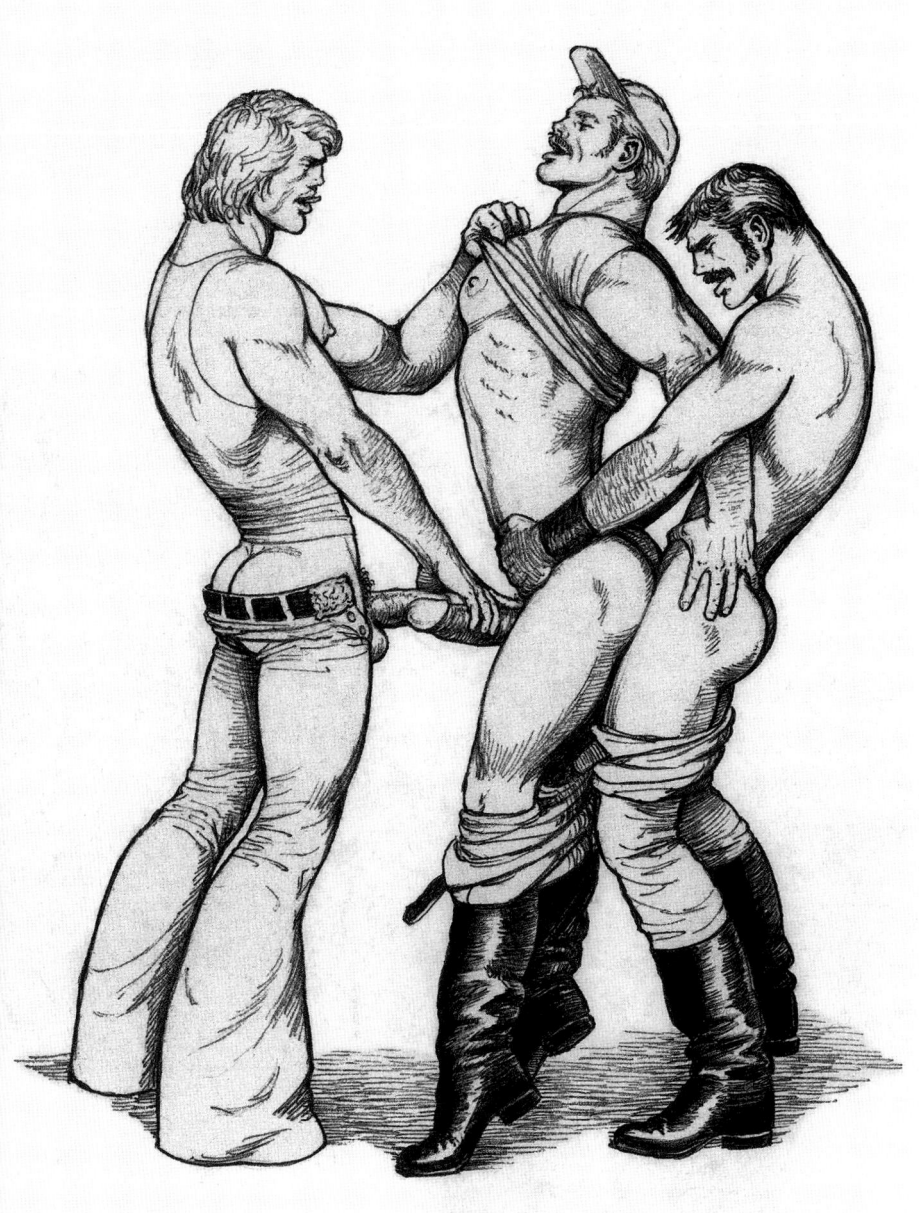

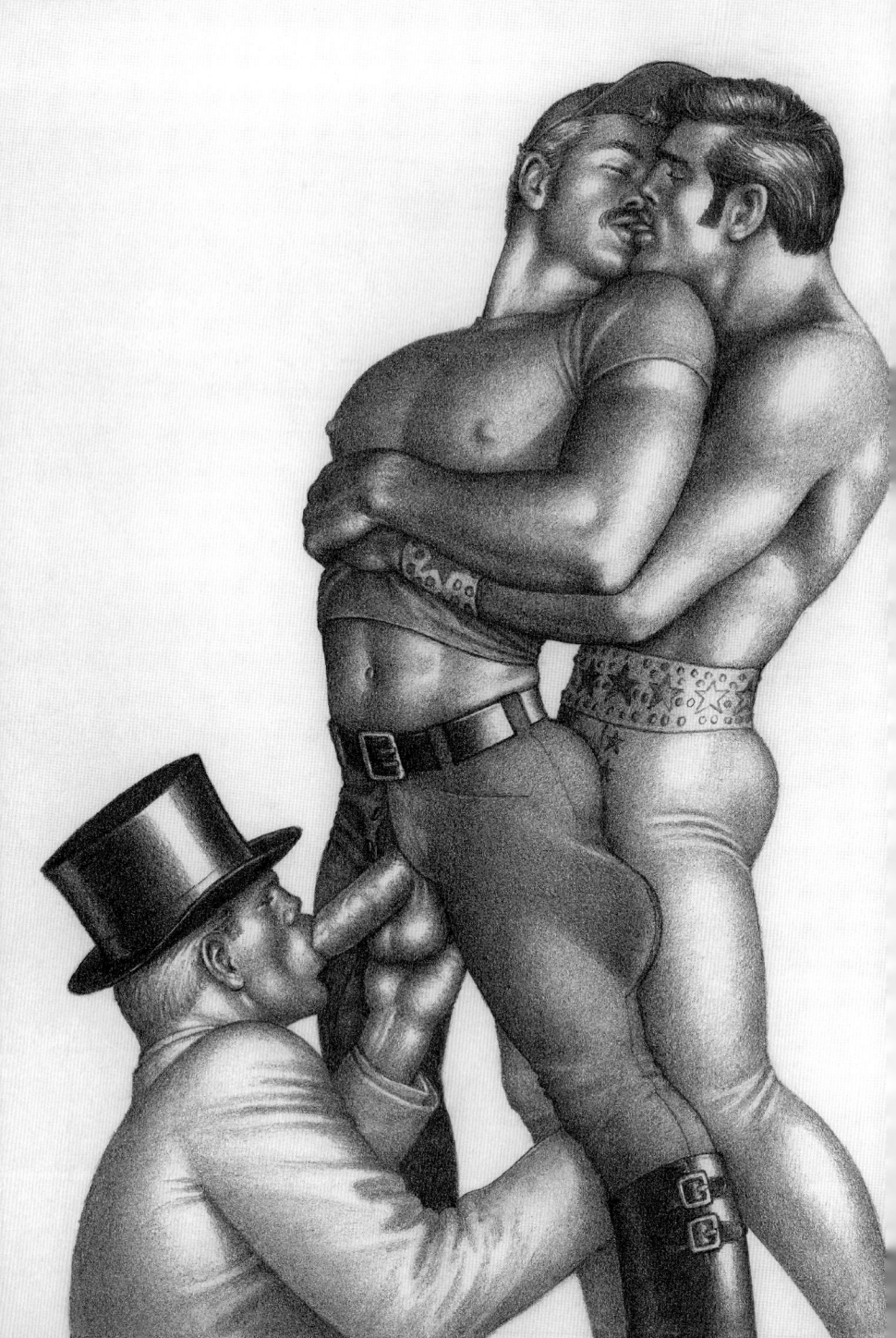

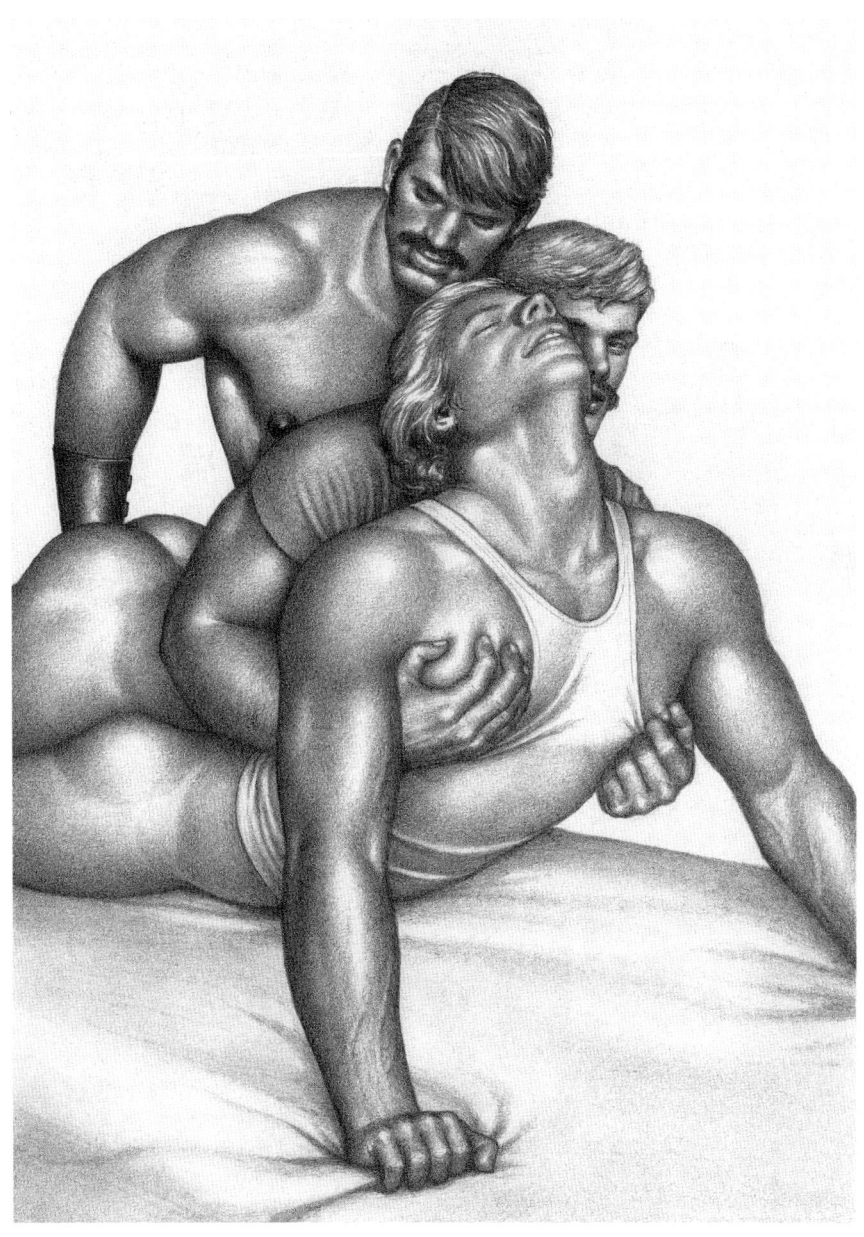

OPPOSITE AND ABOVE 1975, graphite on paper

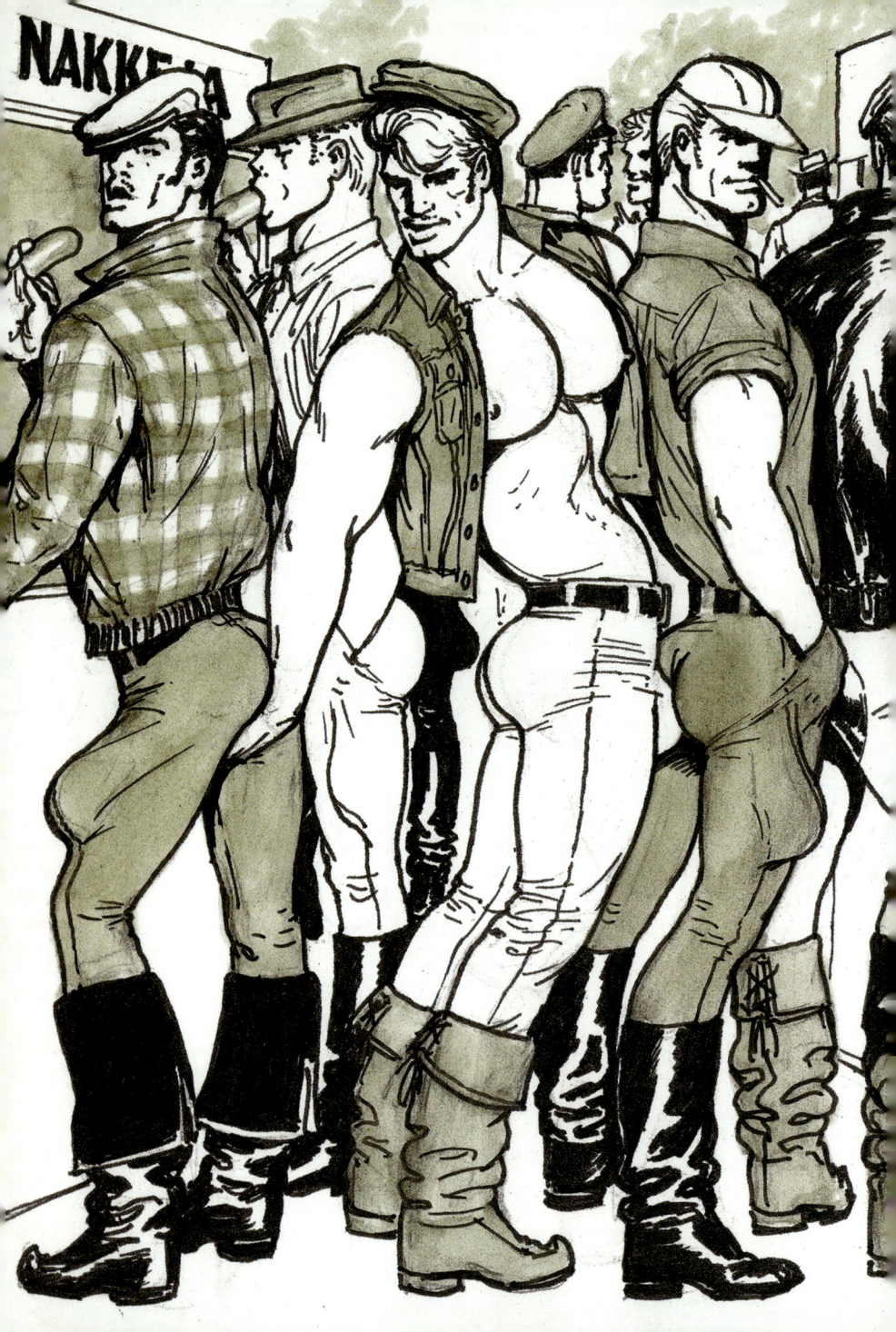

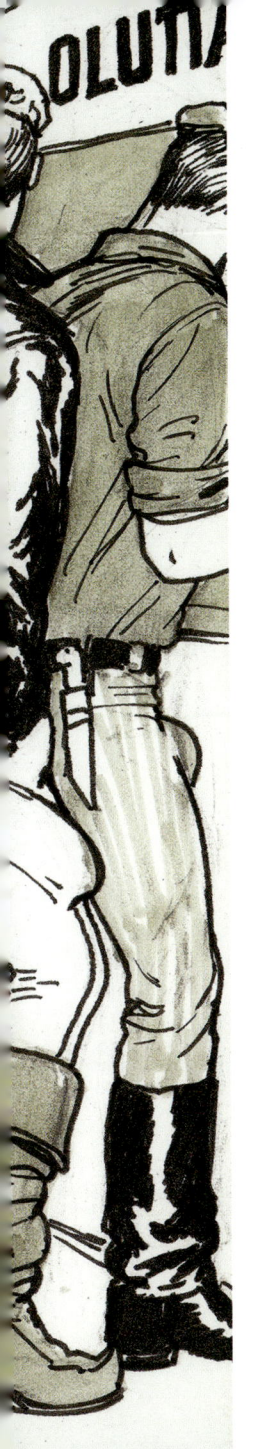

"*The message became not so much that a man wants to fuck another man, but that some men want to live together with other men in a gang of boys, like in their youth.*"
—BERNDT ARELL

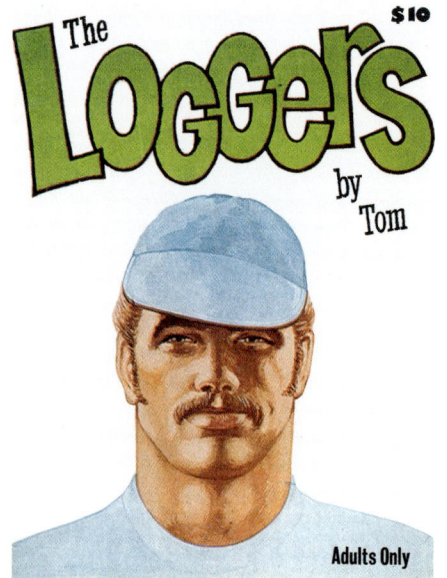

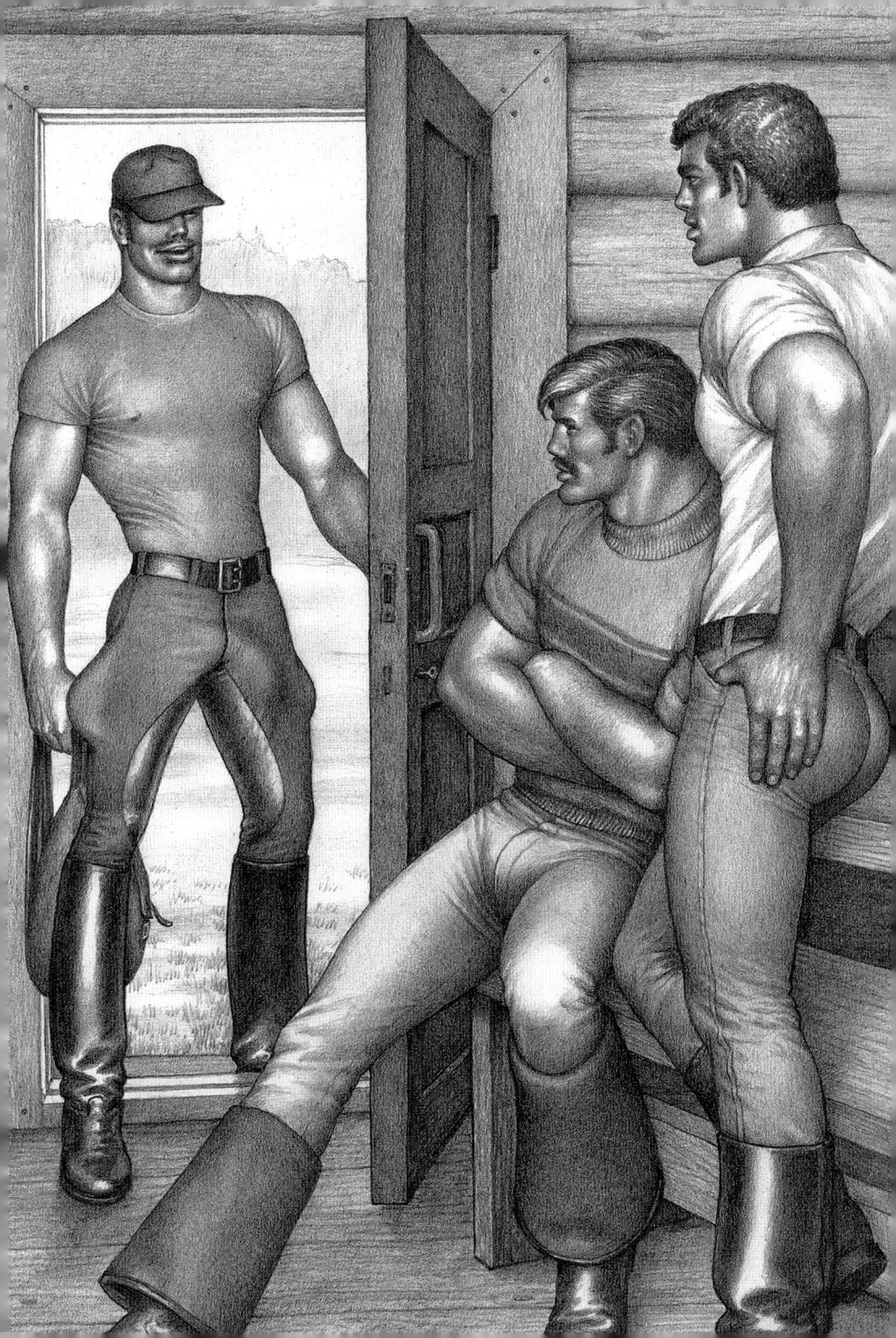

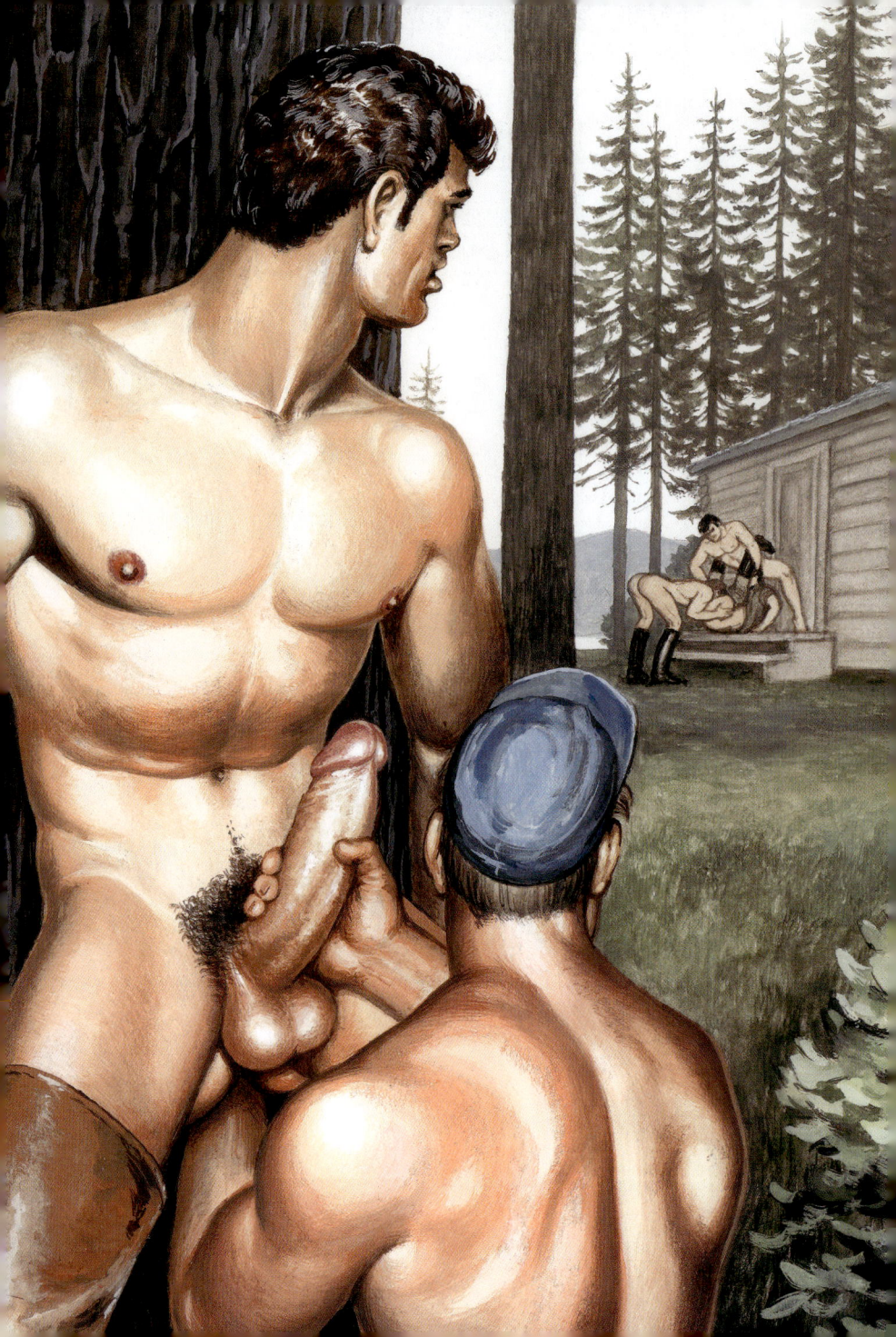

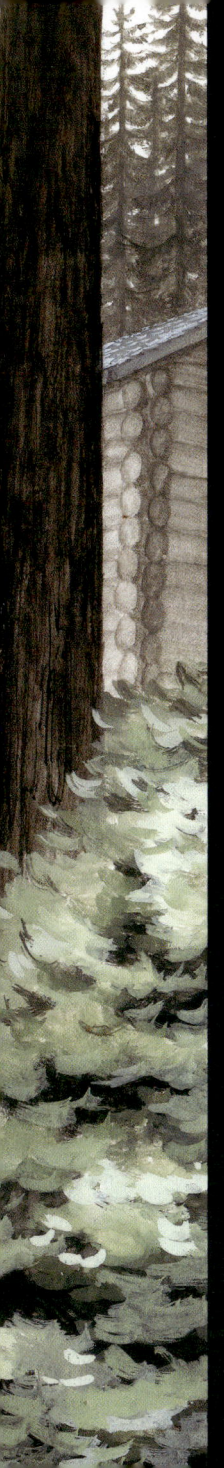

LEFT AND PAGES 78–79 1975, gouache on paper

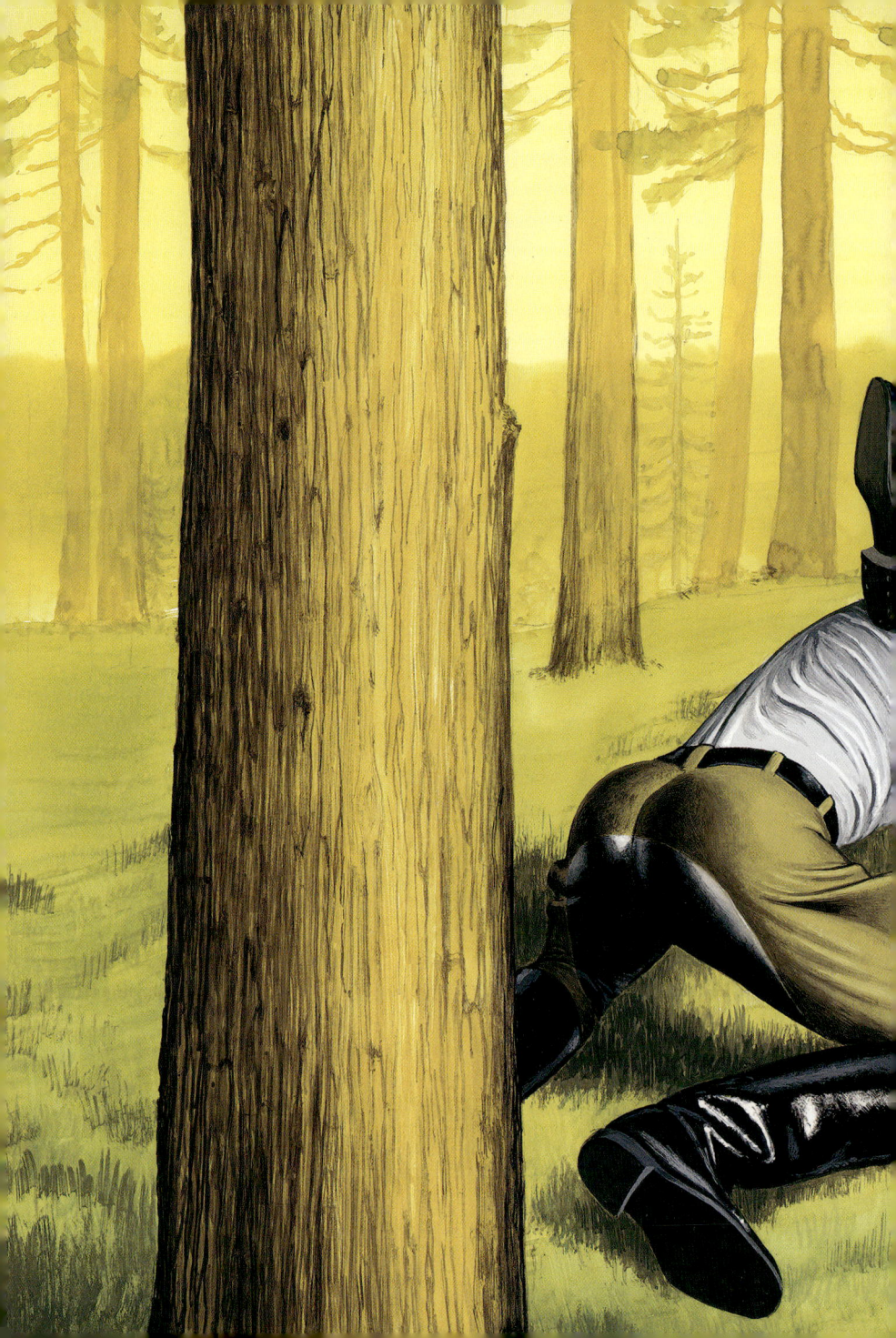

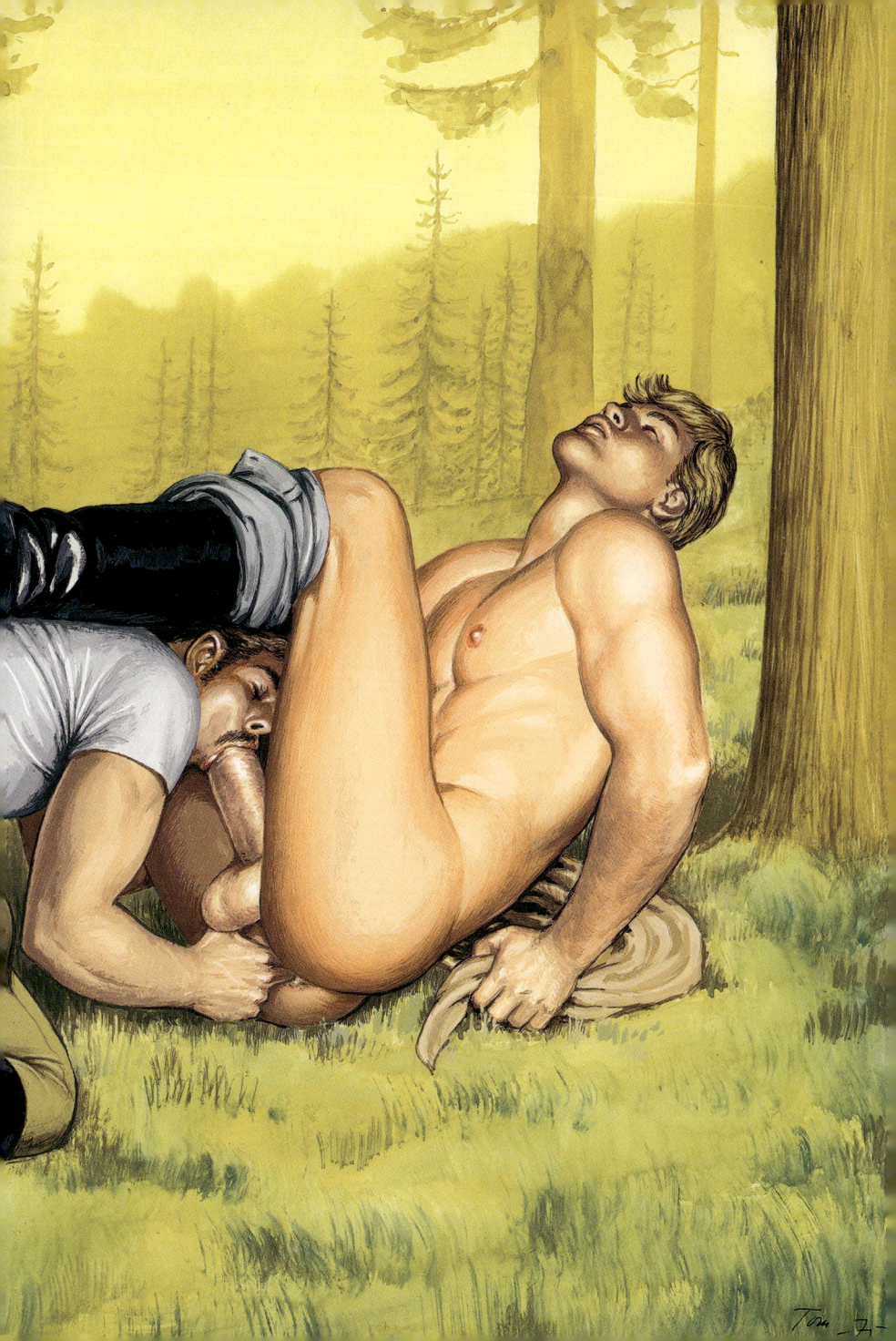

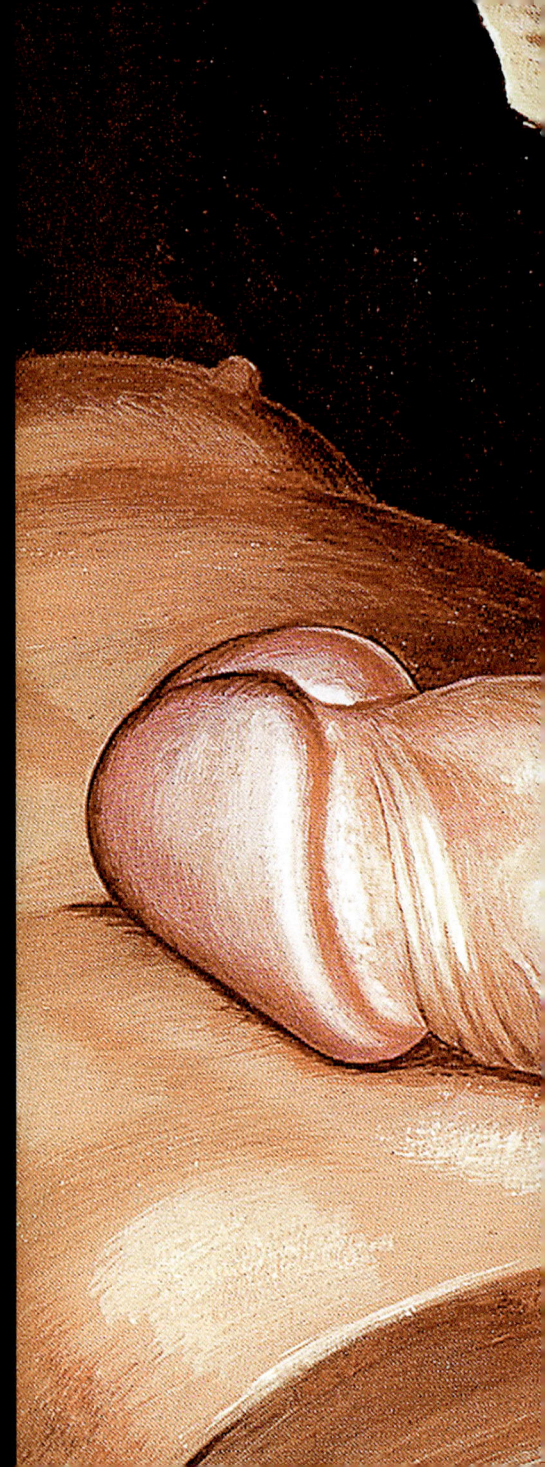

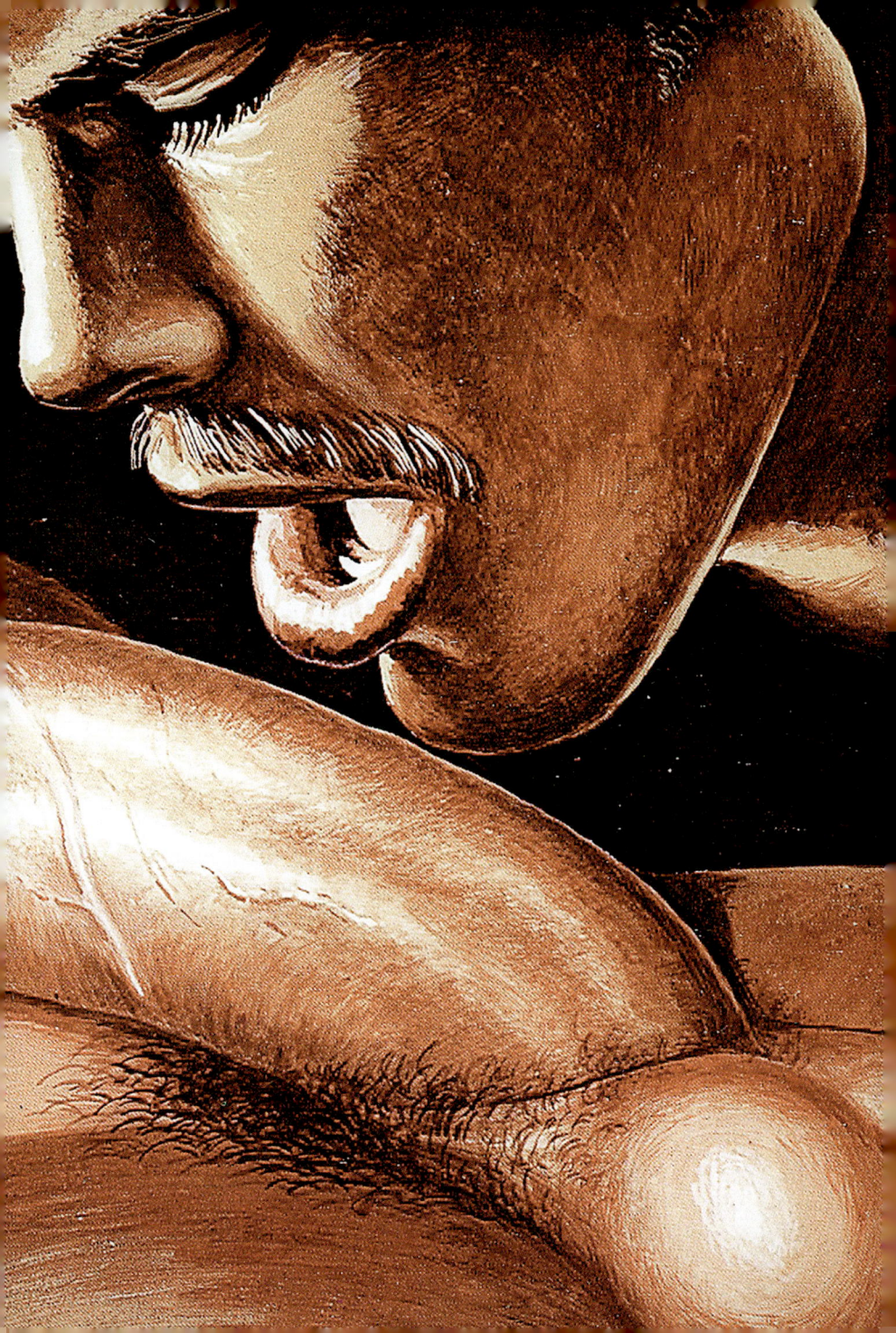

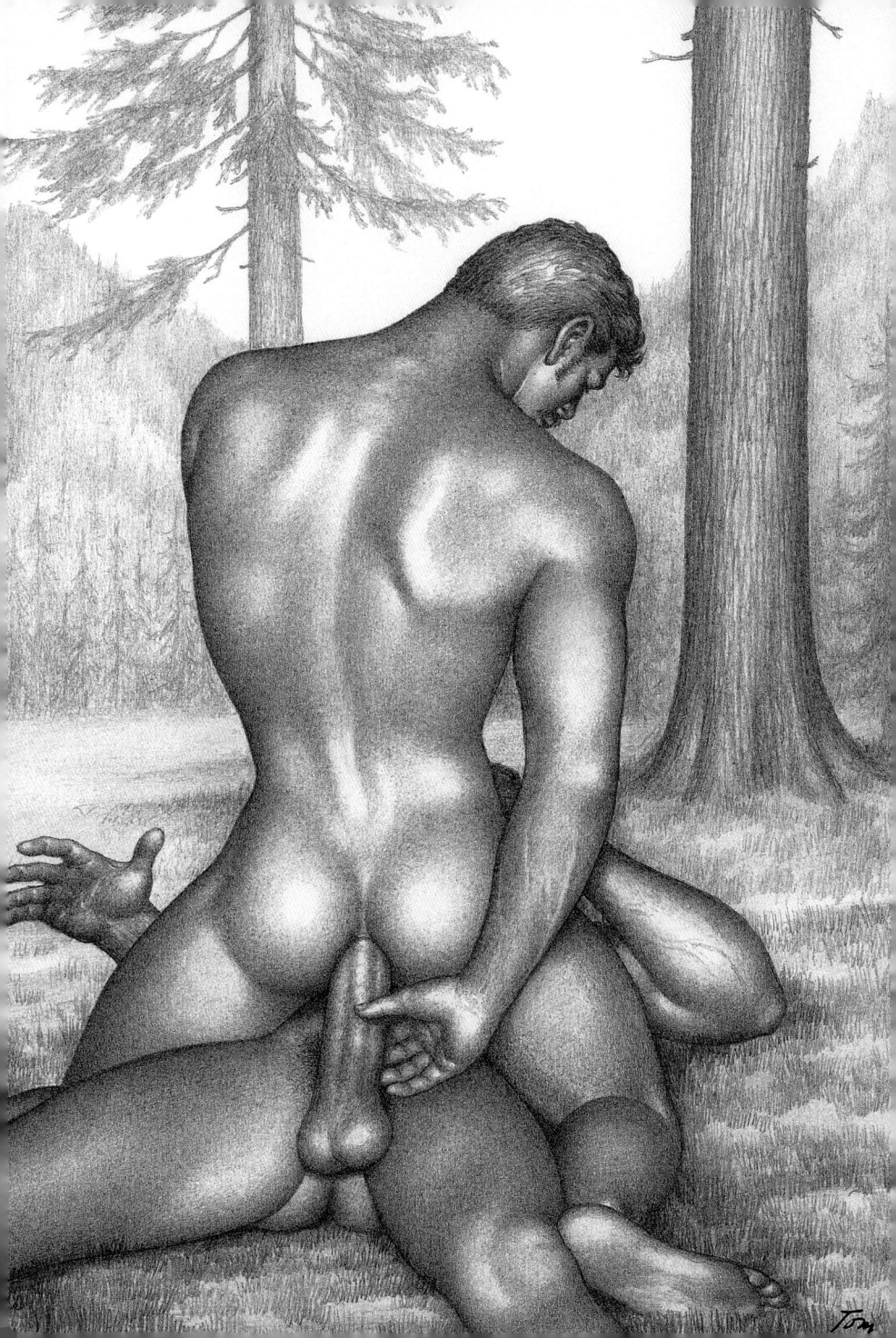

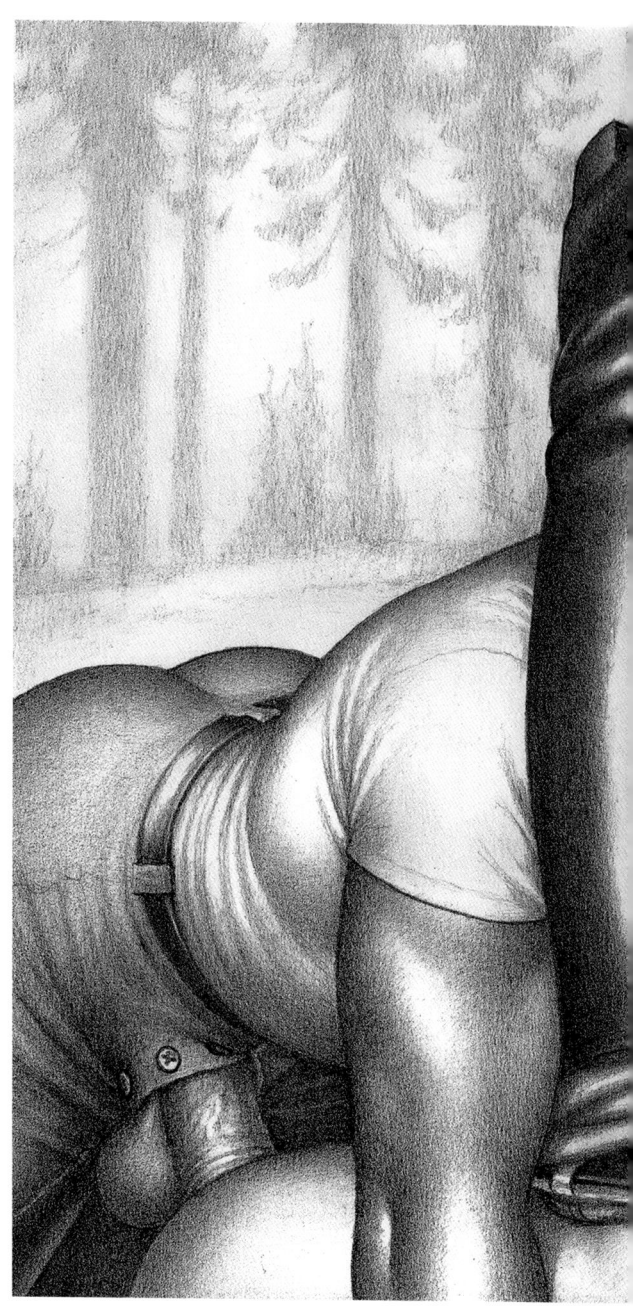

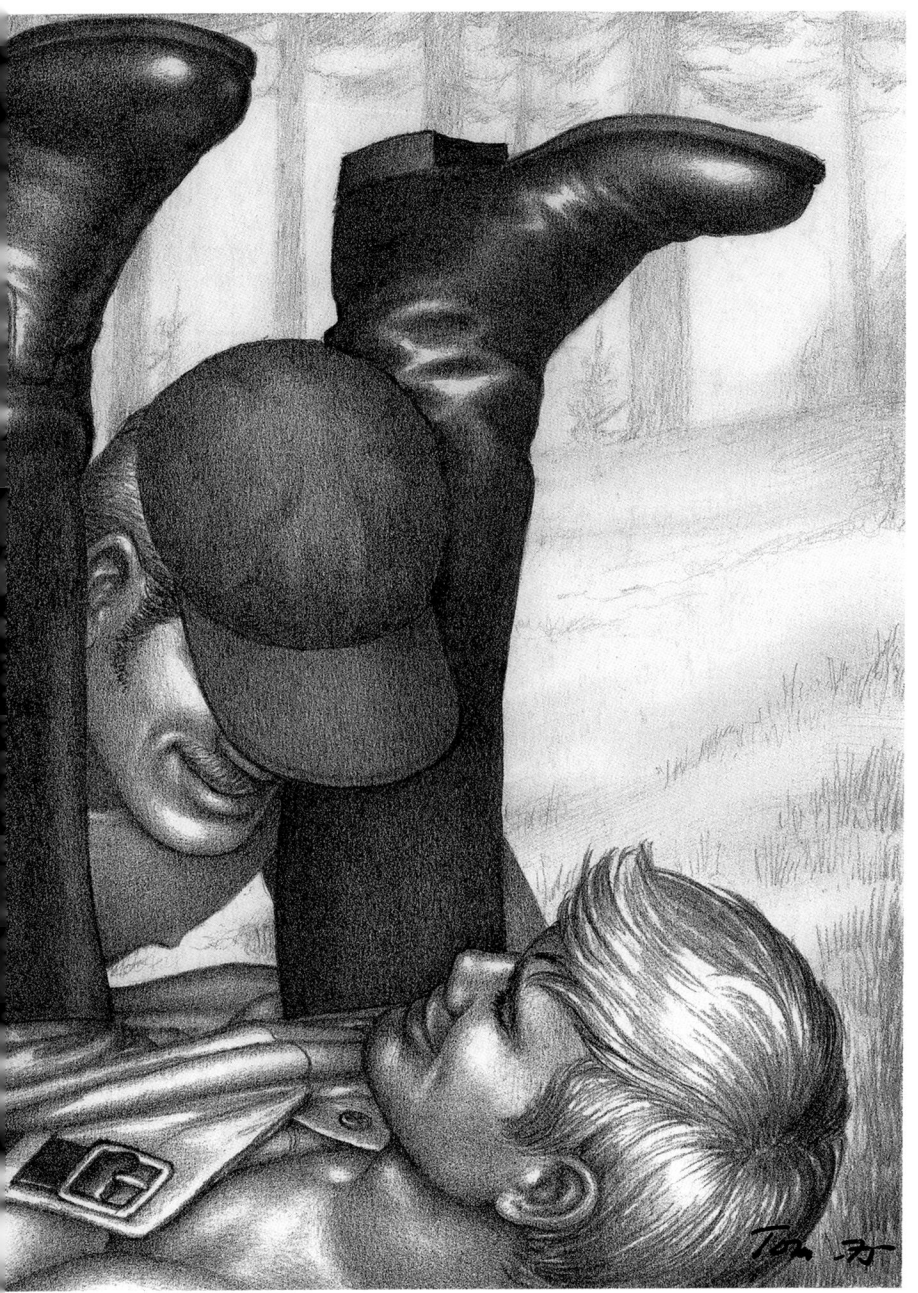

"I had to come up with something you couldn't get in a photograph. So those big cocks are all for the other guys — I'm an ass man myself."
—TOM OF FINLAND

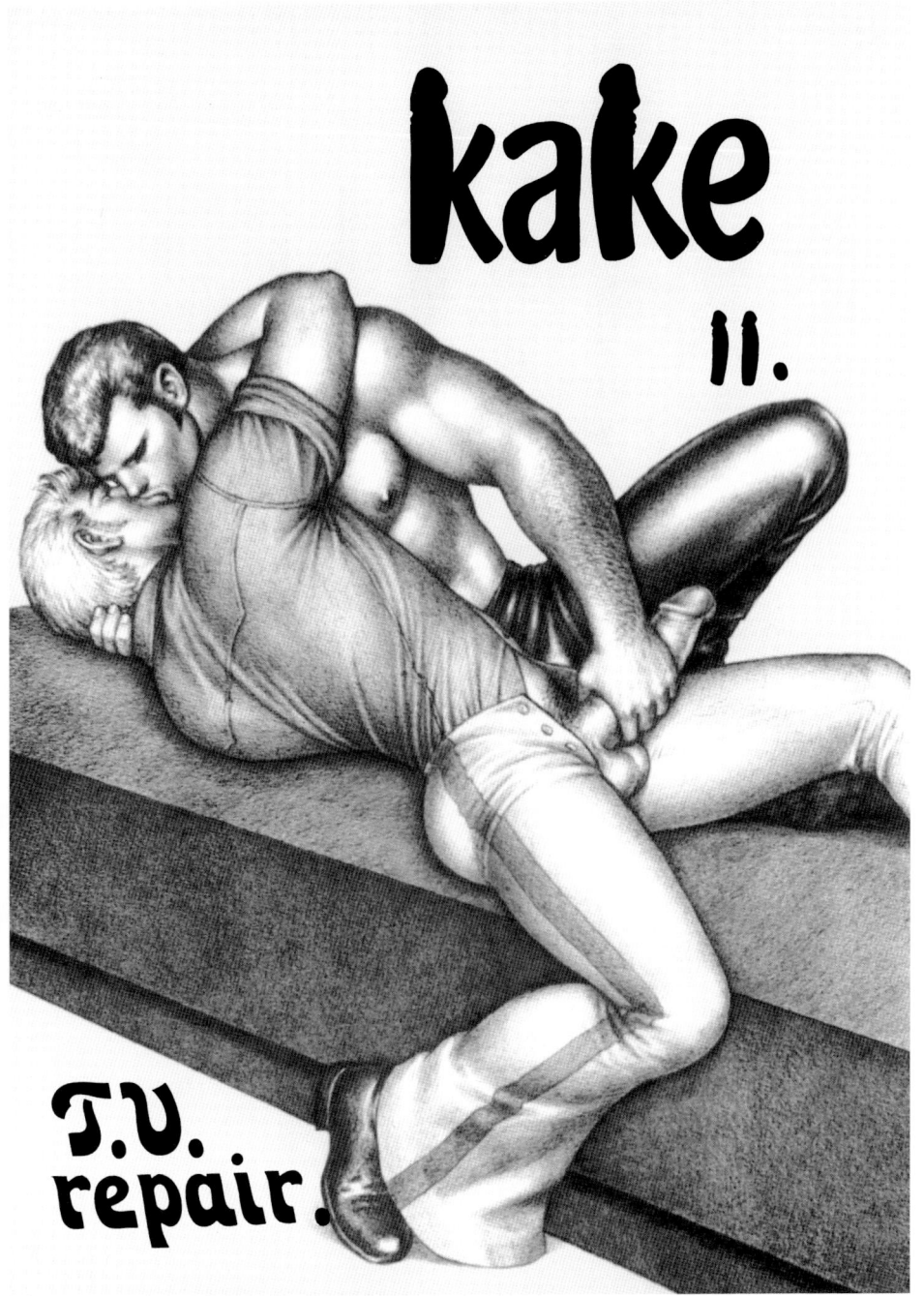

kake

11.

T.V. repair.

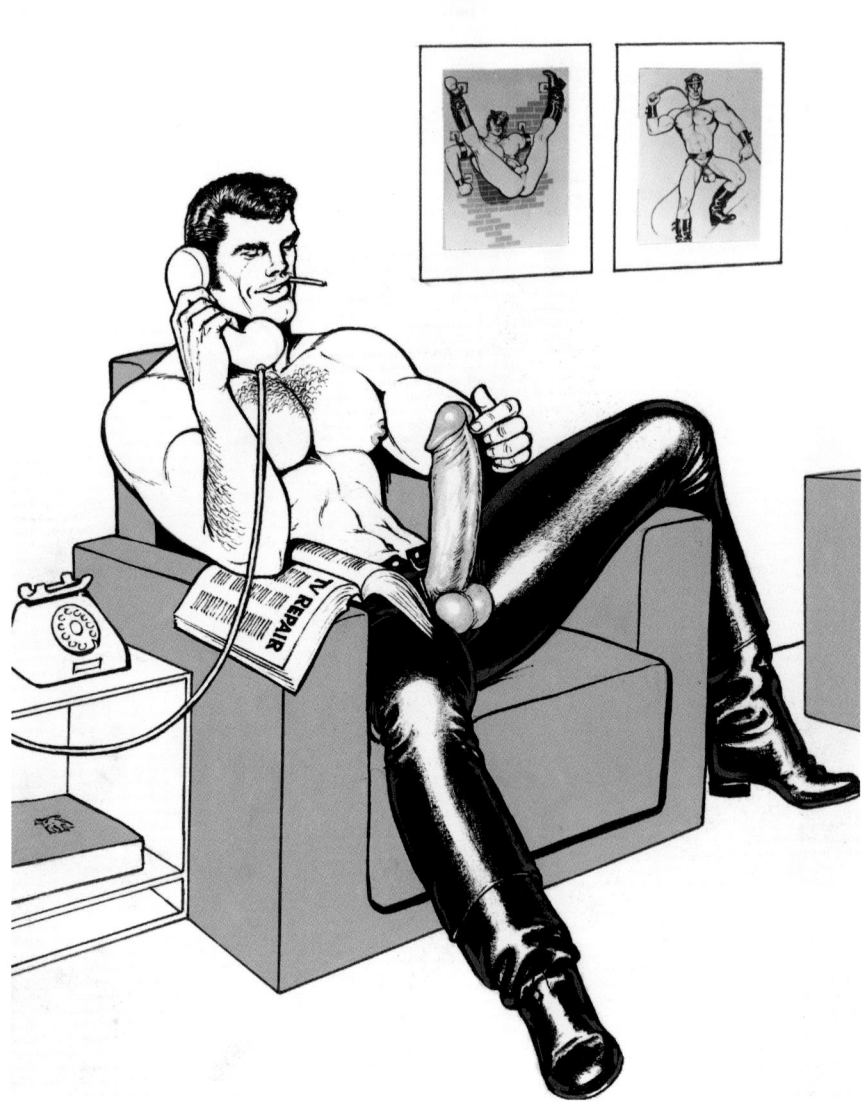

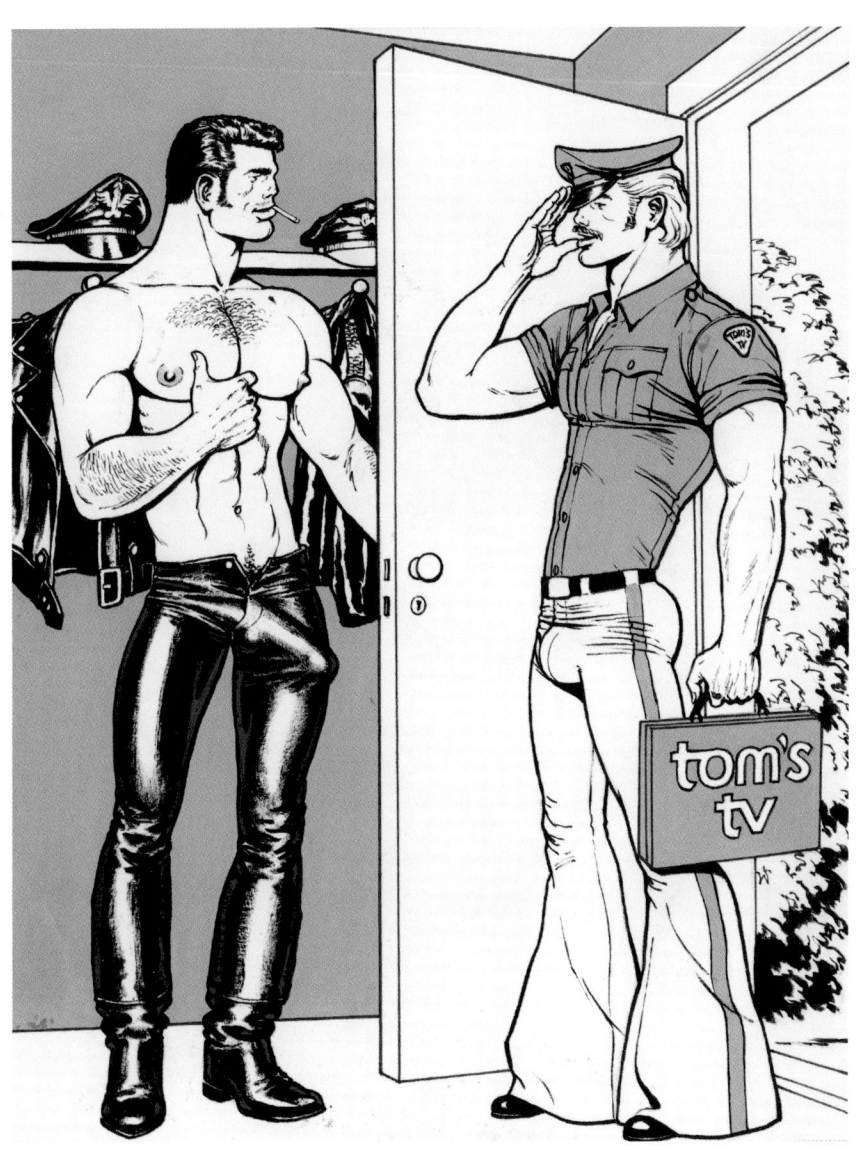

PAGES 88–107 1974, *T.V. Repair*, pen and ink and ink wash

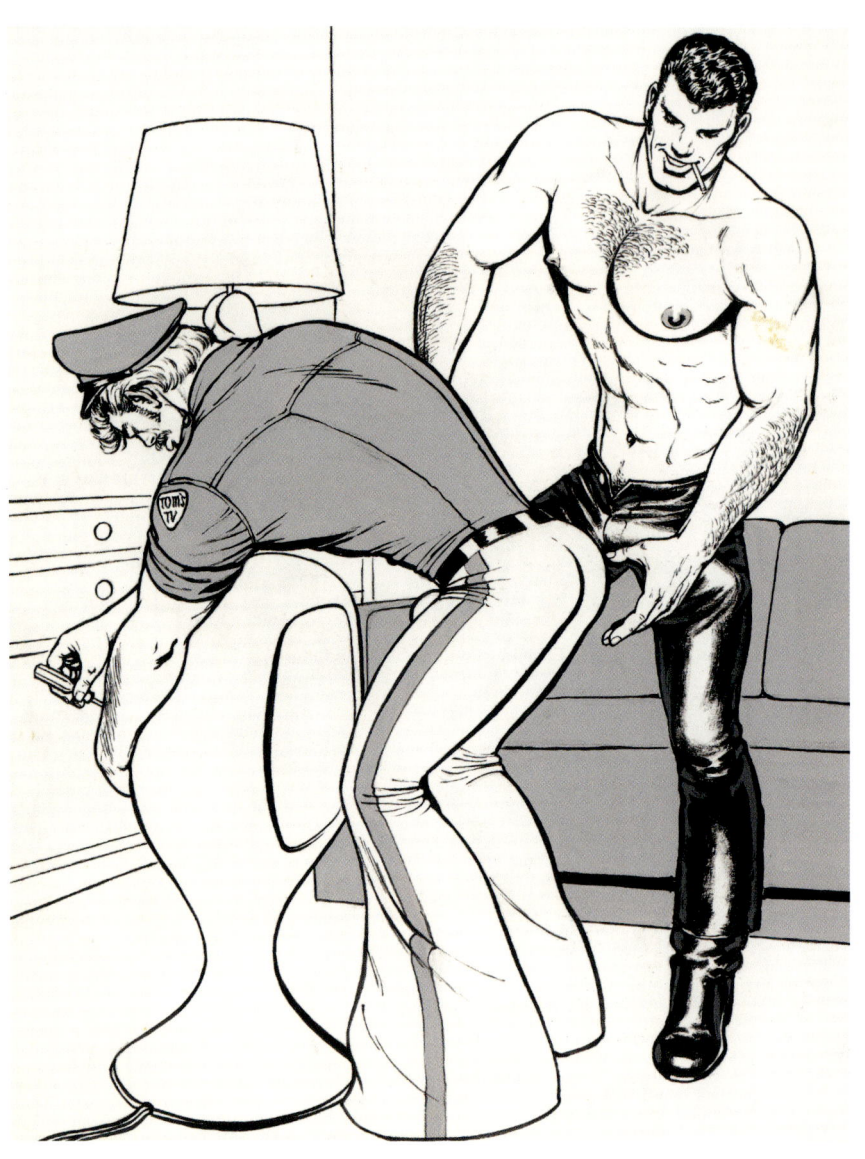

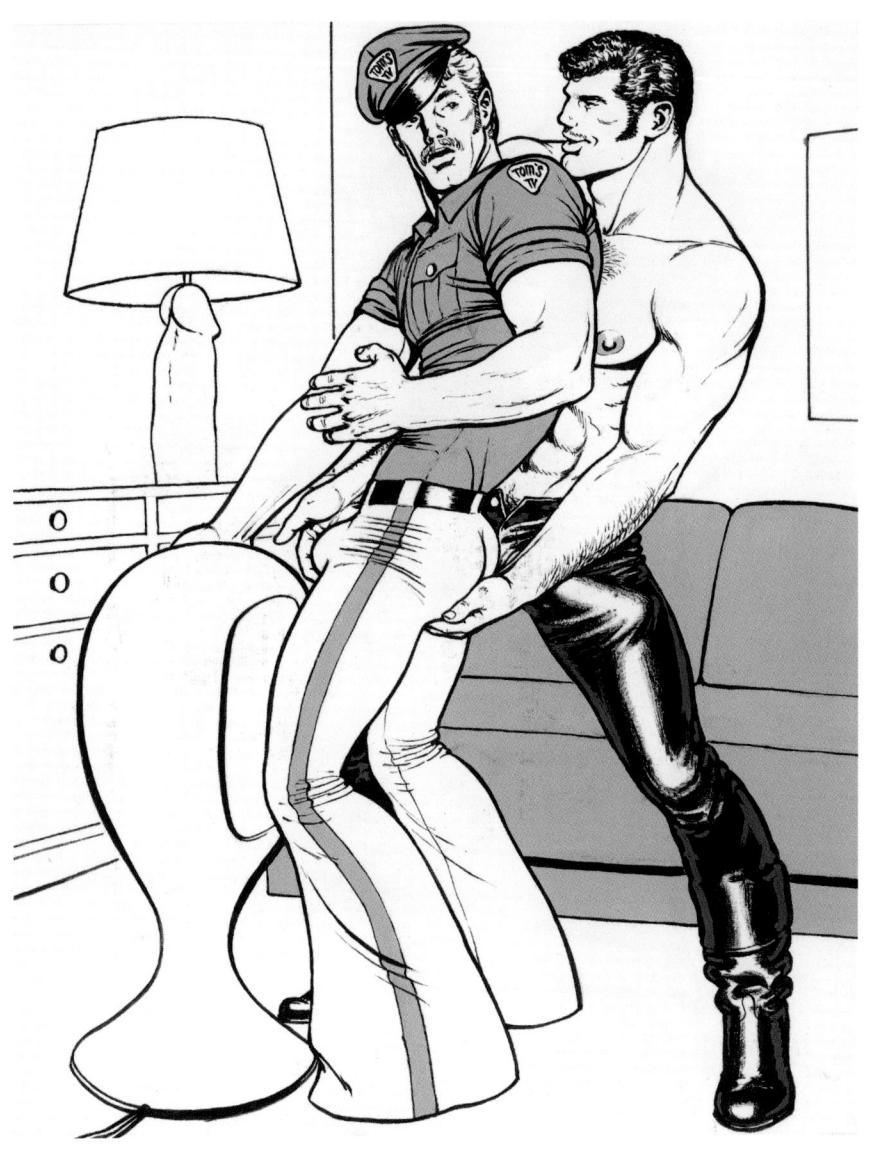

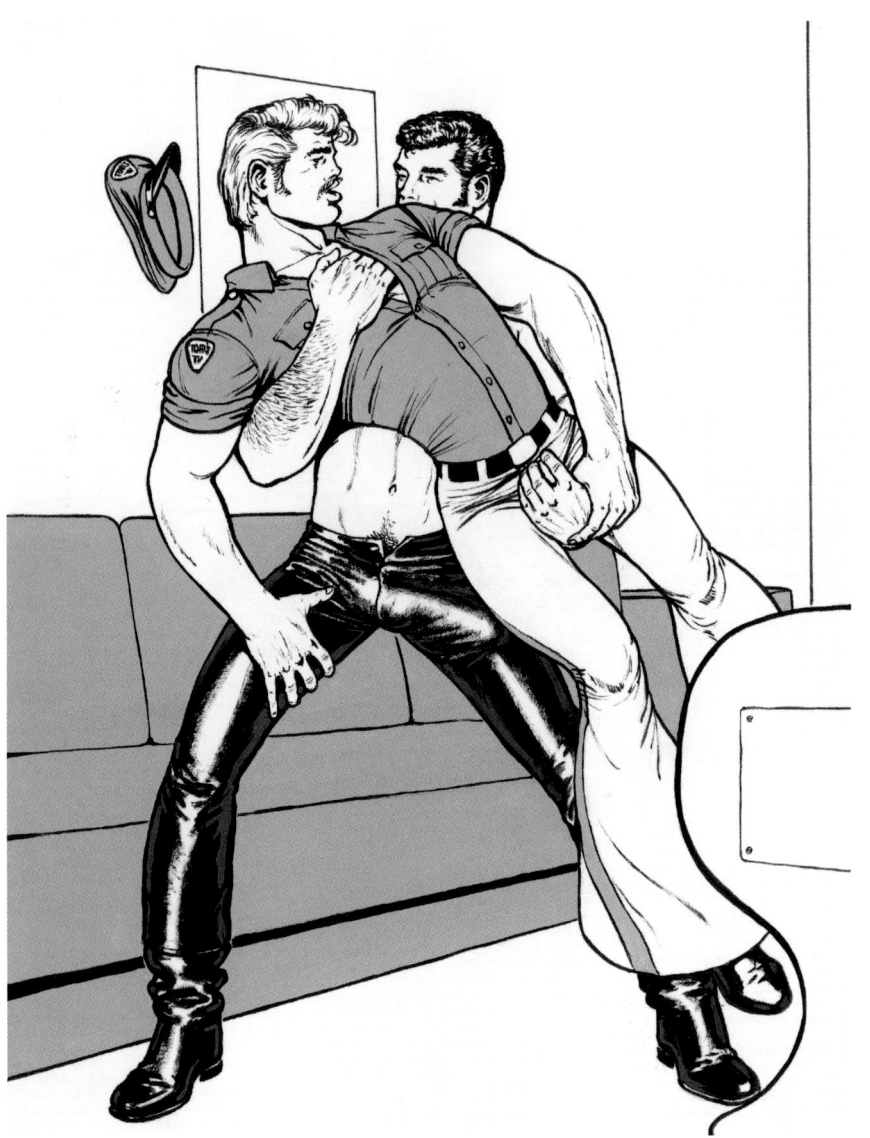

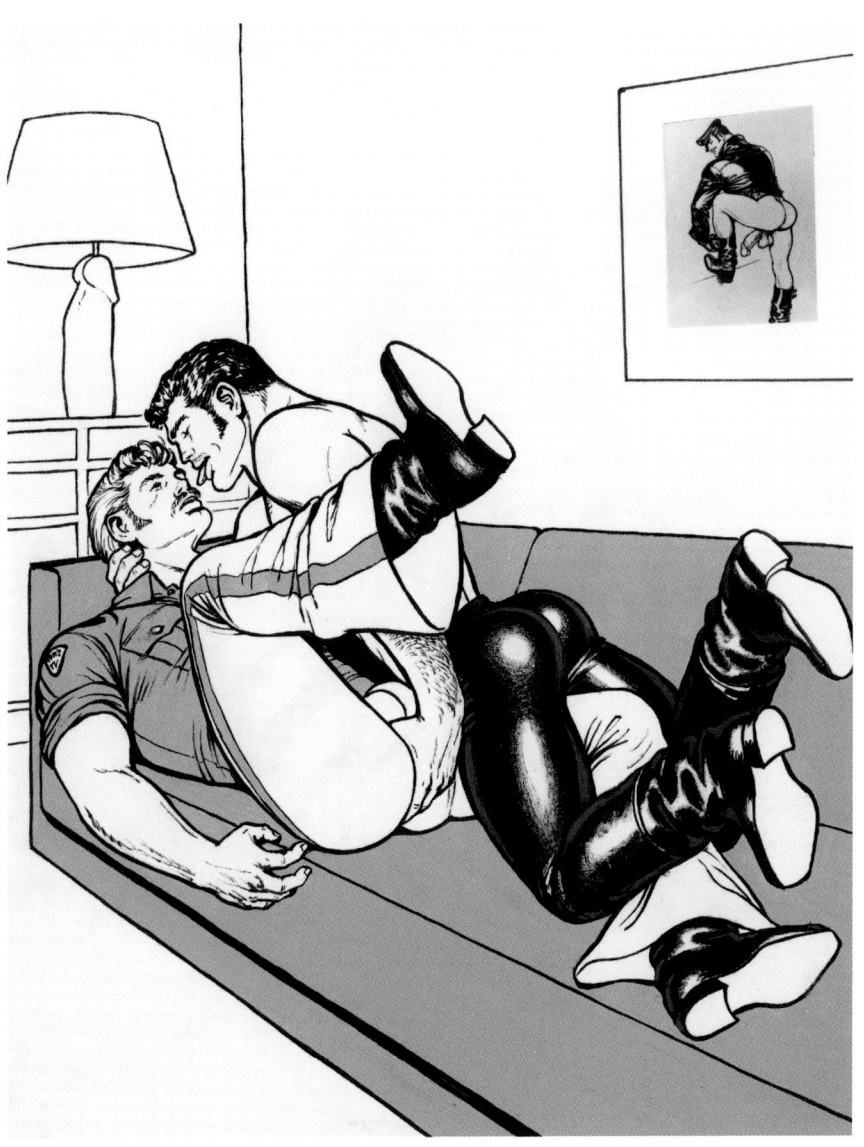

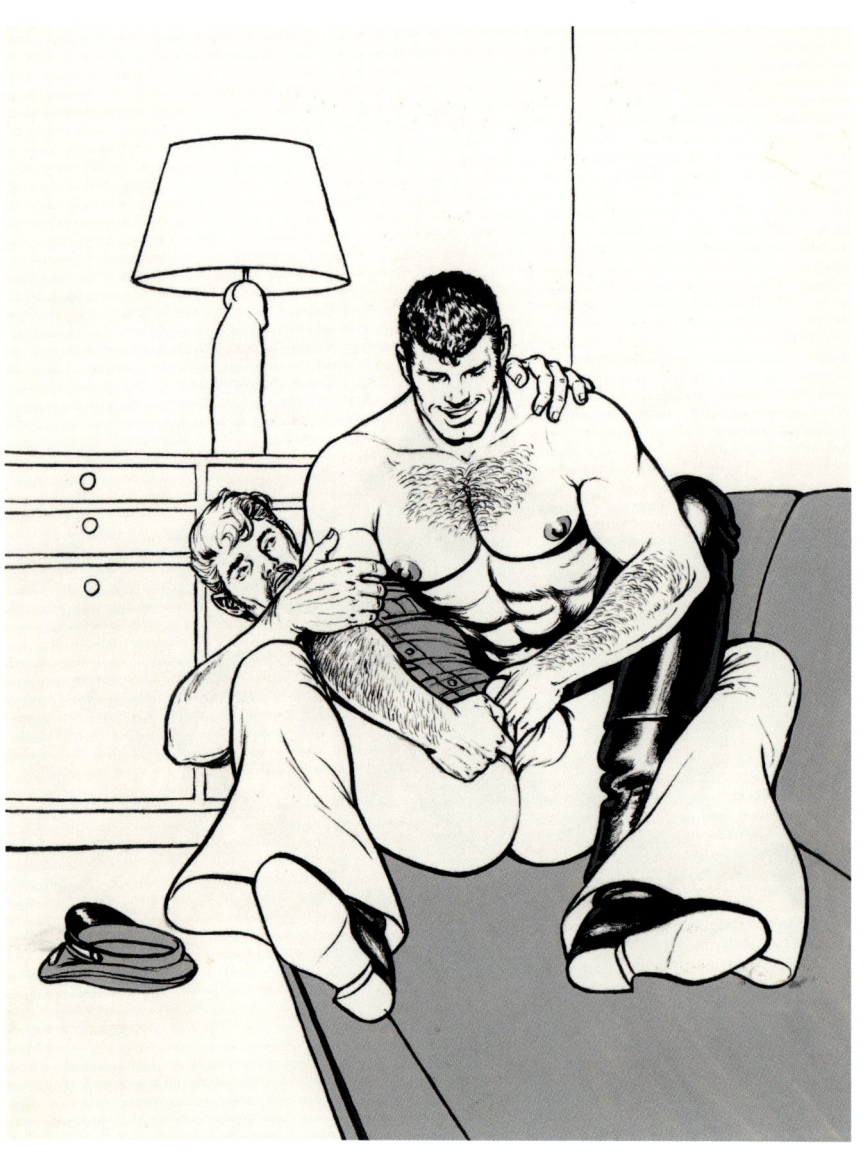

94

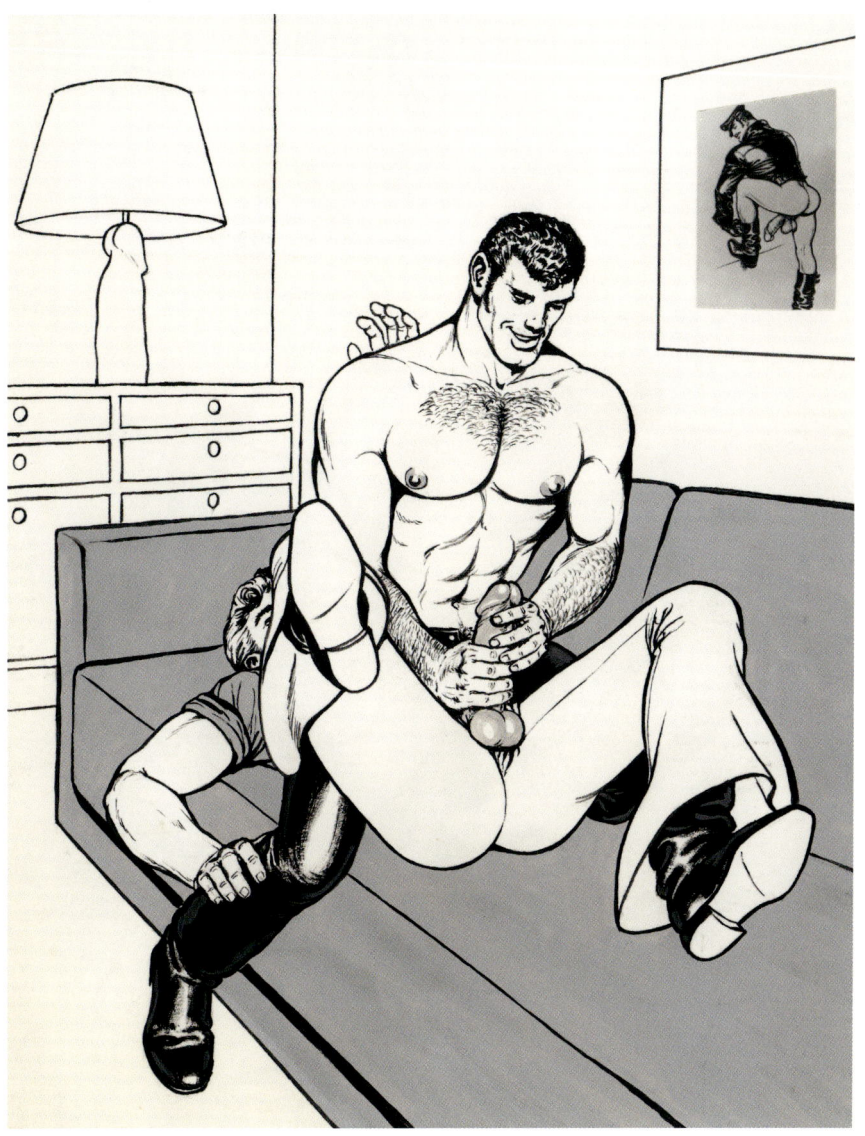

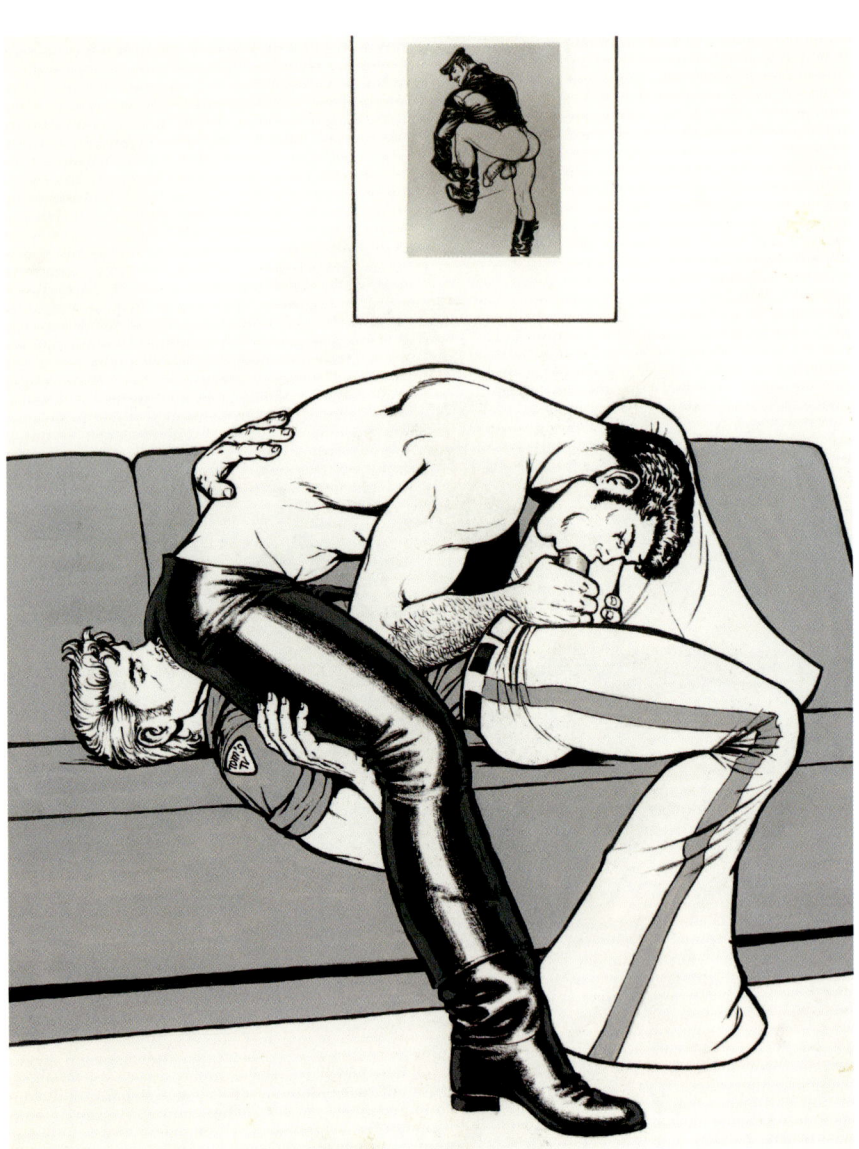

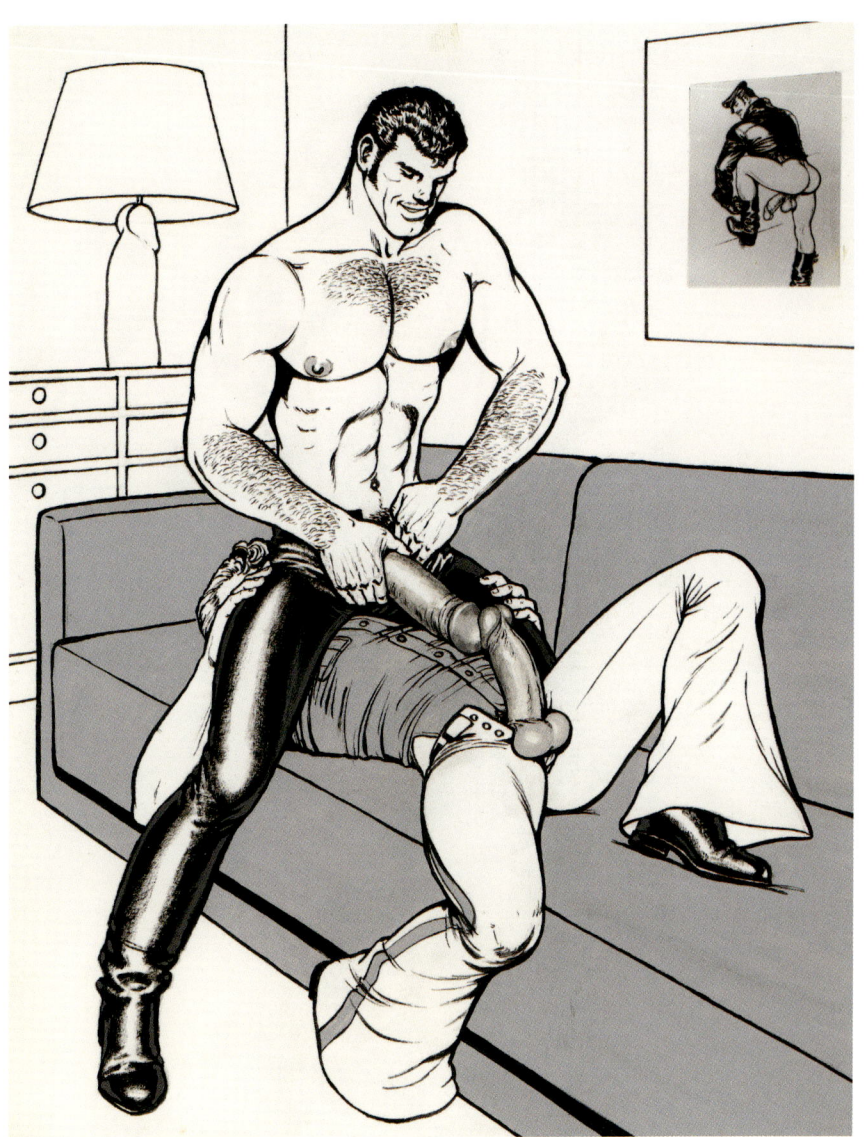

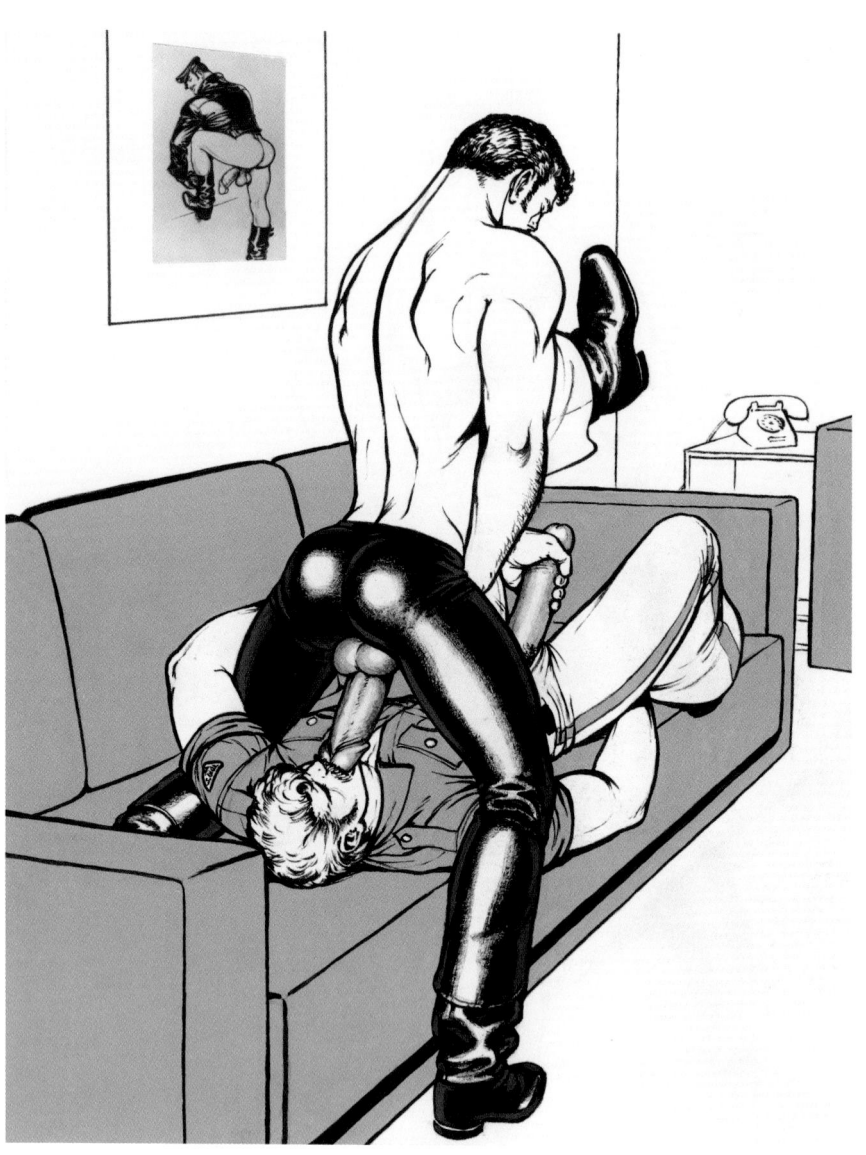

98

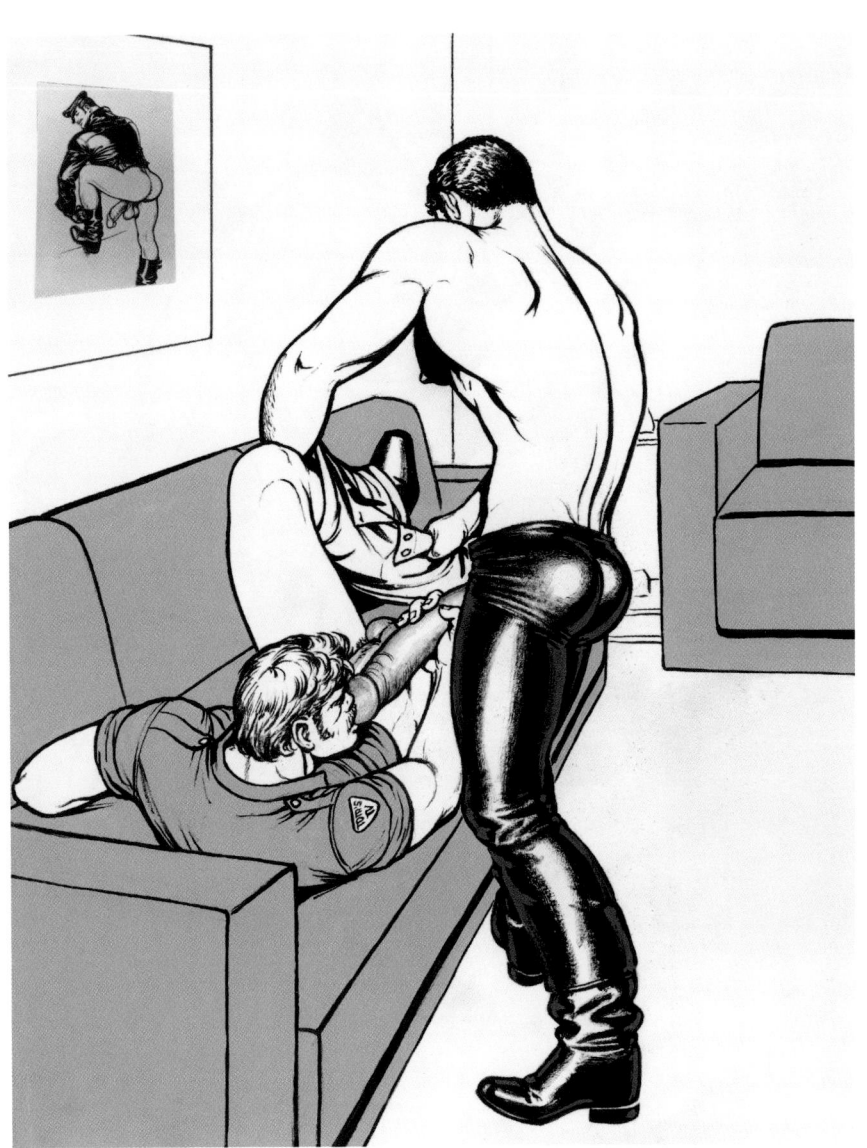

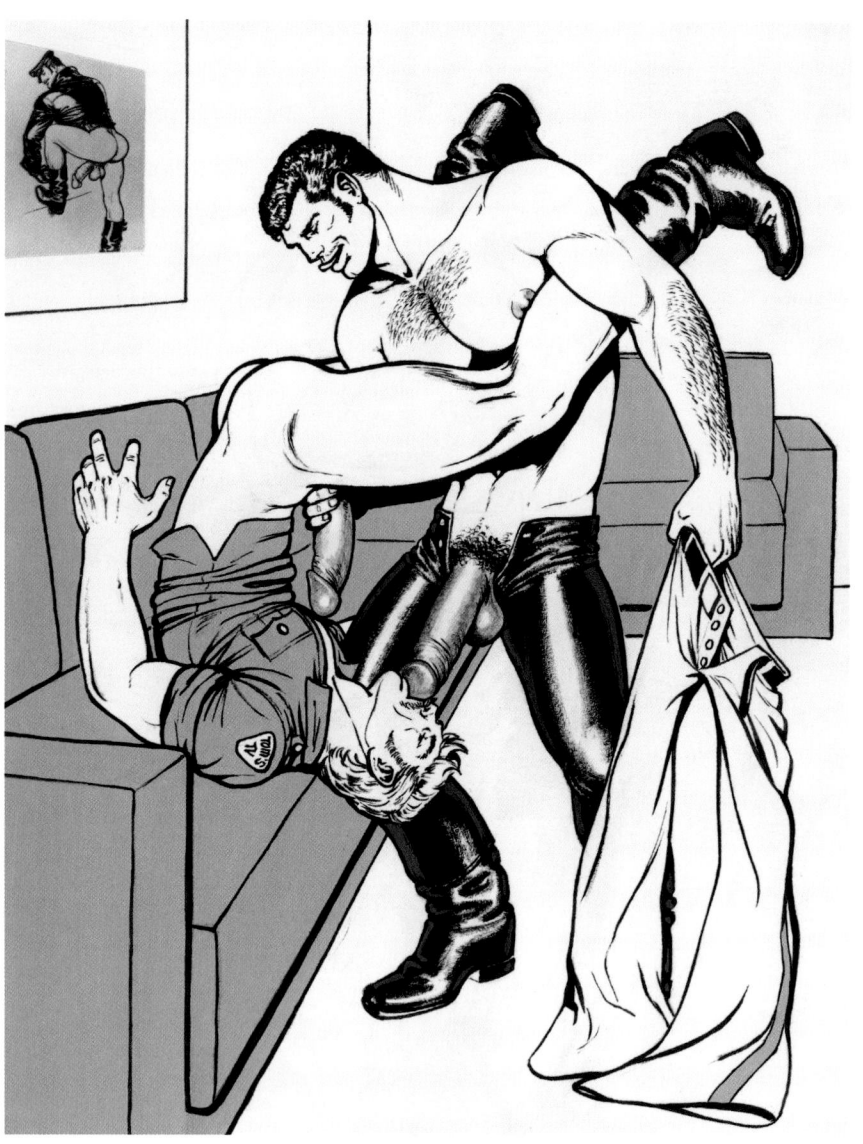

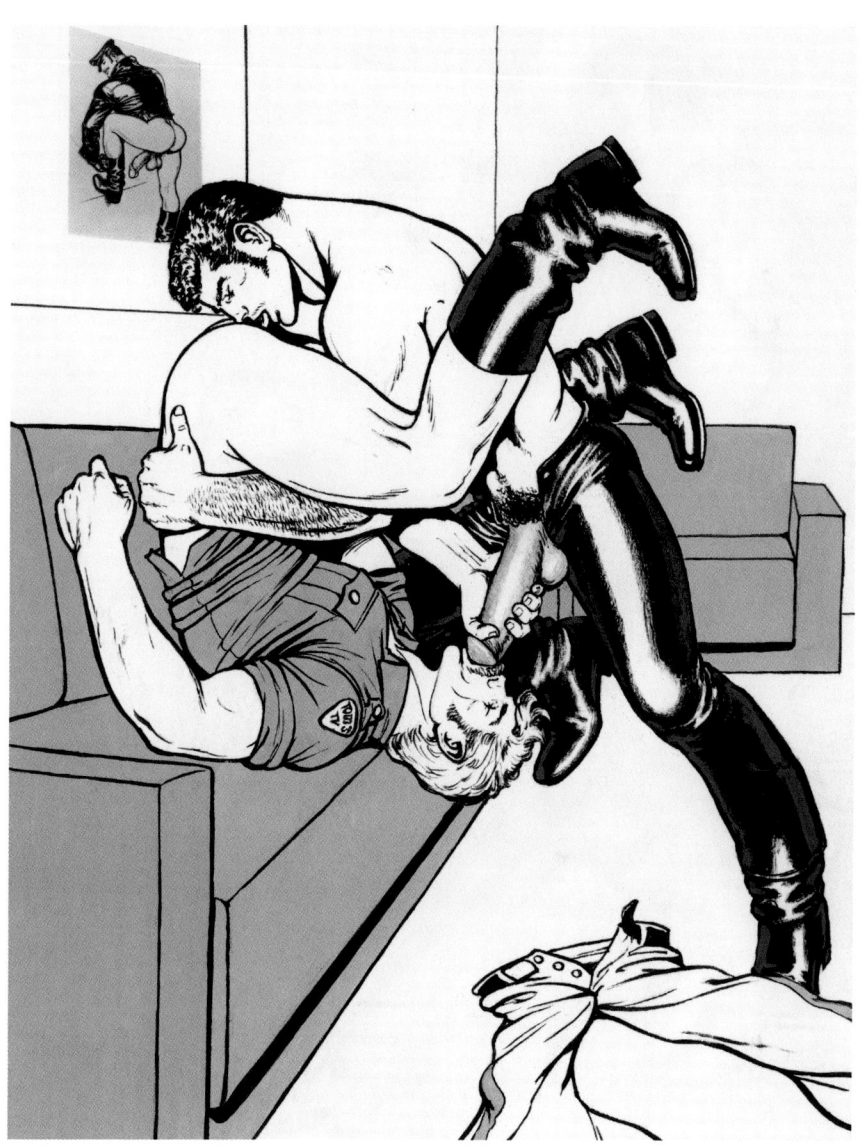

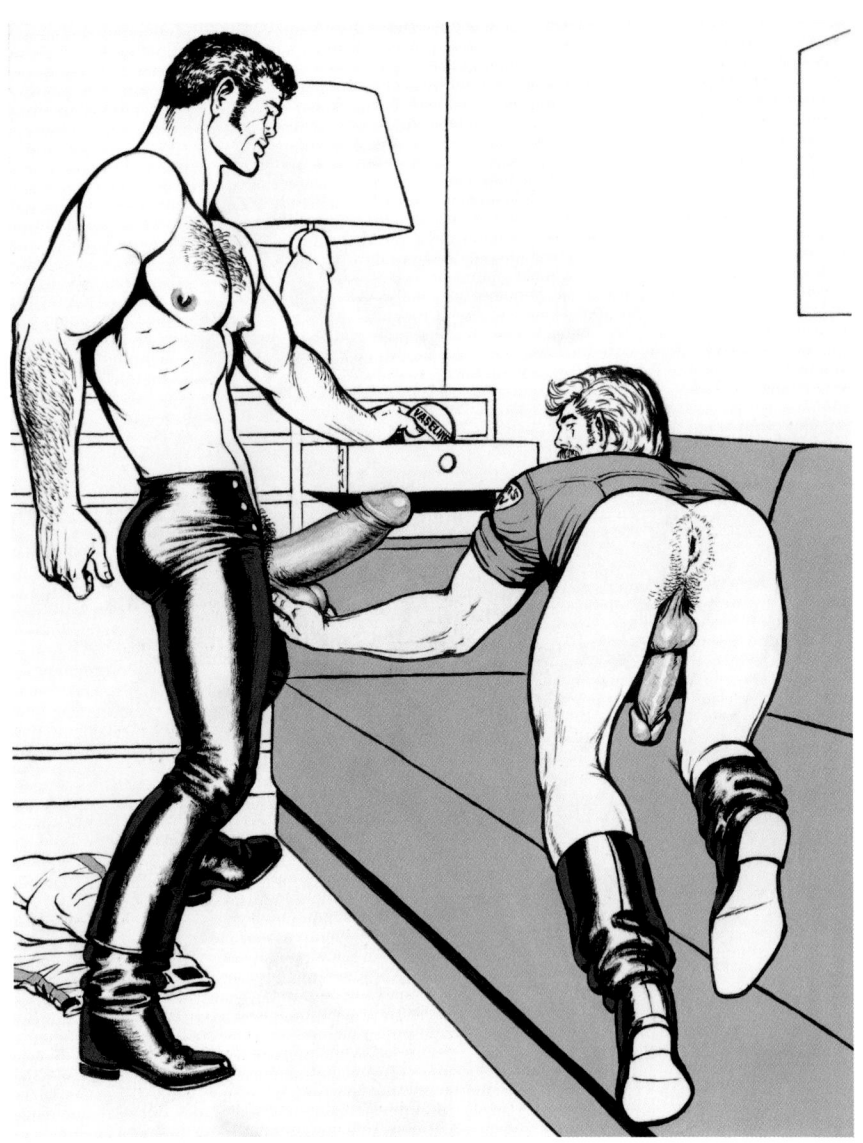

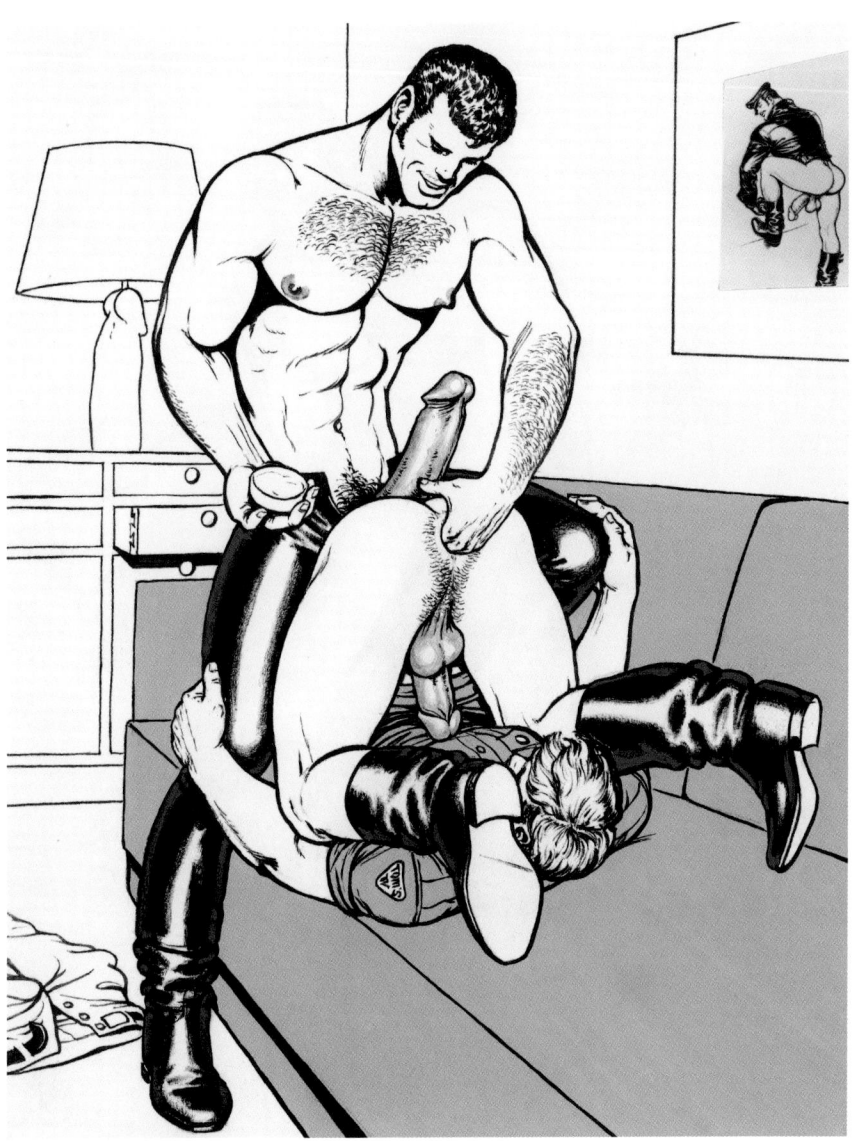

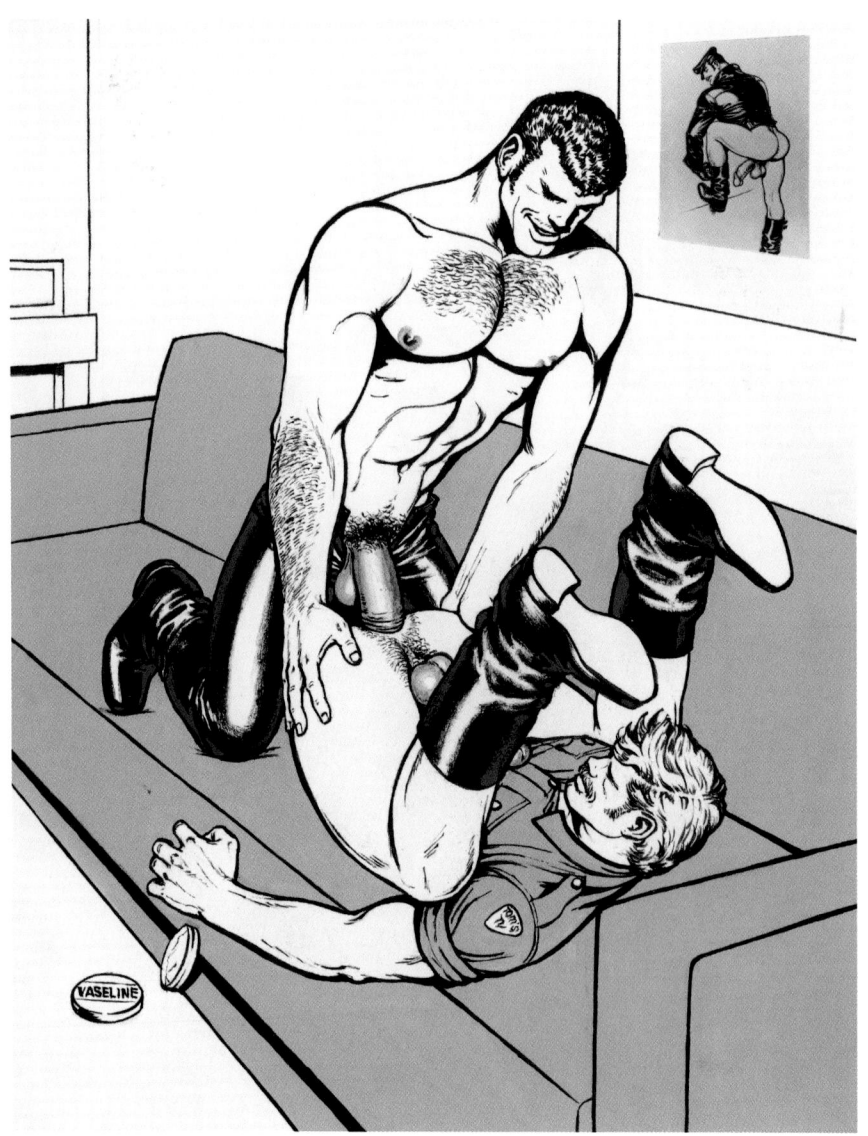

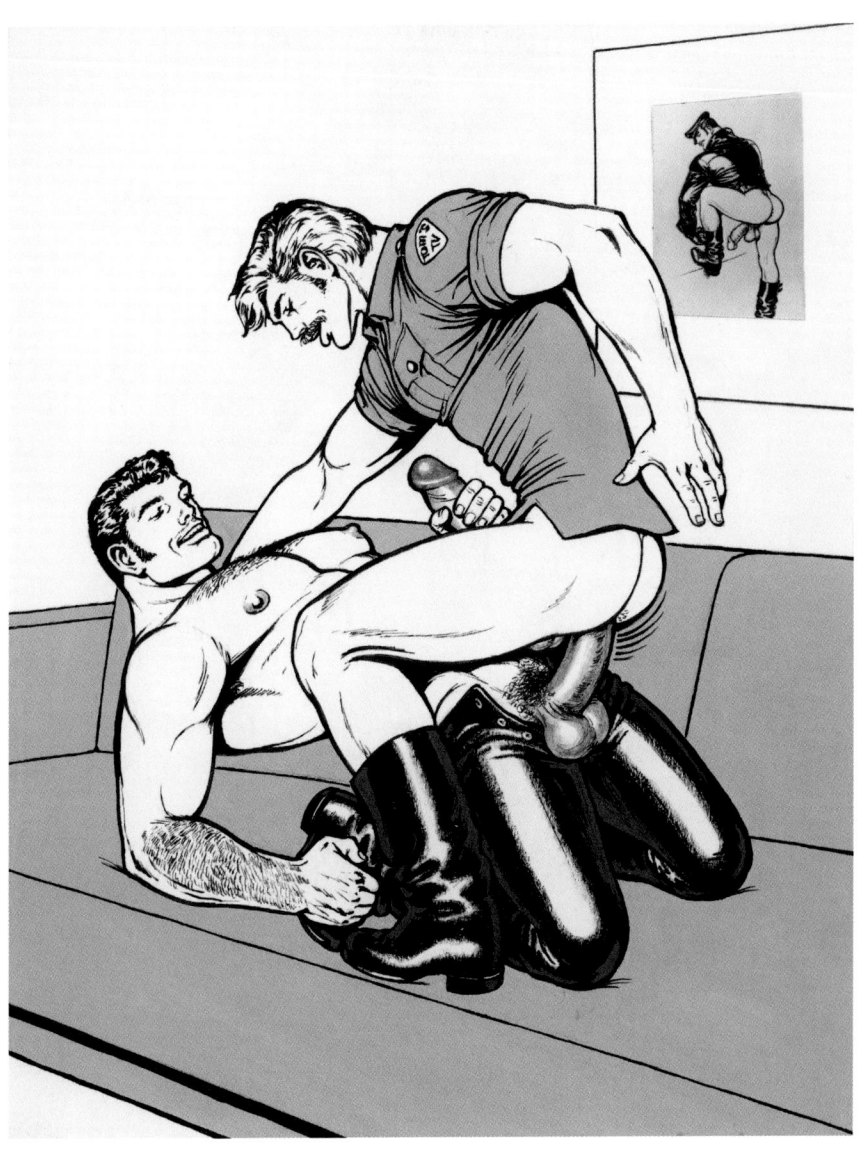

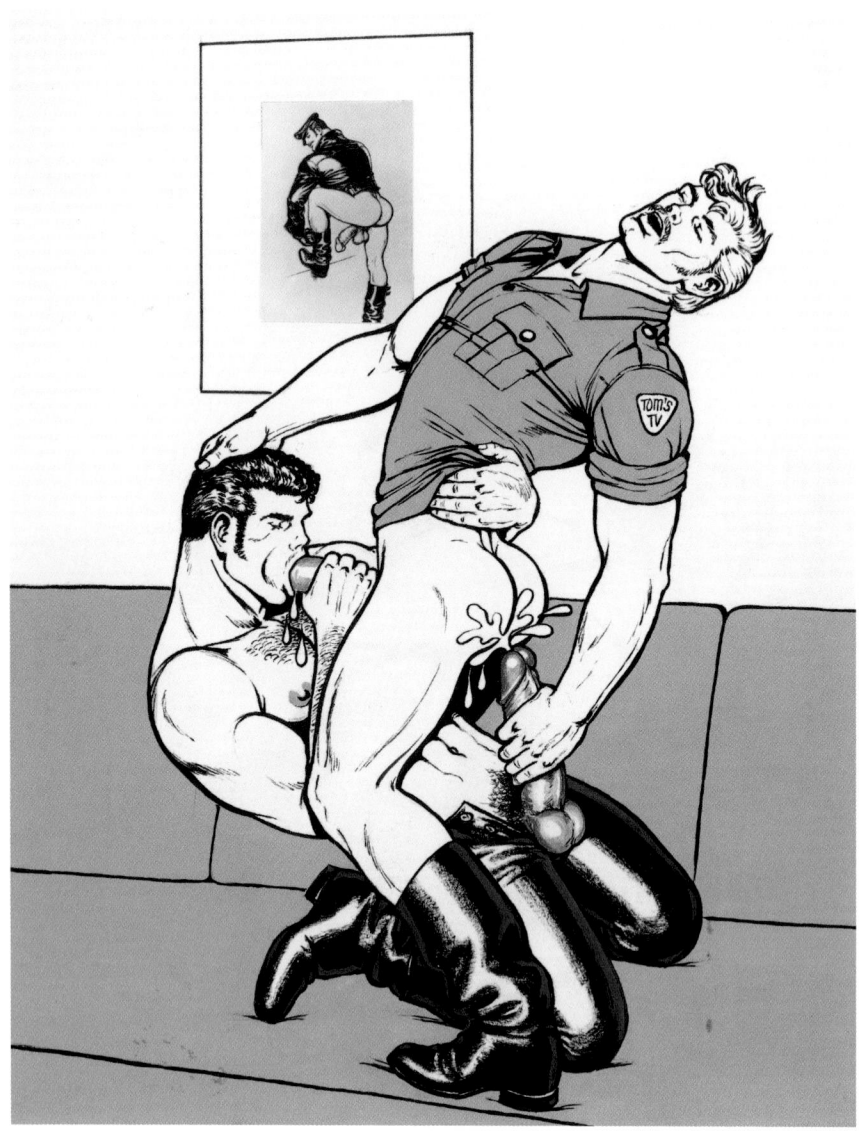

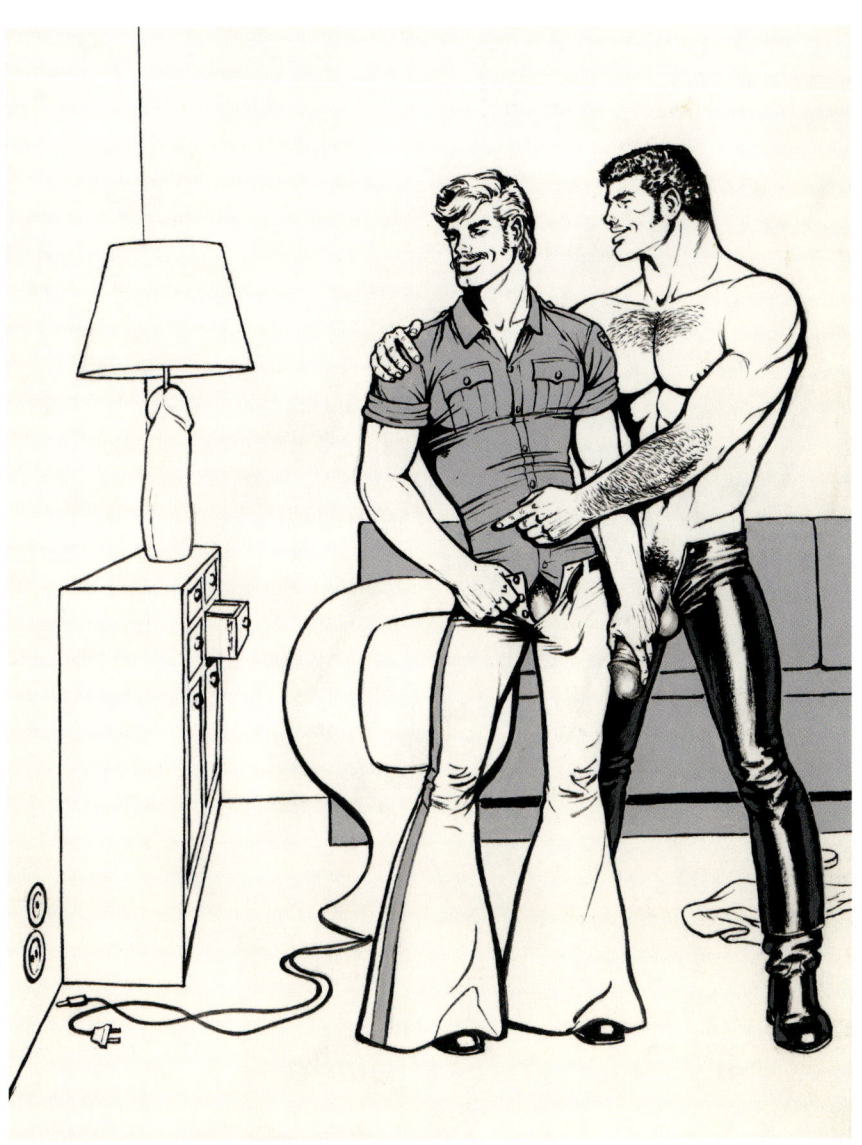

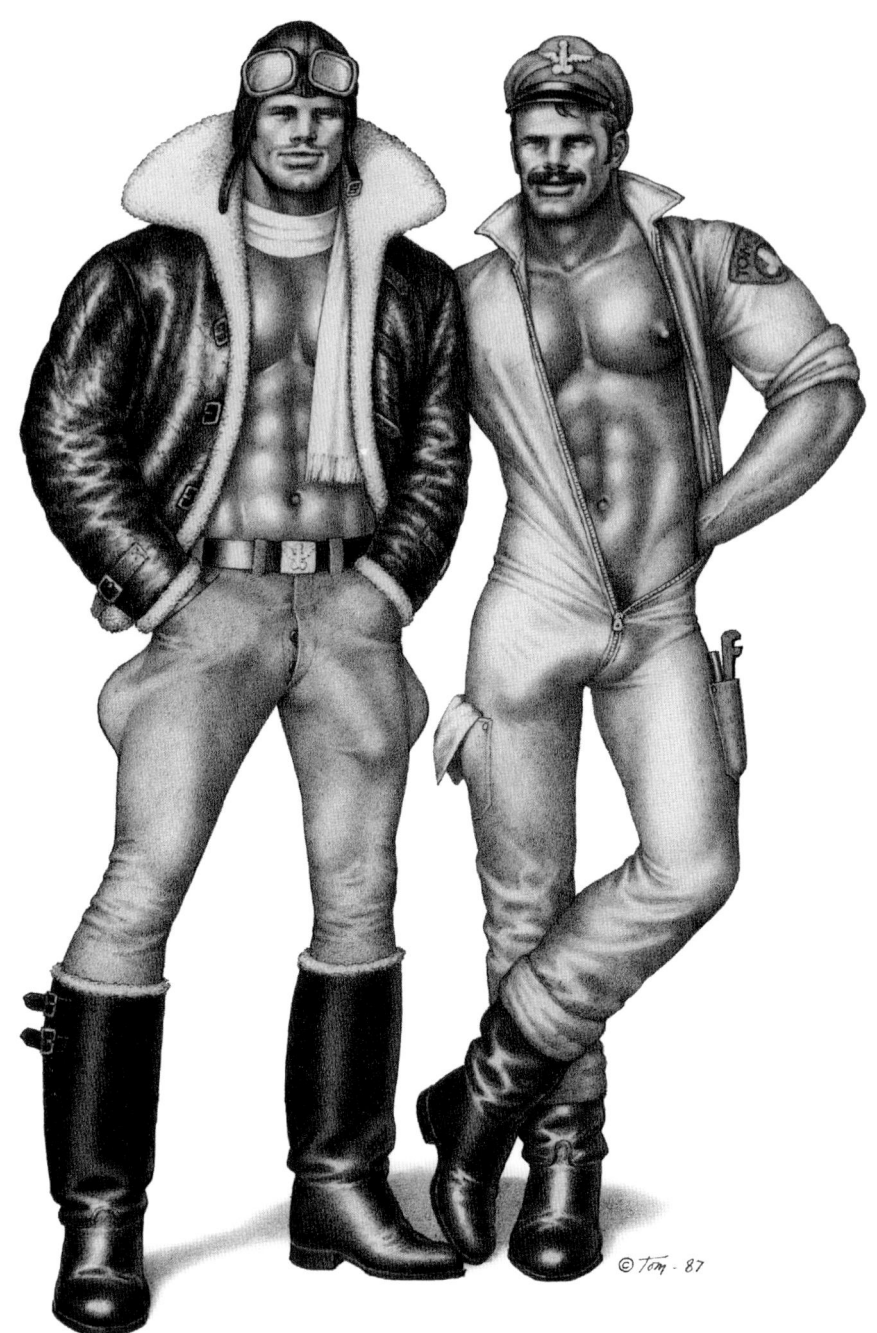

©Tom · 87

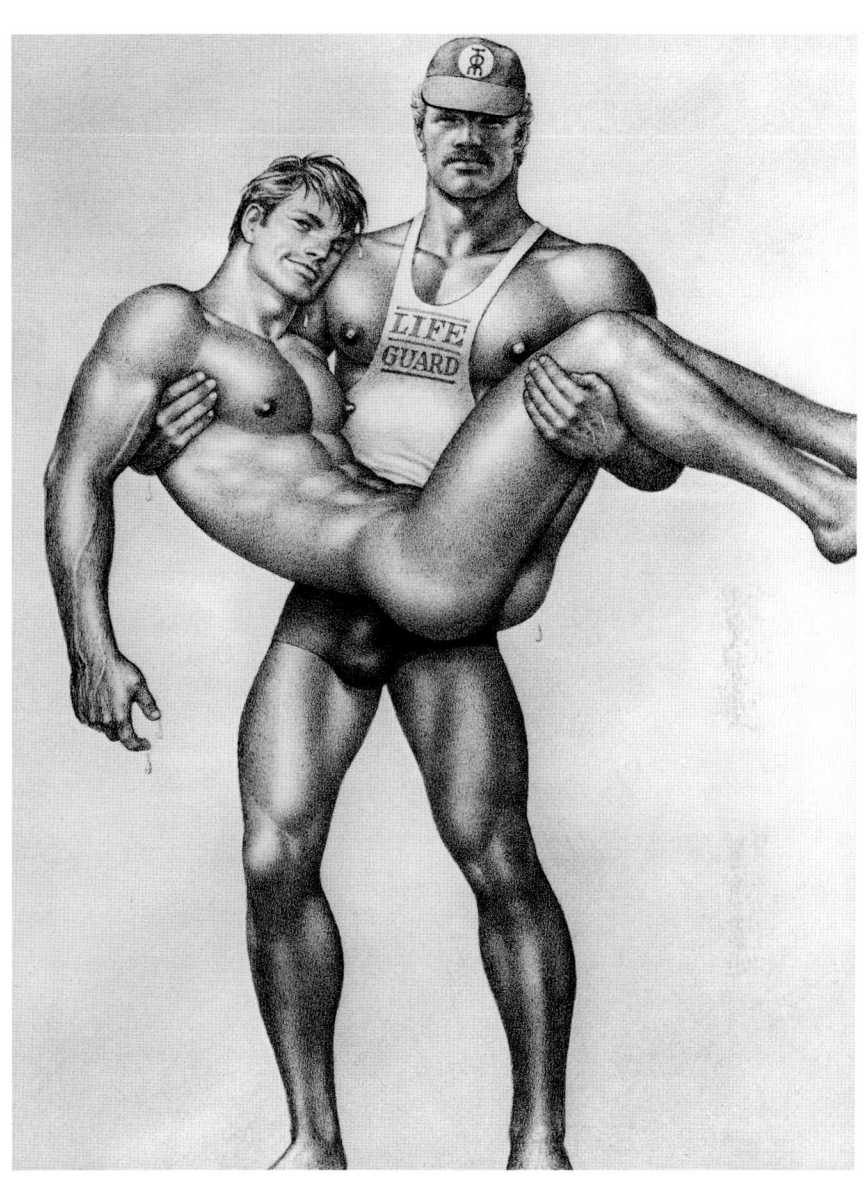

OPPOSITE 1987, graphite on paper
ABOVE 1977, graphite on paper

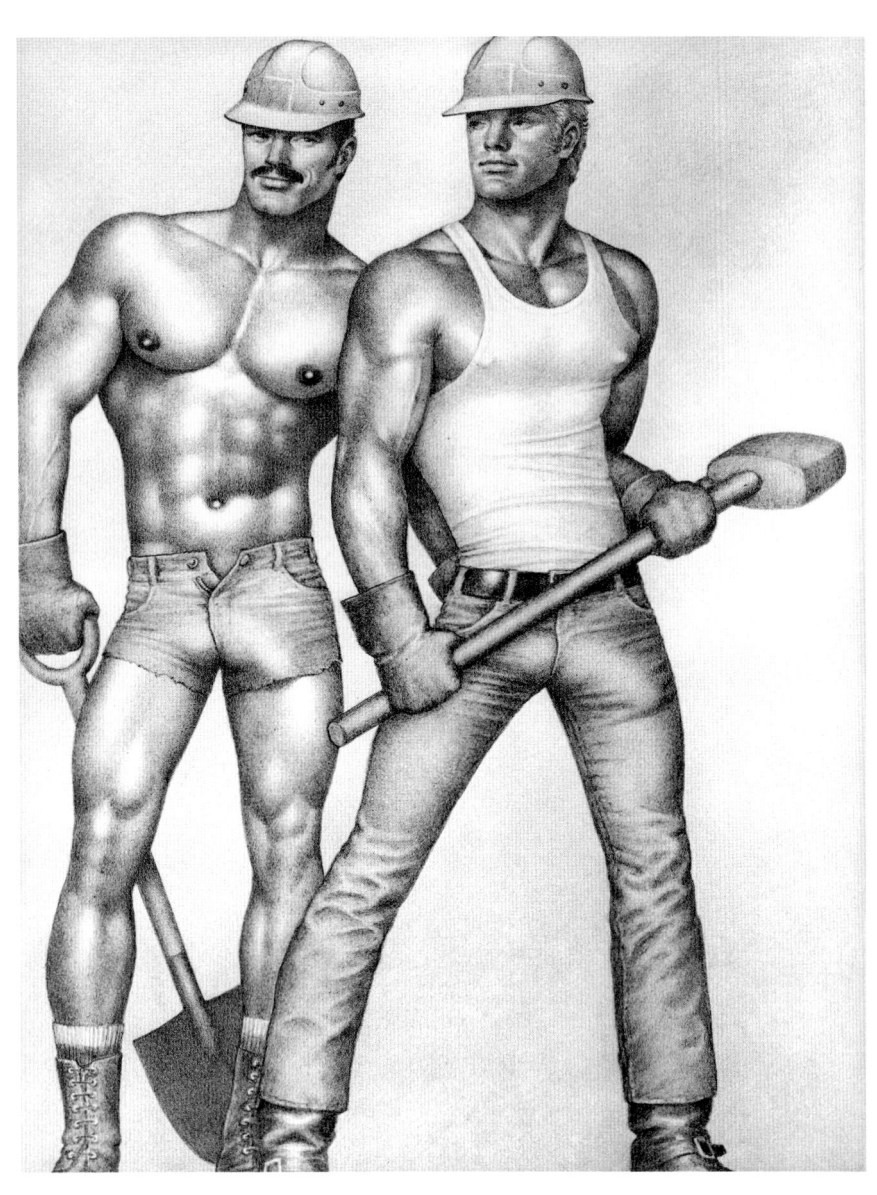

ABOVE 1977, graphite on paper
OPPOSITE 1980, graphite on paper

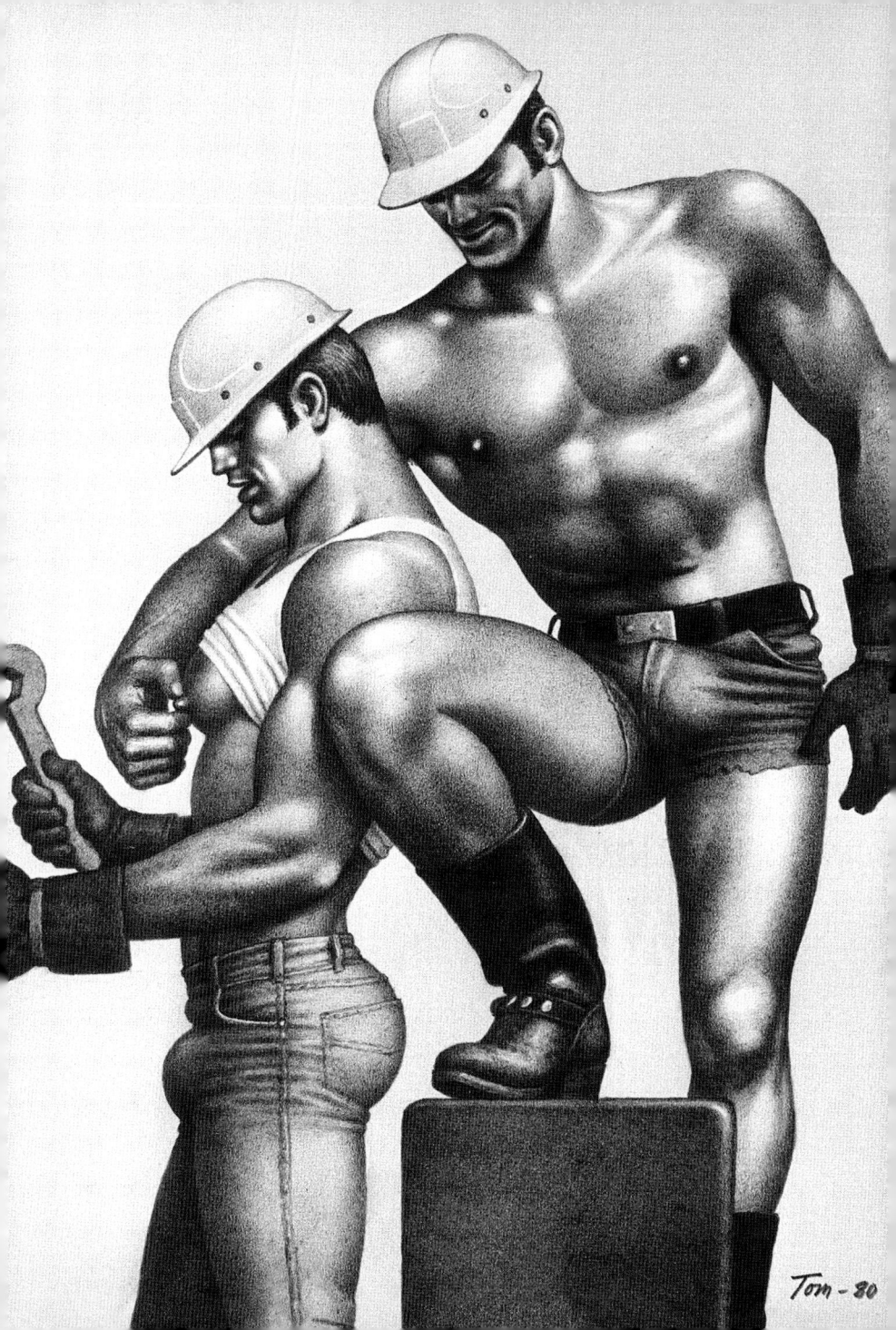

"The drawings by Tom...stress the blue collar aspect of gay sexuality — not only the attraction felt by many middle-class homosexual men for working-class roughnecks, but the idea of the working class as a sexual secret society, characterized by total lack of inhibition. "
—EDWARD LUCIE-SMITH

OPPOSITE Cover for *Service Station,* 1972, graphite on paper

kake

12.

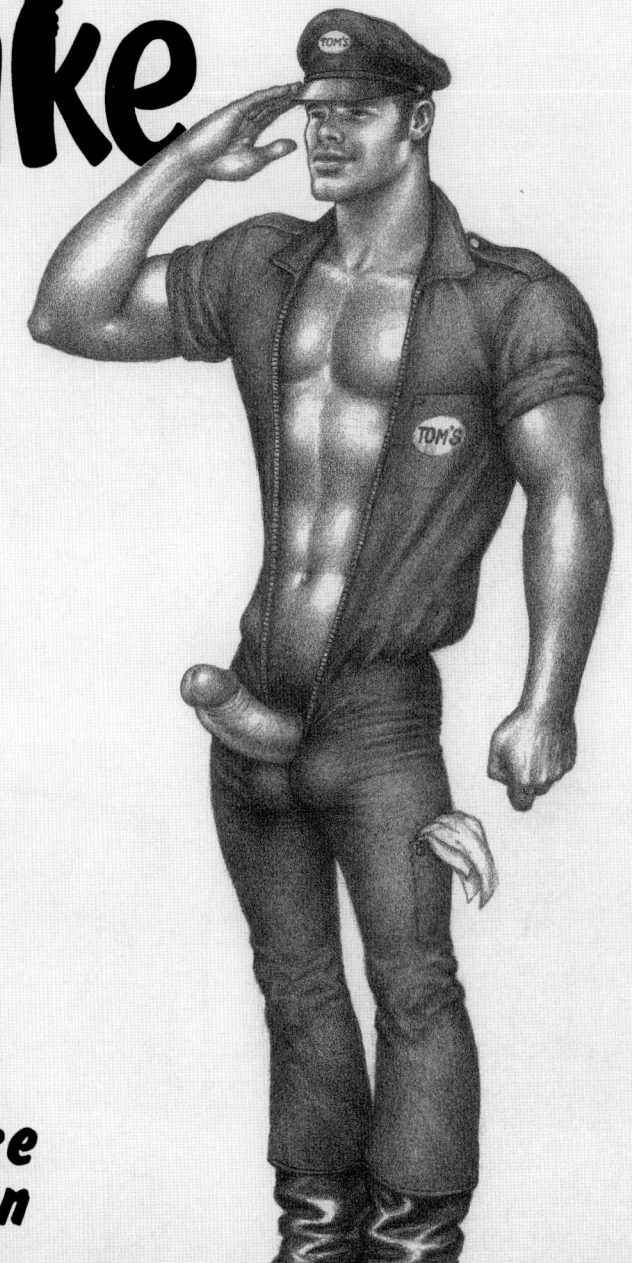

Service
Station

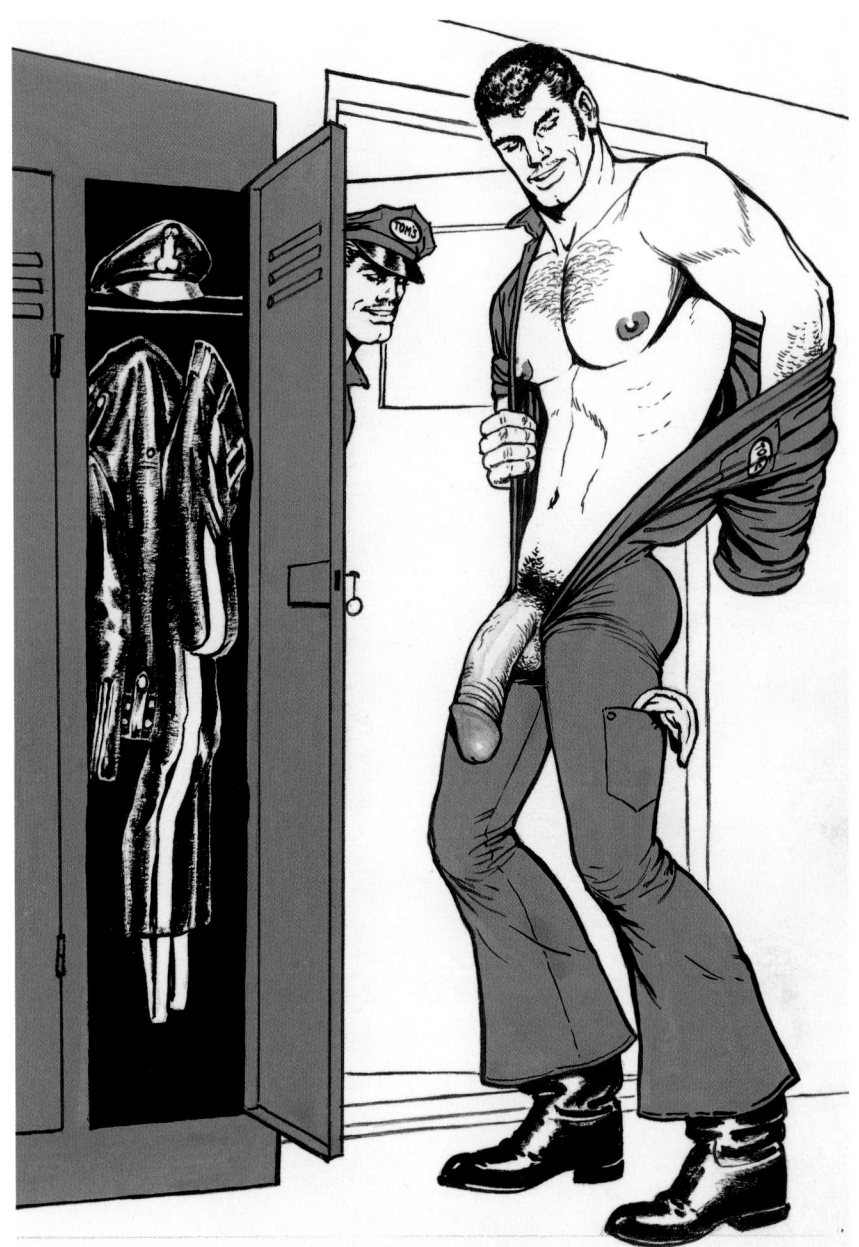

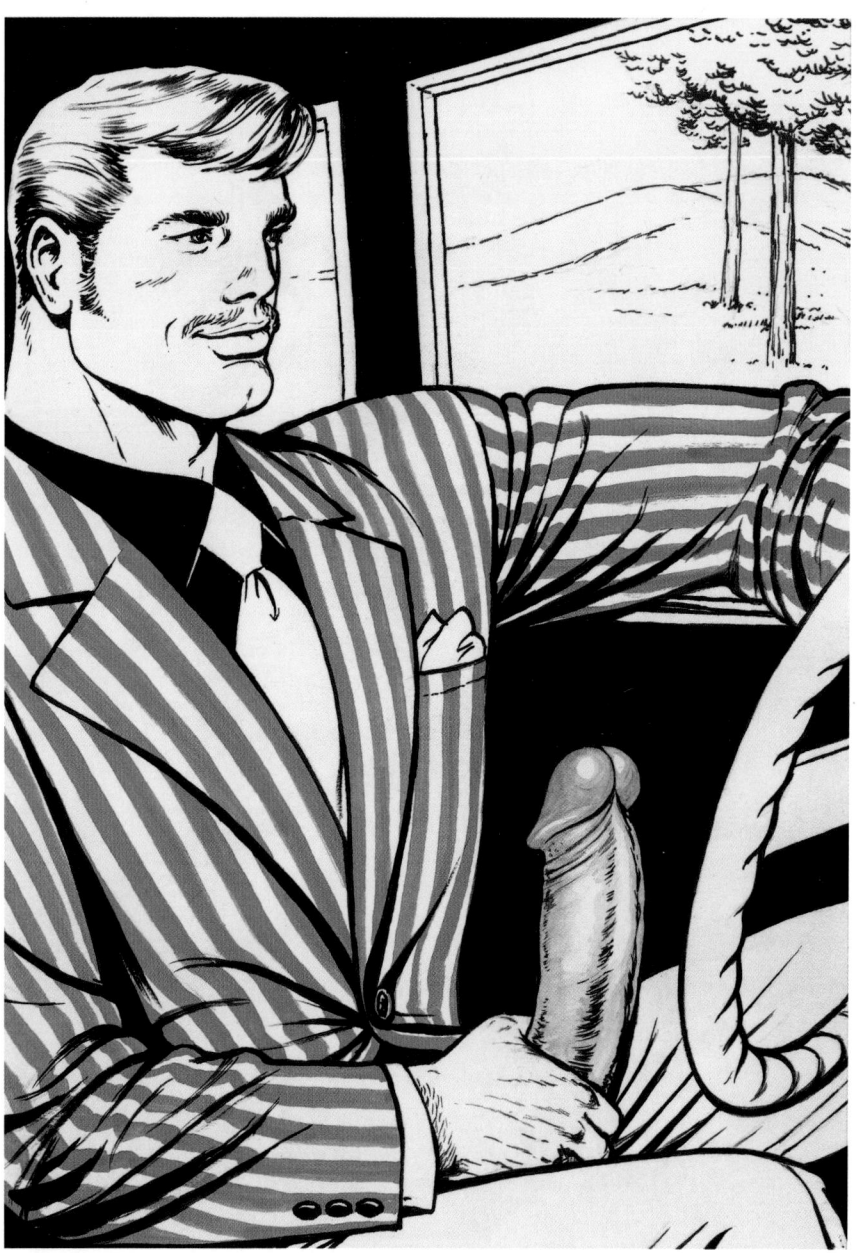

PAGES 114–133 1972, *Service Station*, pen and ink and ink wash

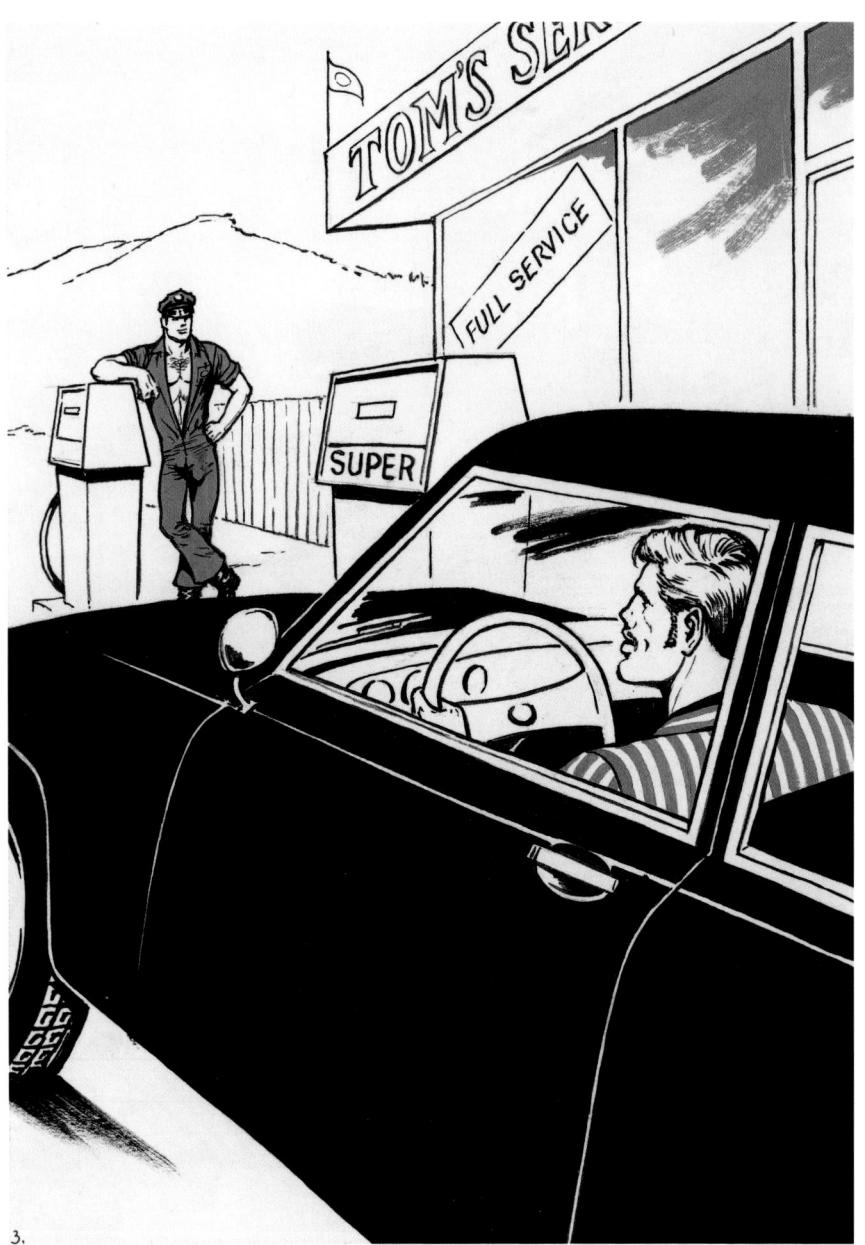

3.

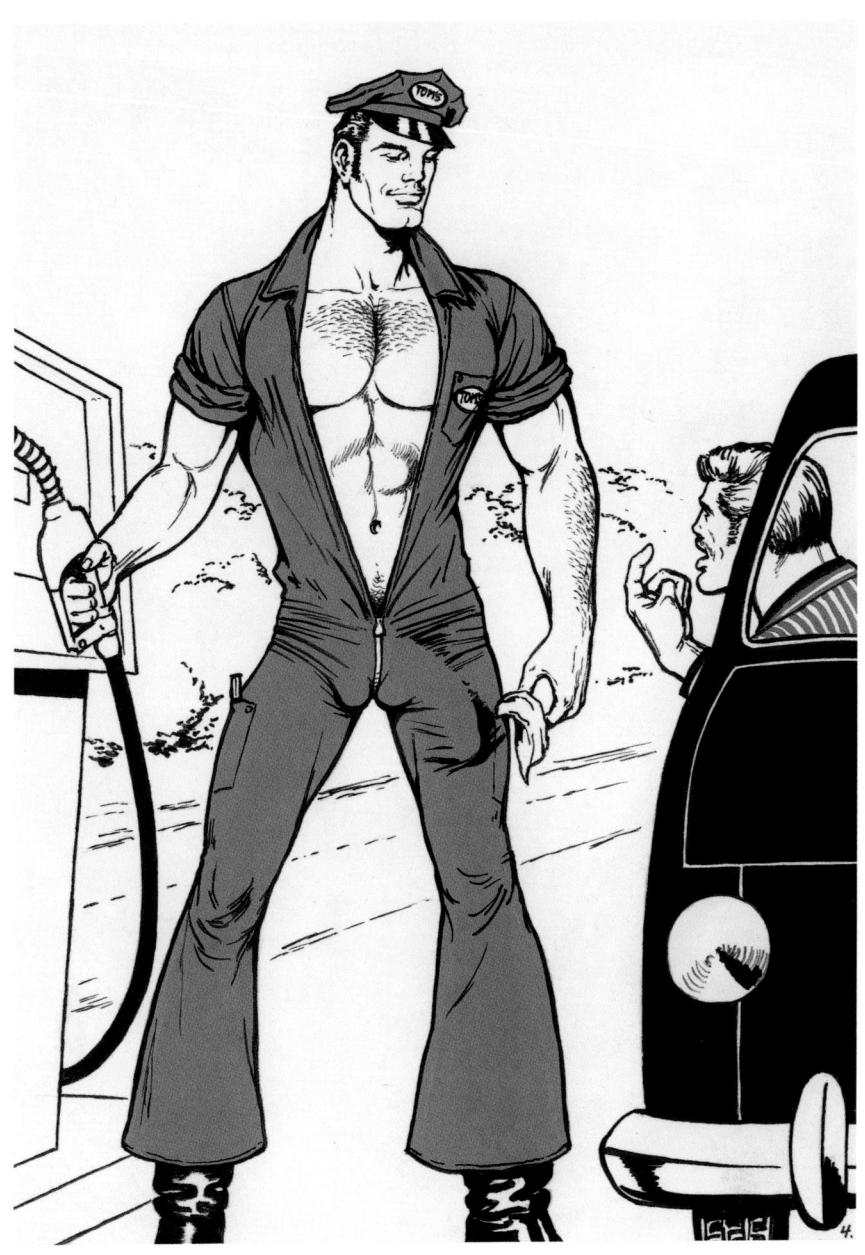

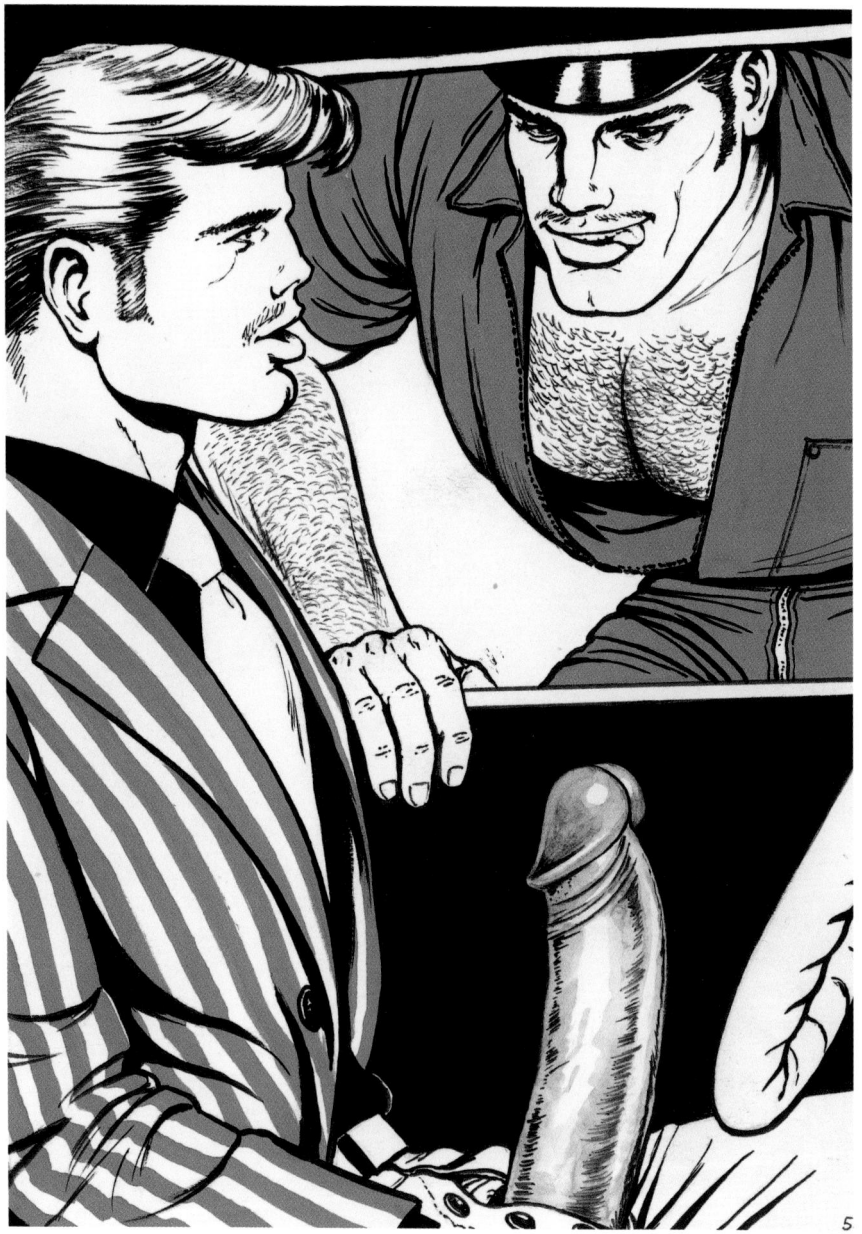

5

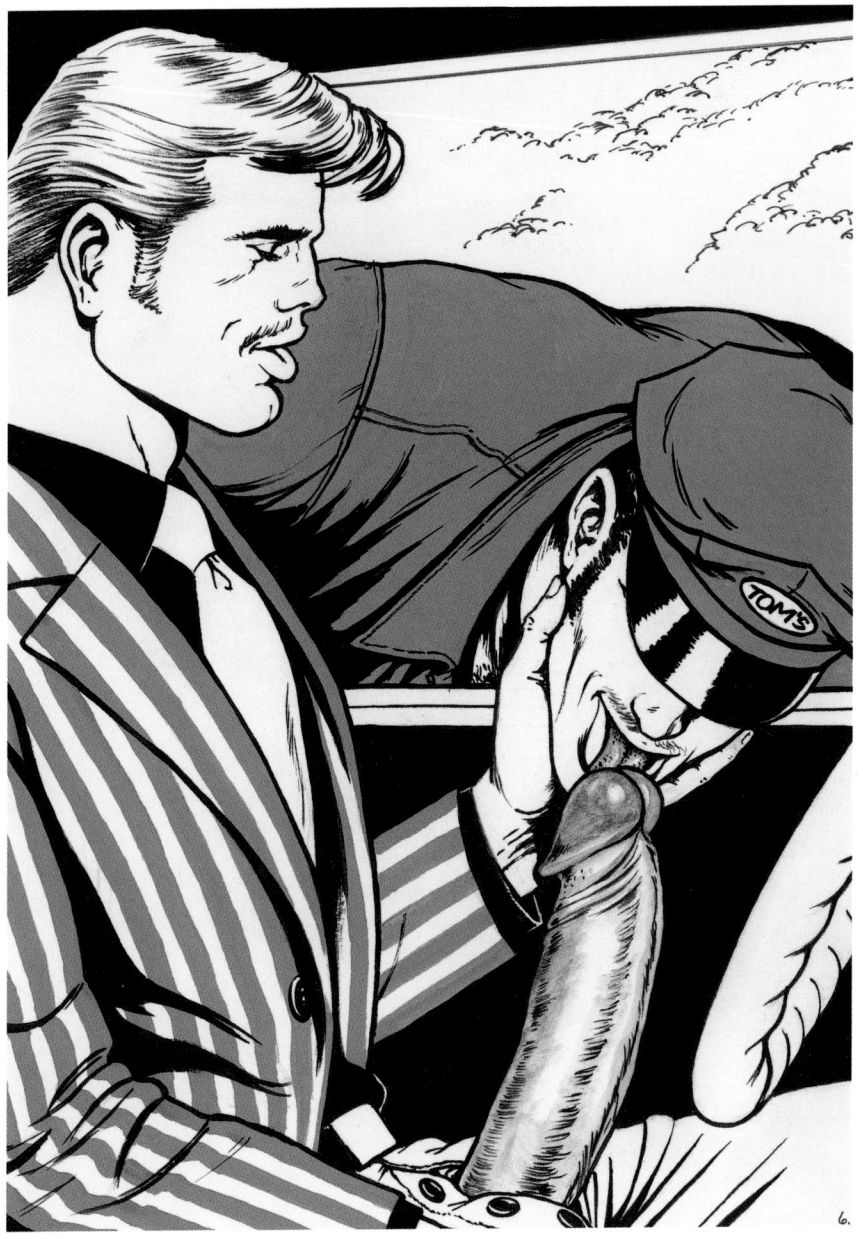

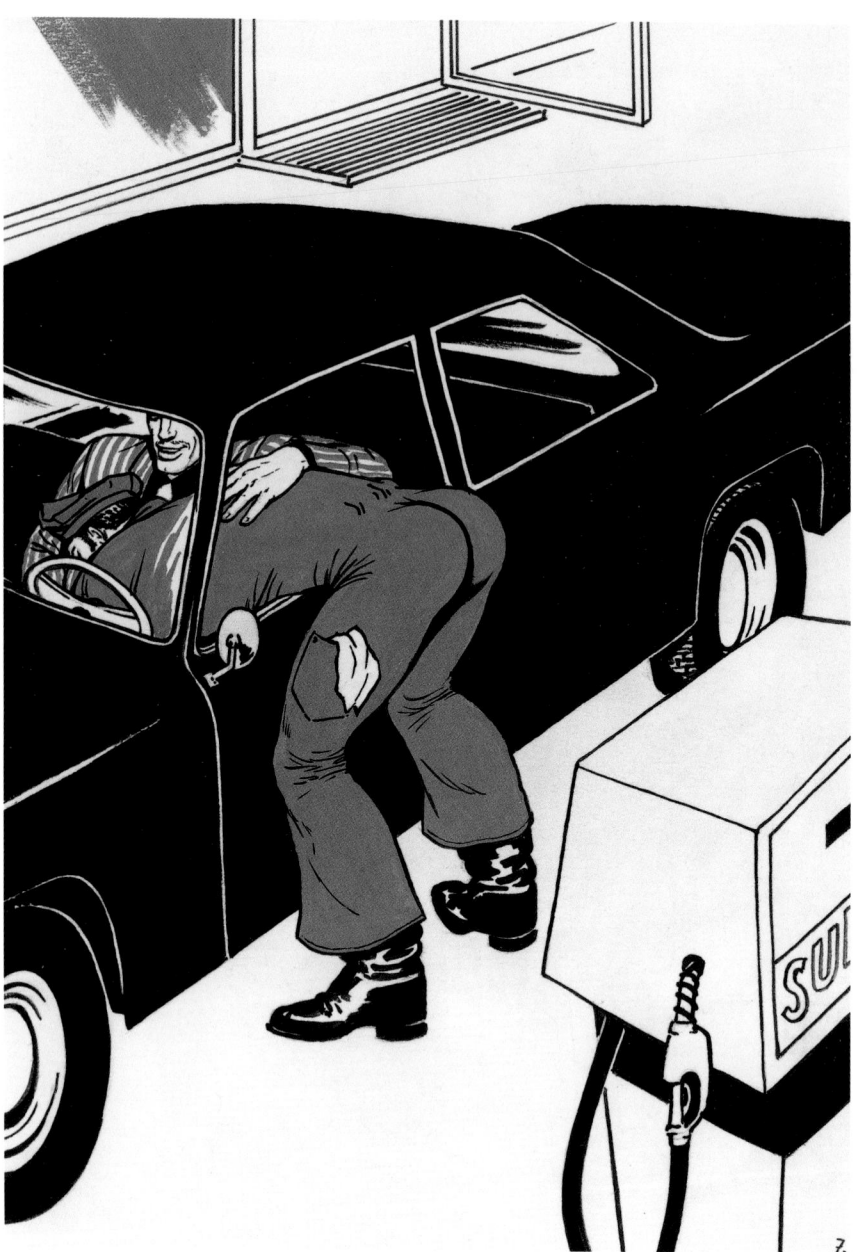

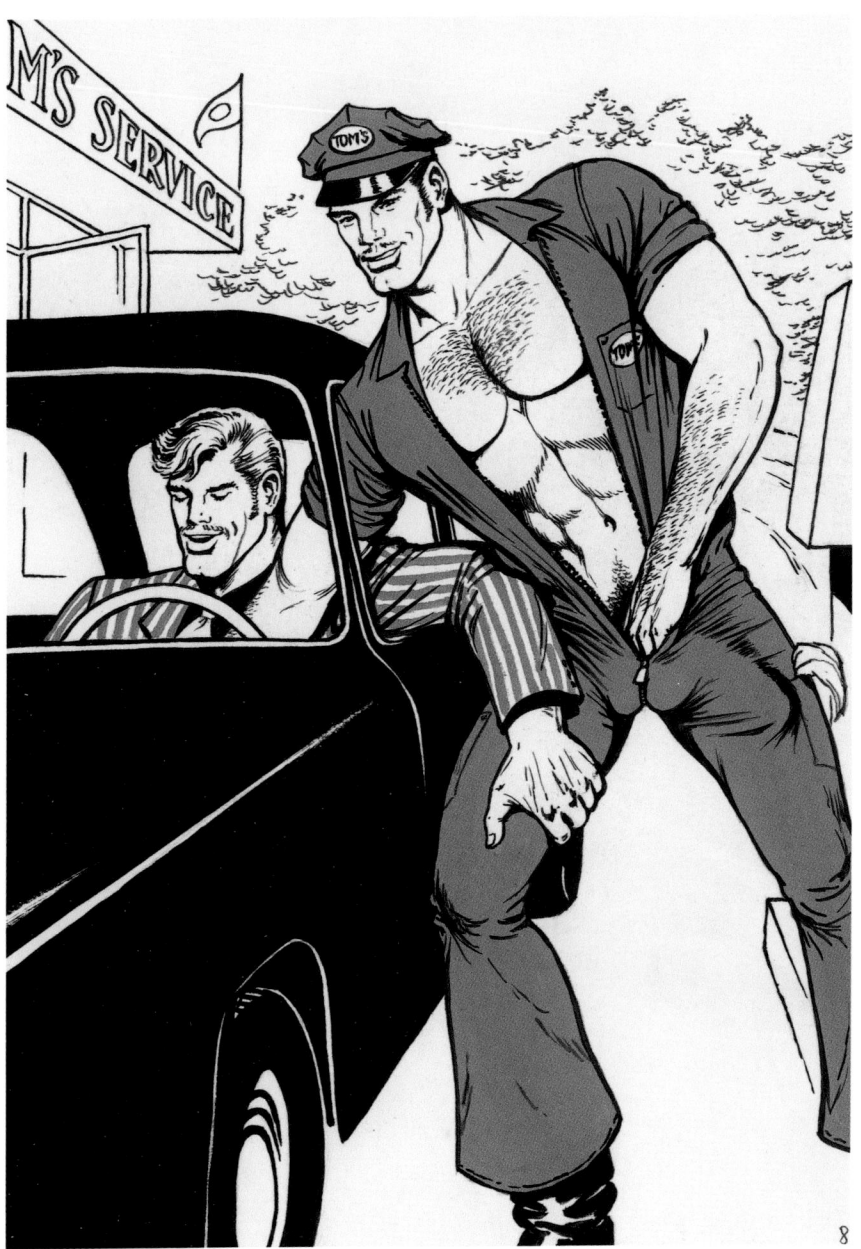

8

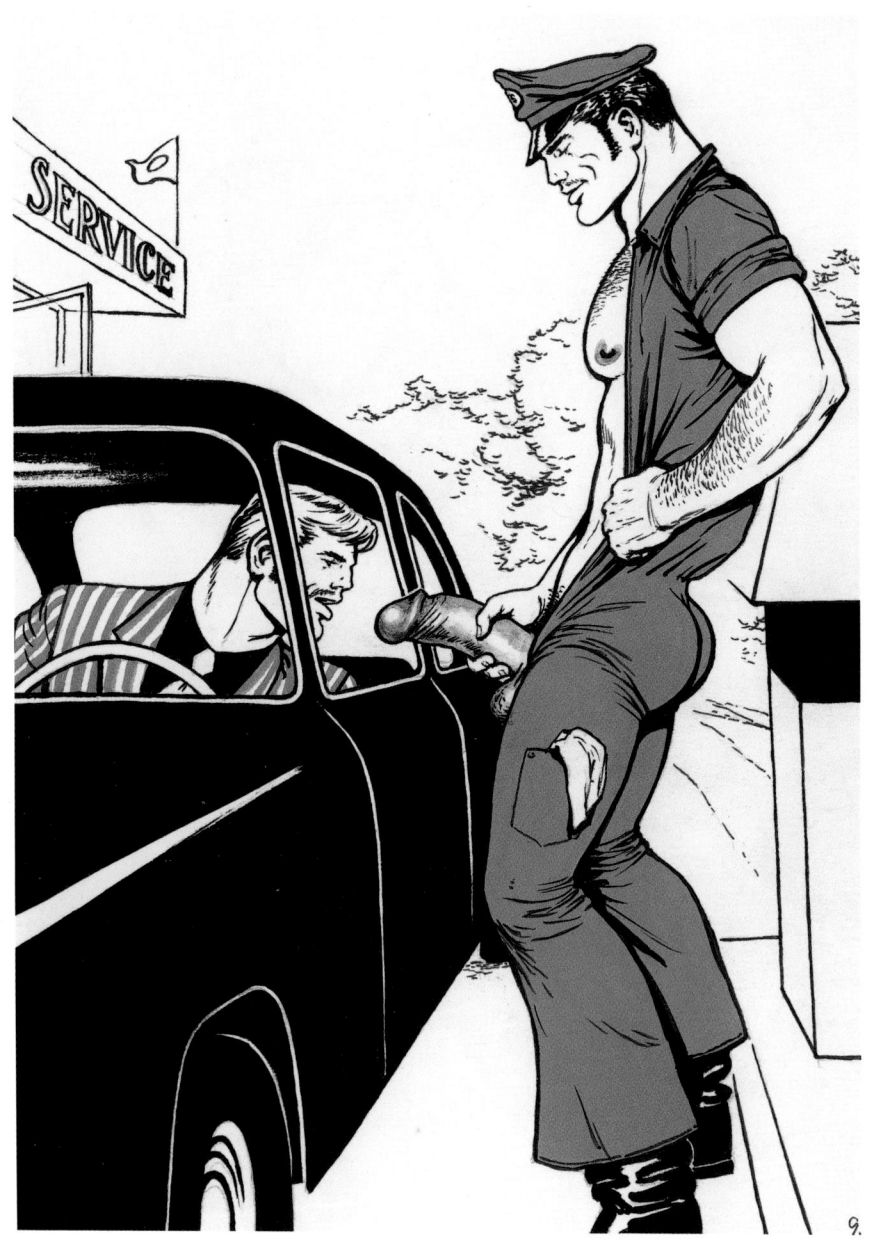

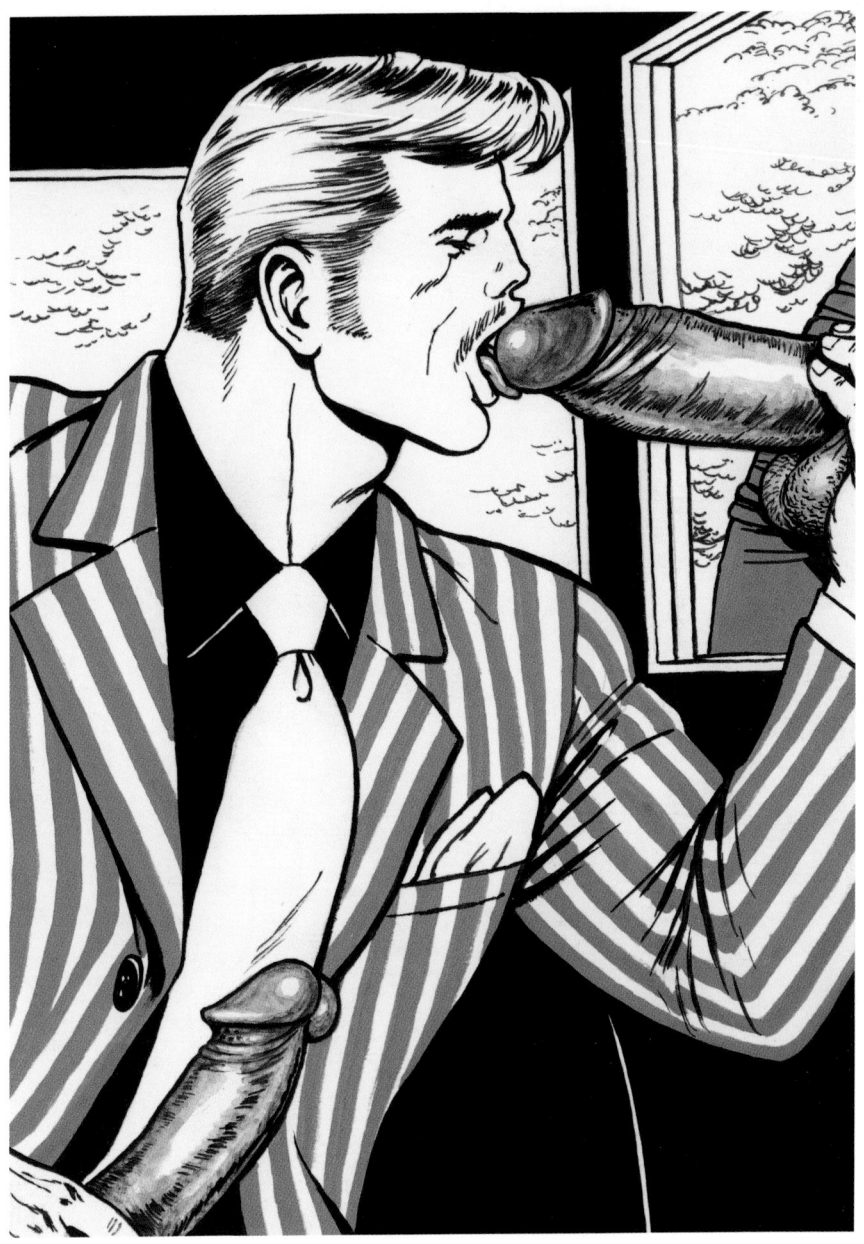

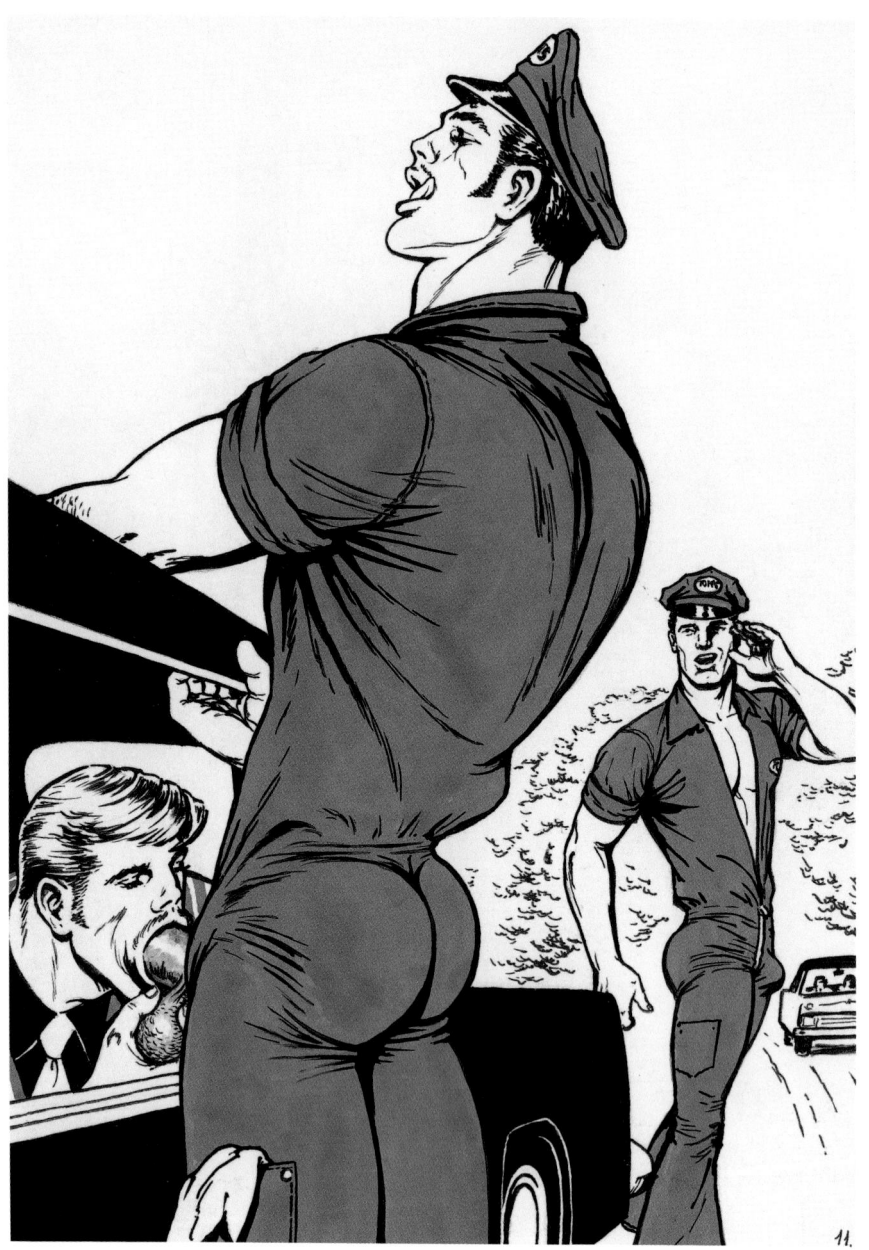

11.

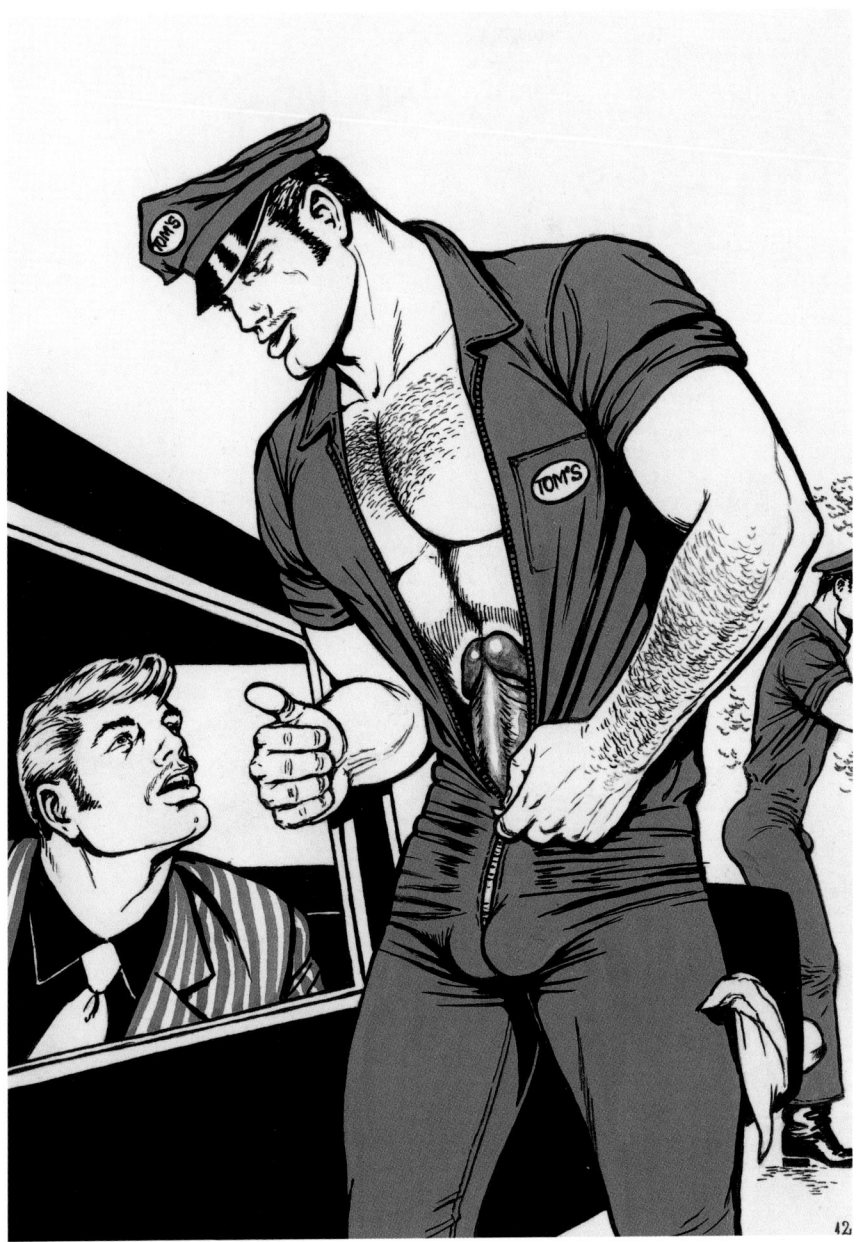

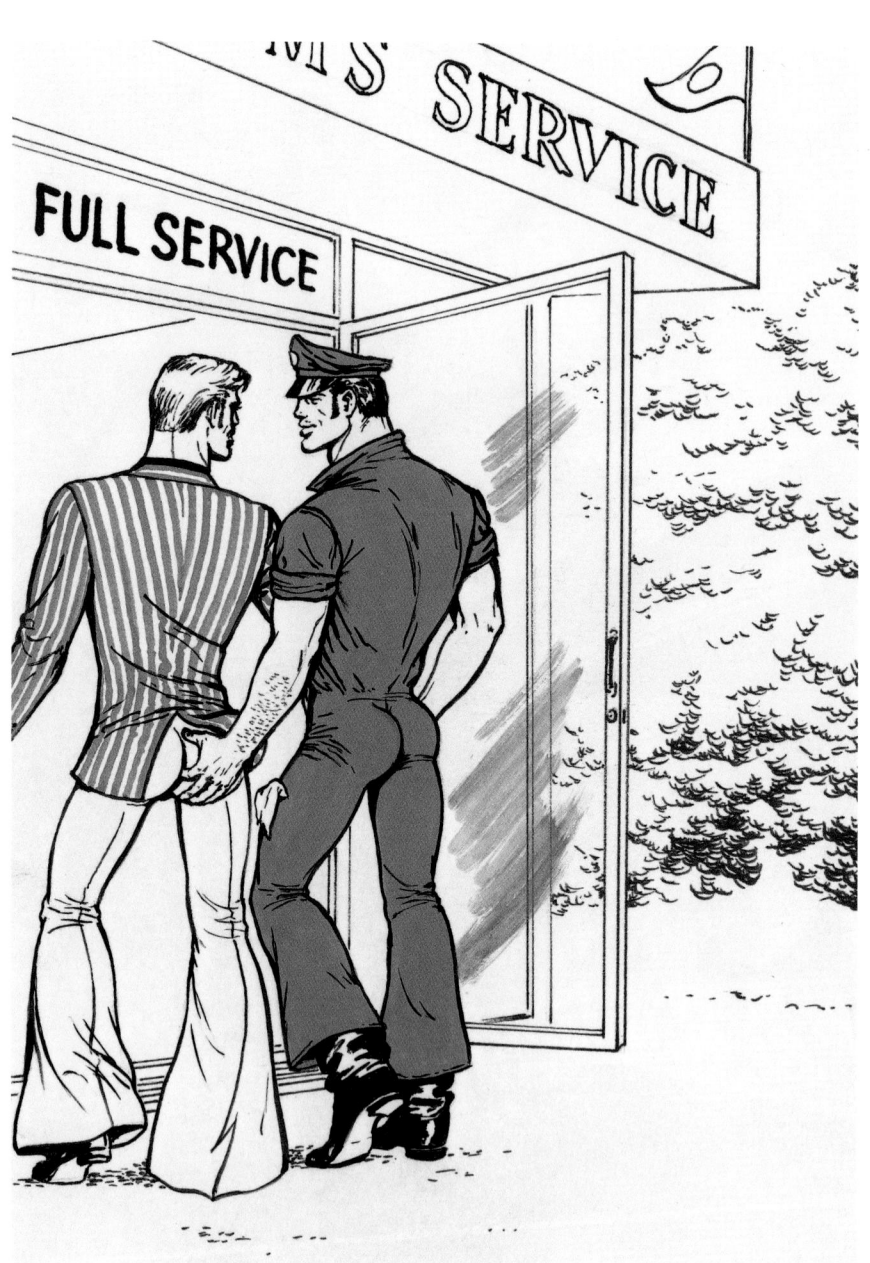

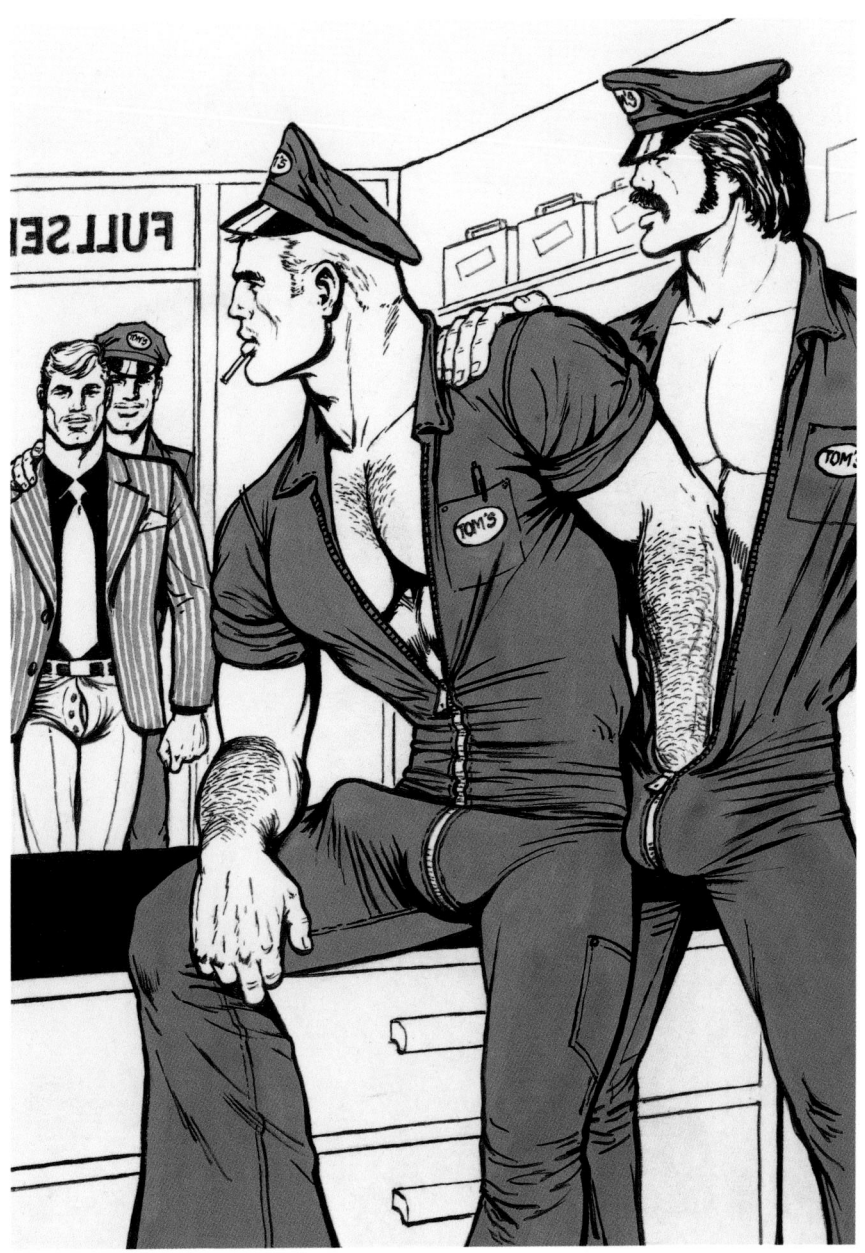

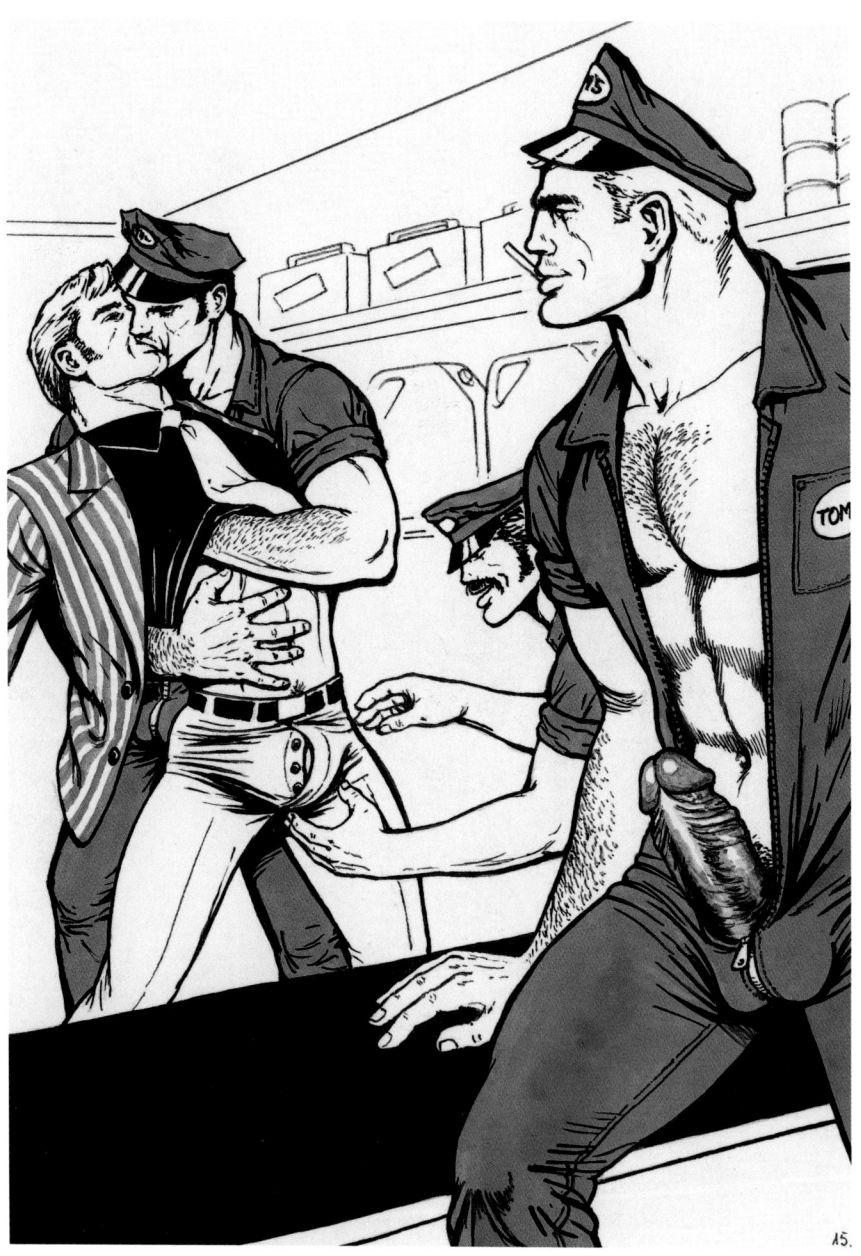

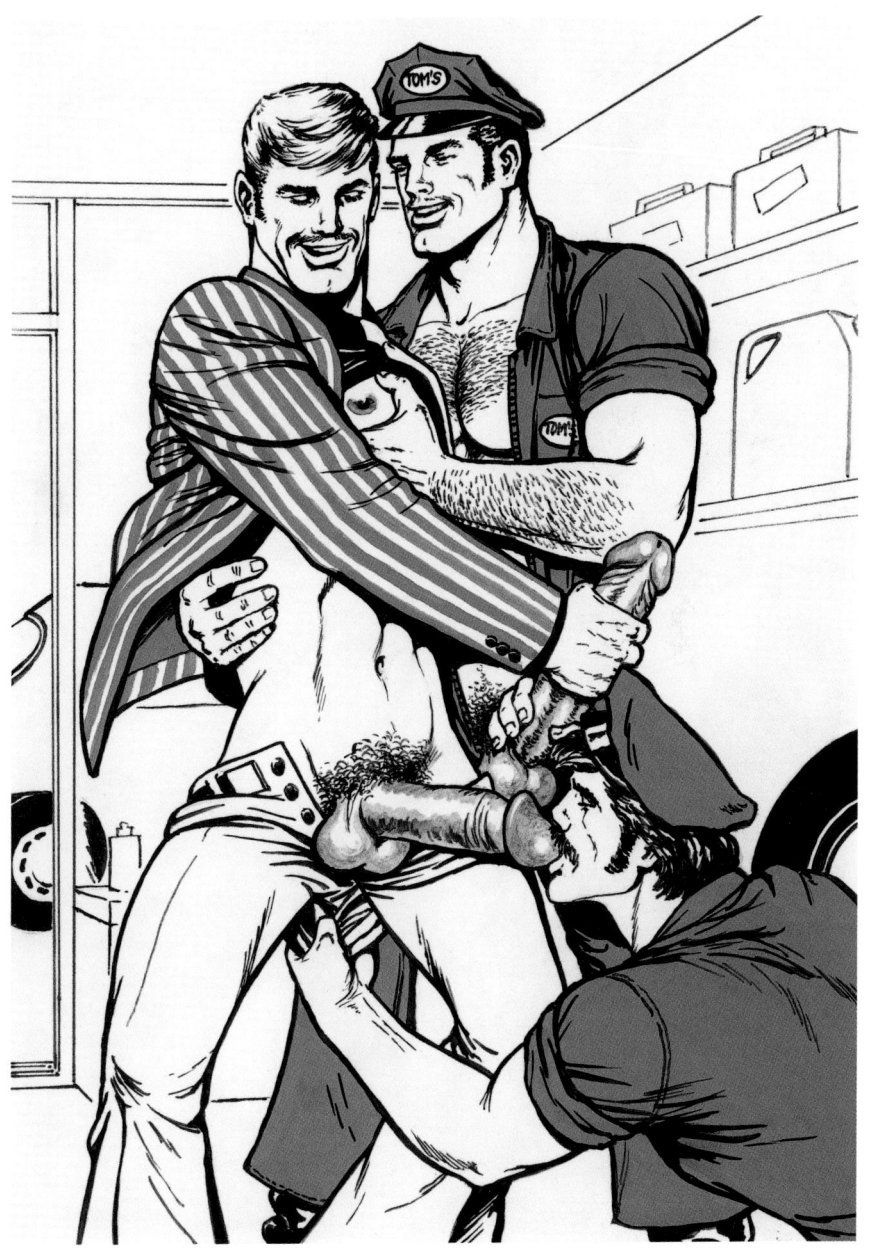

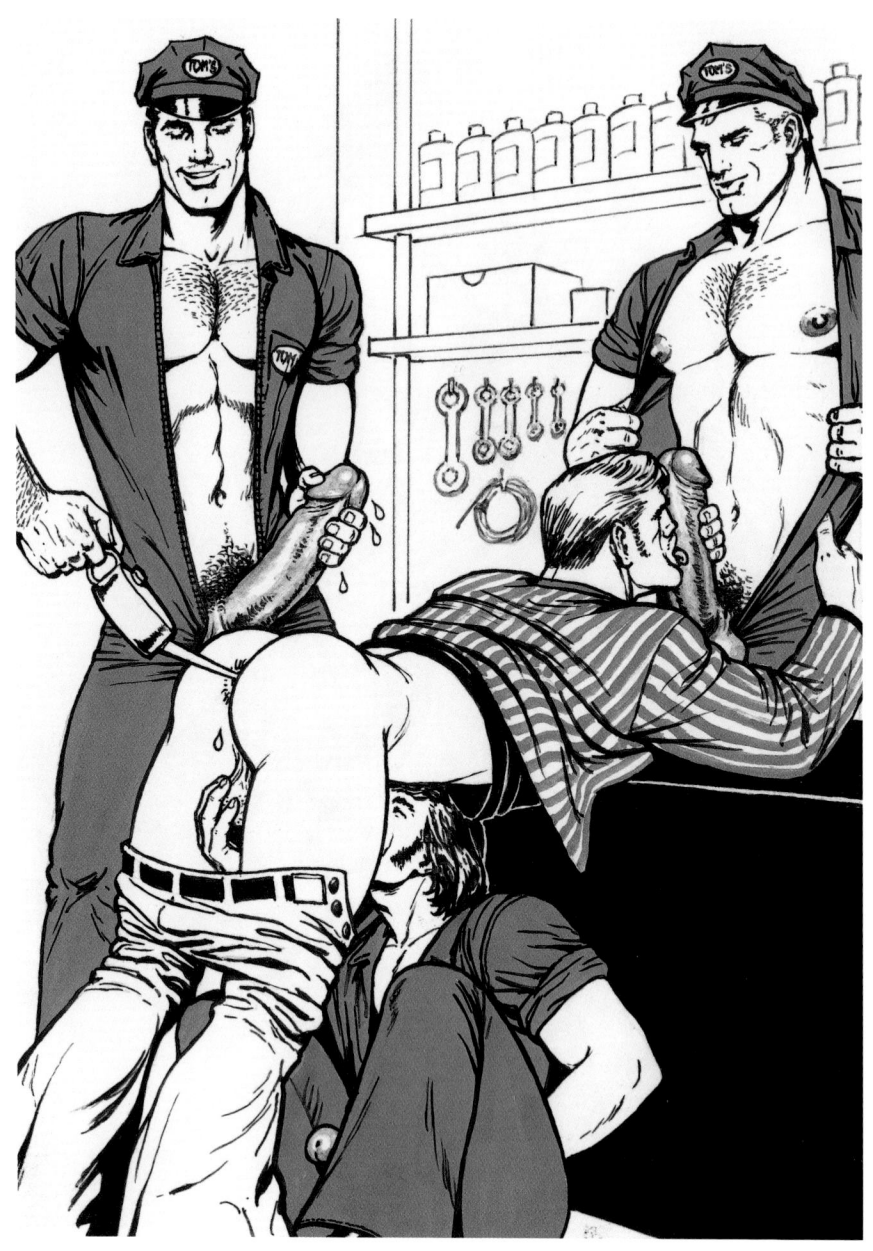

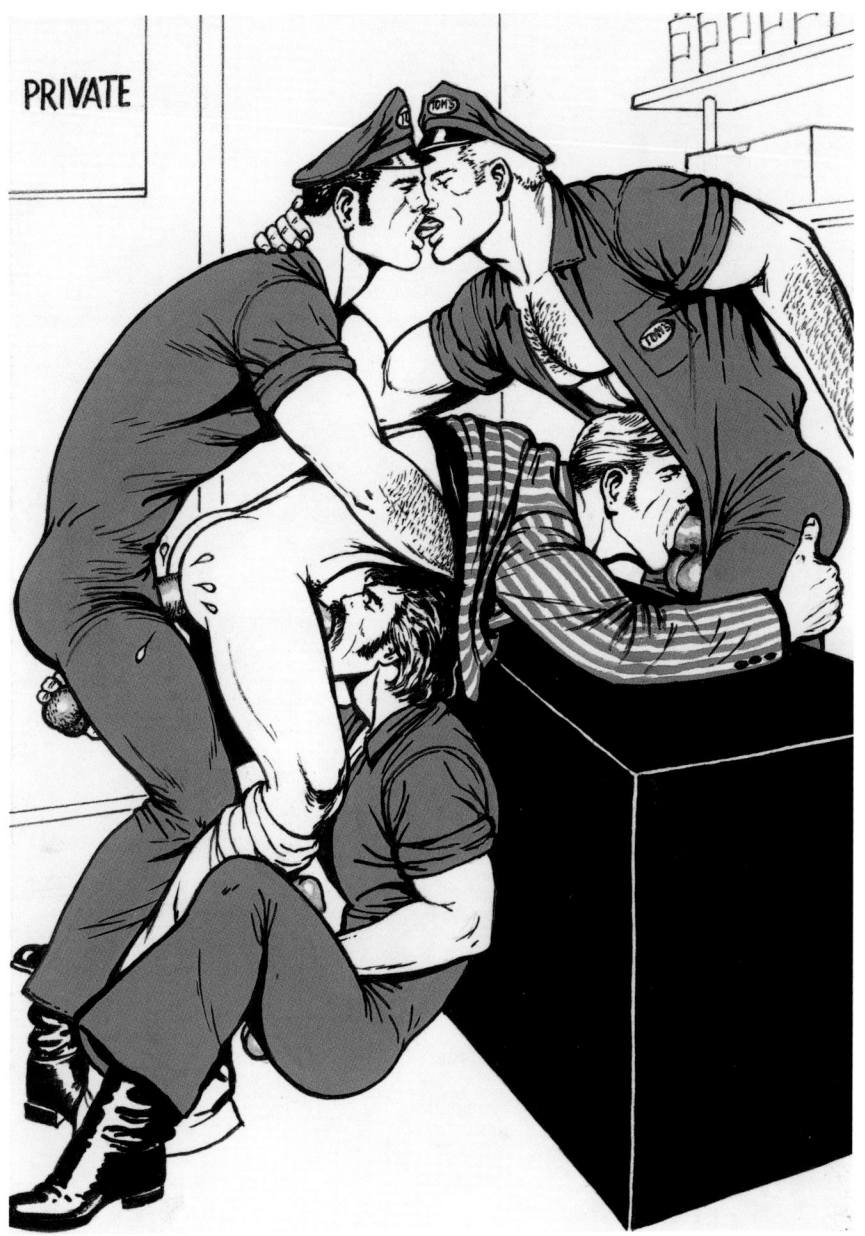

PRIVATE

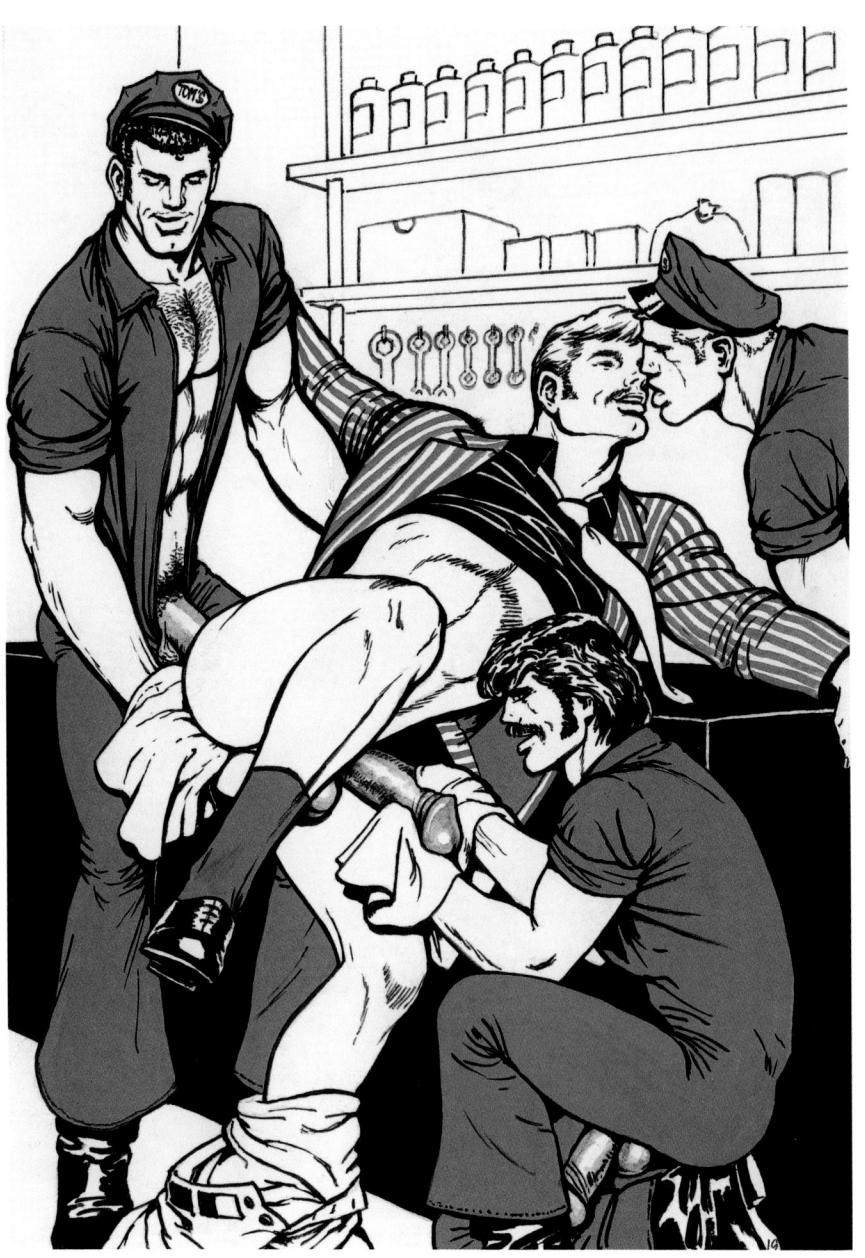

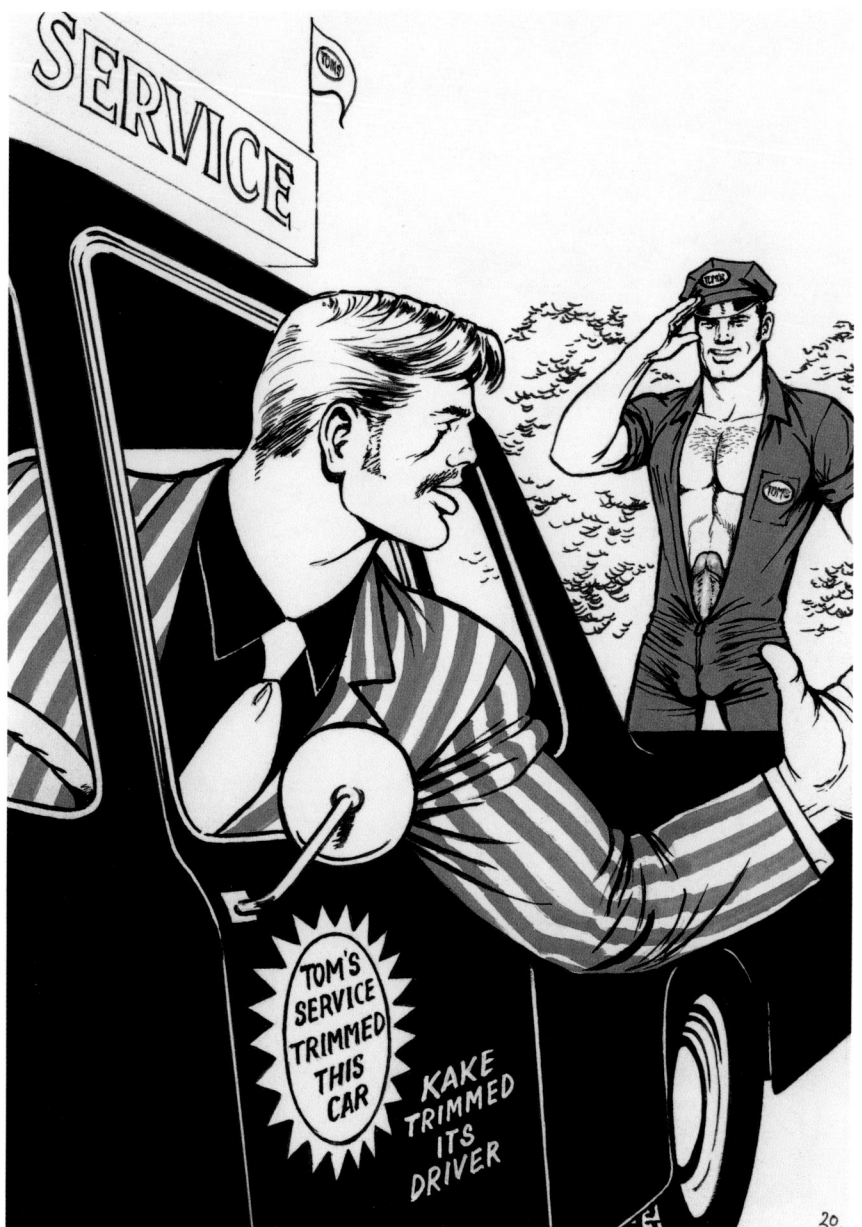

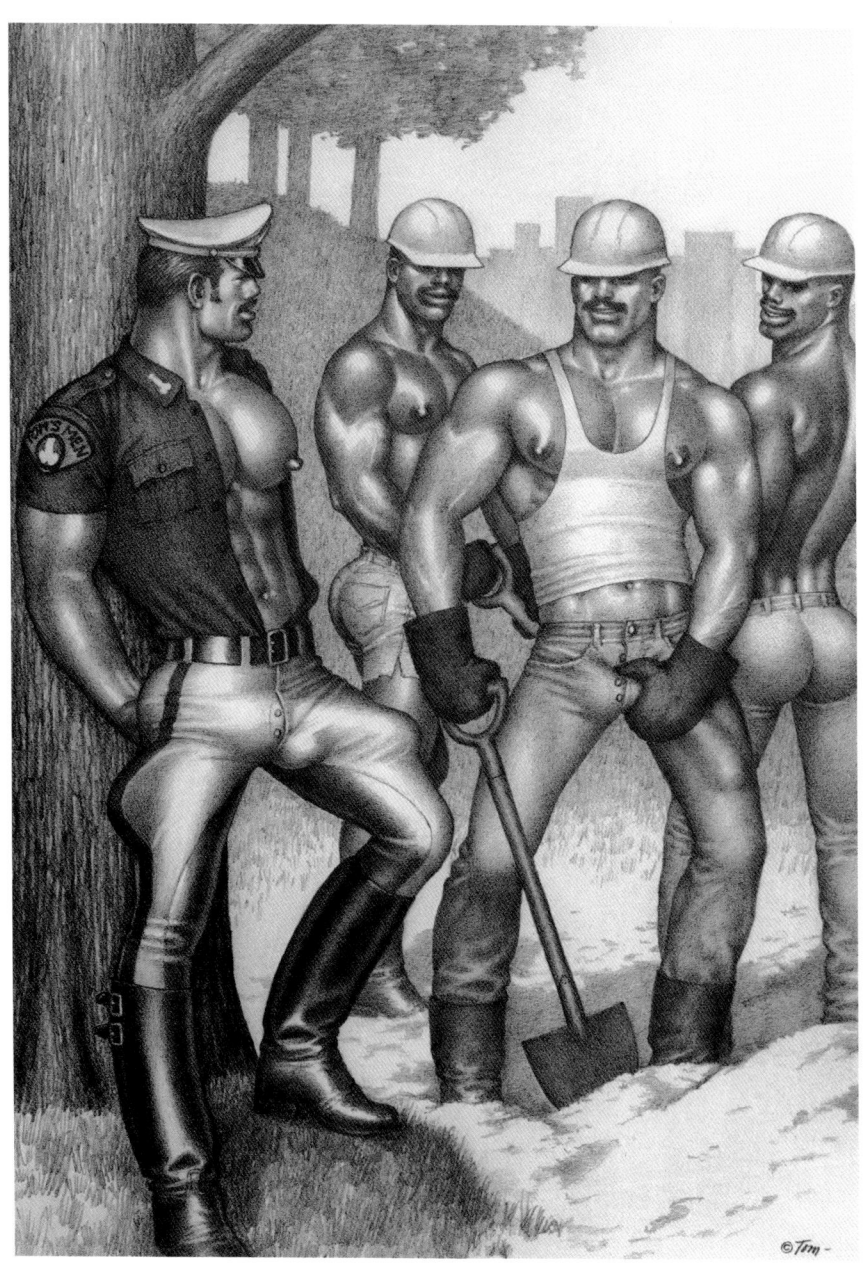

ABOVE 1988, graphite on paper, permanent collection of the Art Institute of Chicago

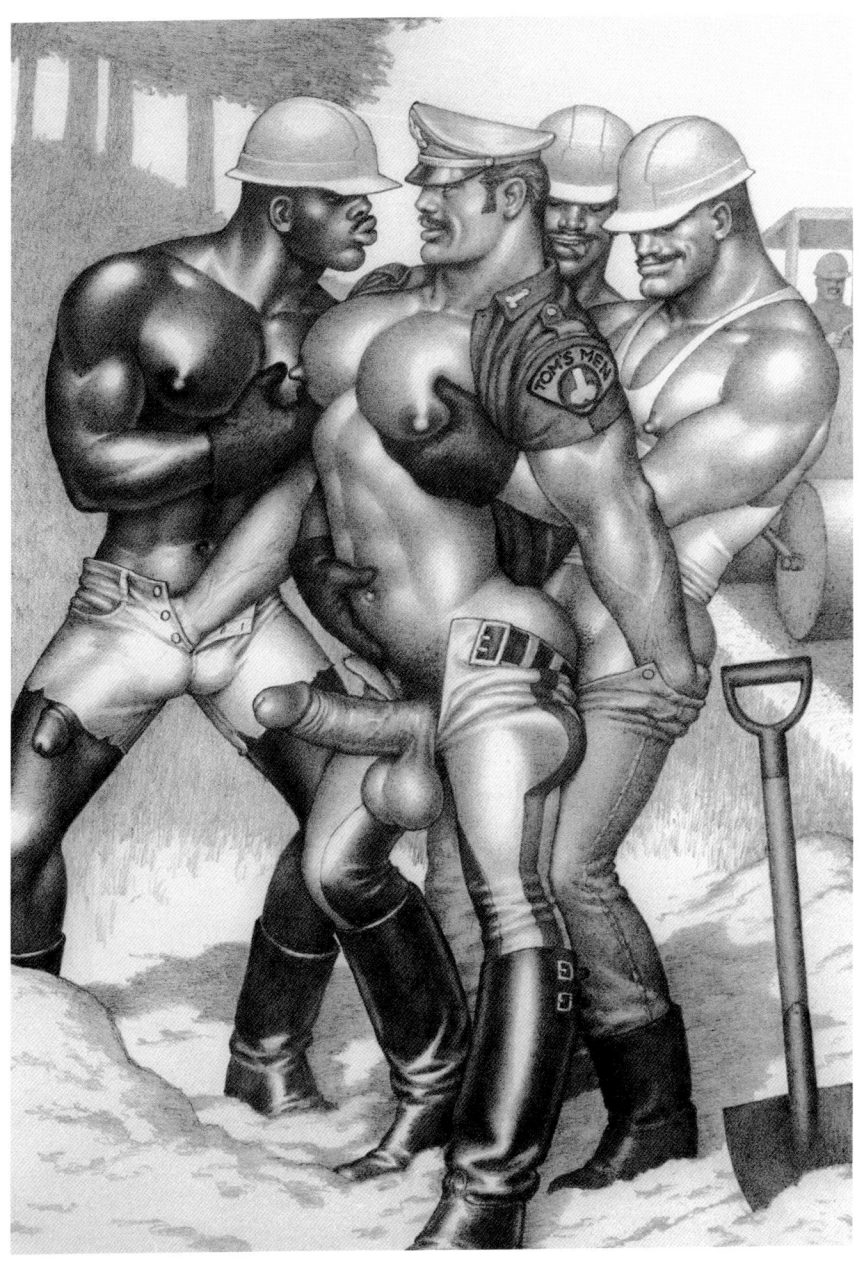

ABOVE 1988, graphite on paper

"*I know my little 'dirty drawings' are never going to hang in the main salons of the Louvre, but if our world learns to accept all the different ways of loving, then maybe I could have a place in one of the smaller side rooms.*"

—TOM OF FINLAND

OPPOSITE Cover for *Loading Zone*, 1975, pen and ink on paper

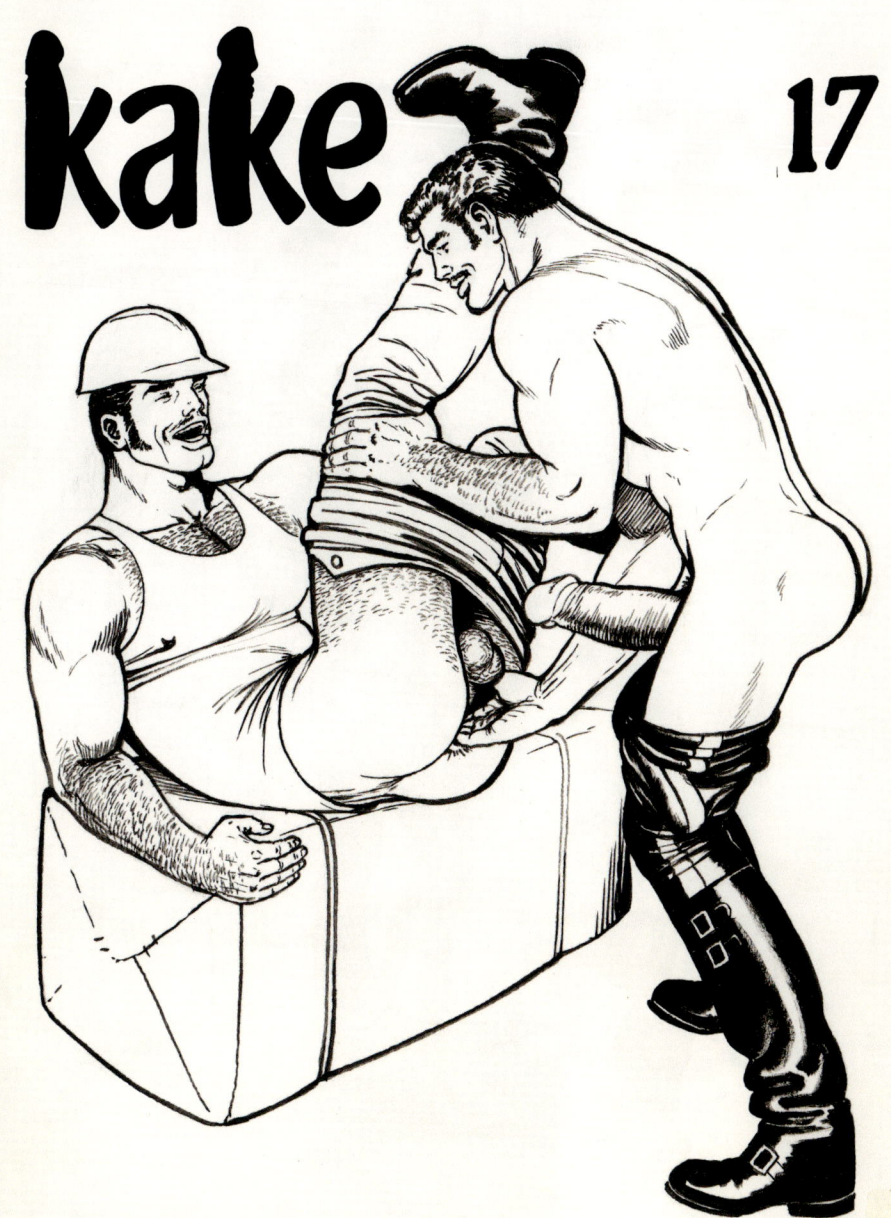

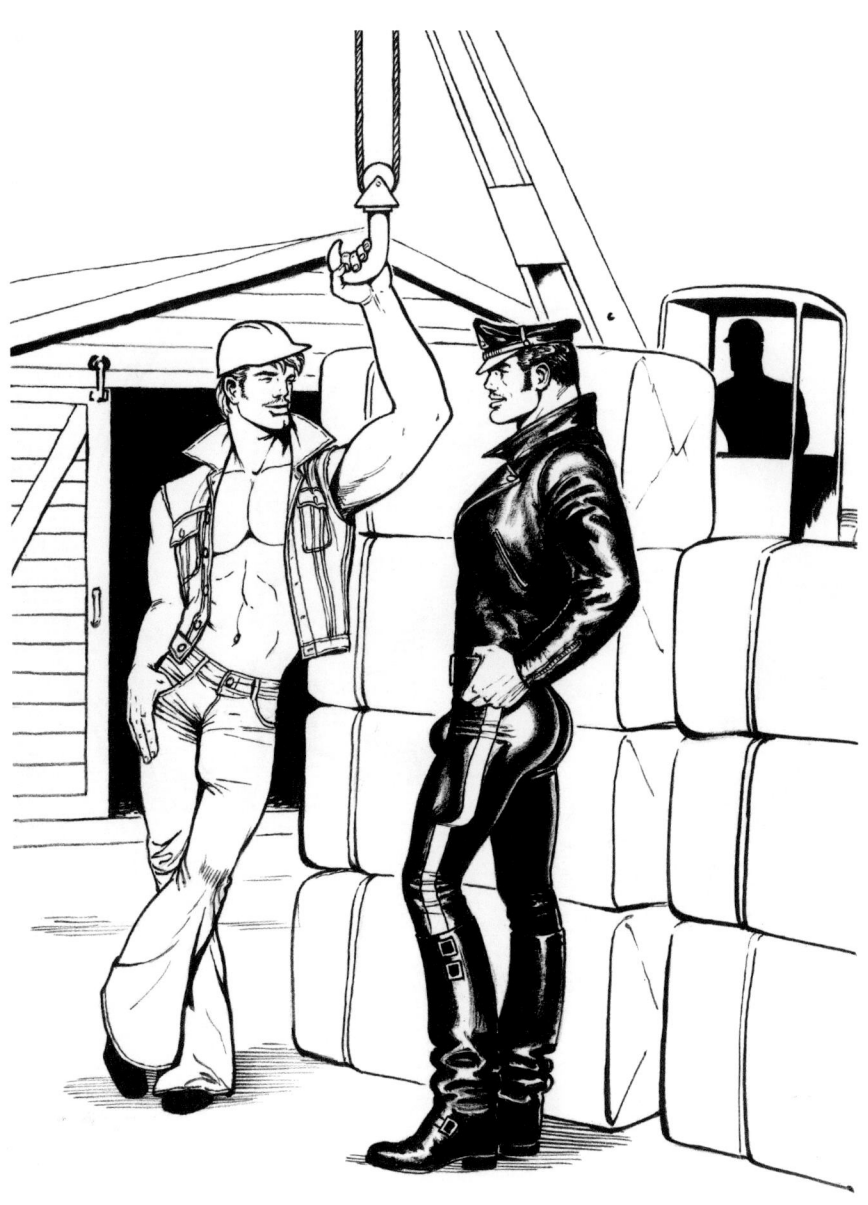

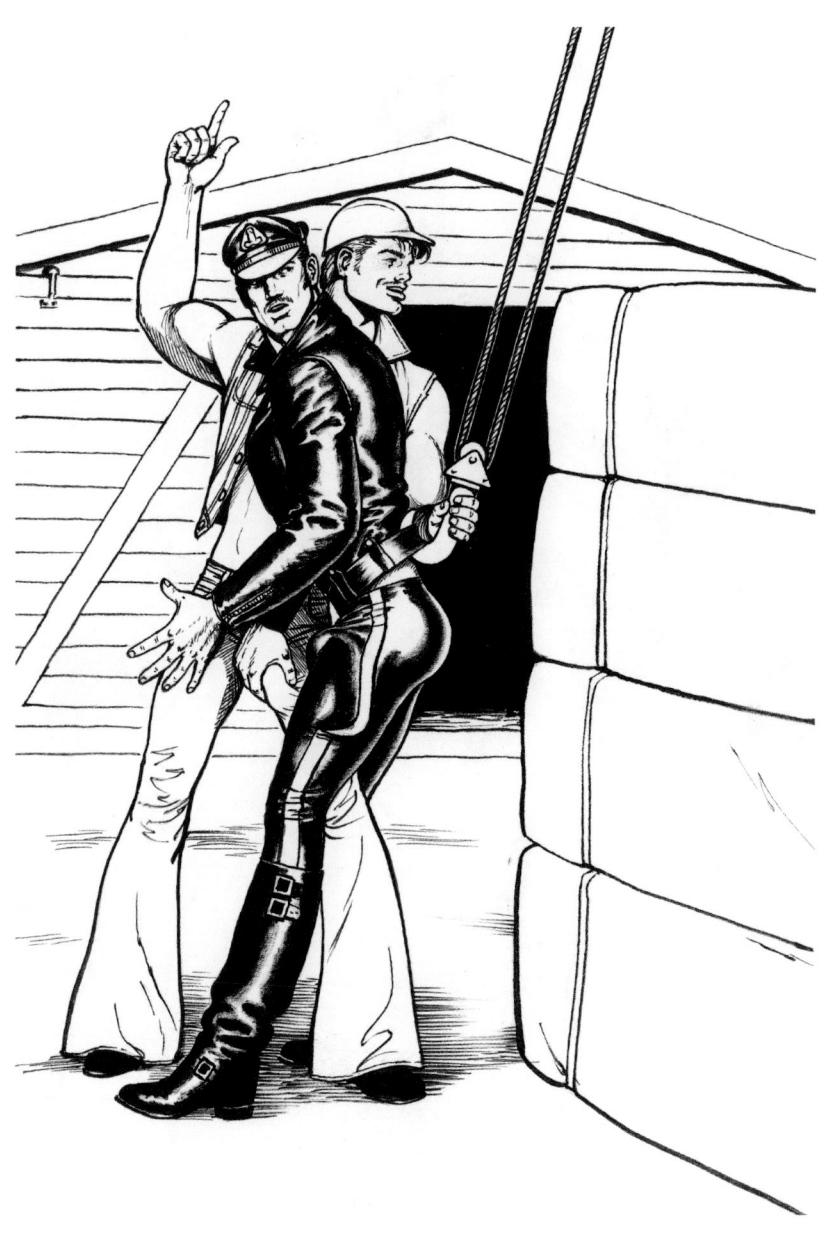

PAGES 138–157 1975, *Loading Zone*, pen and ink on paper

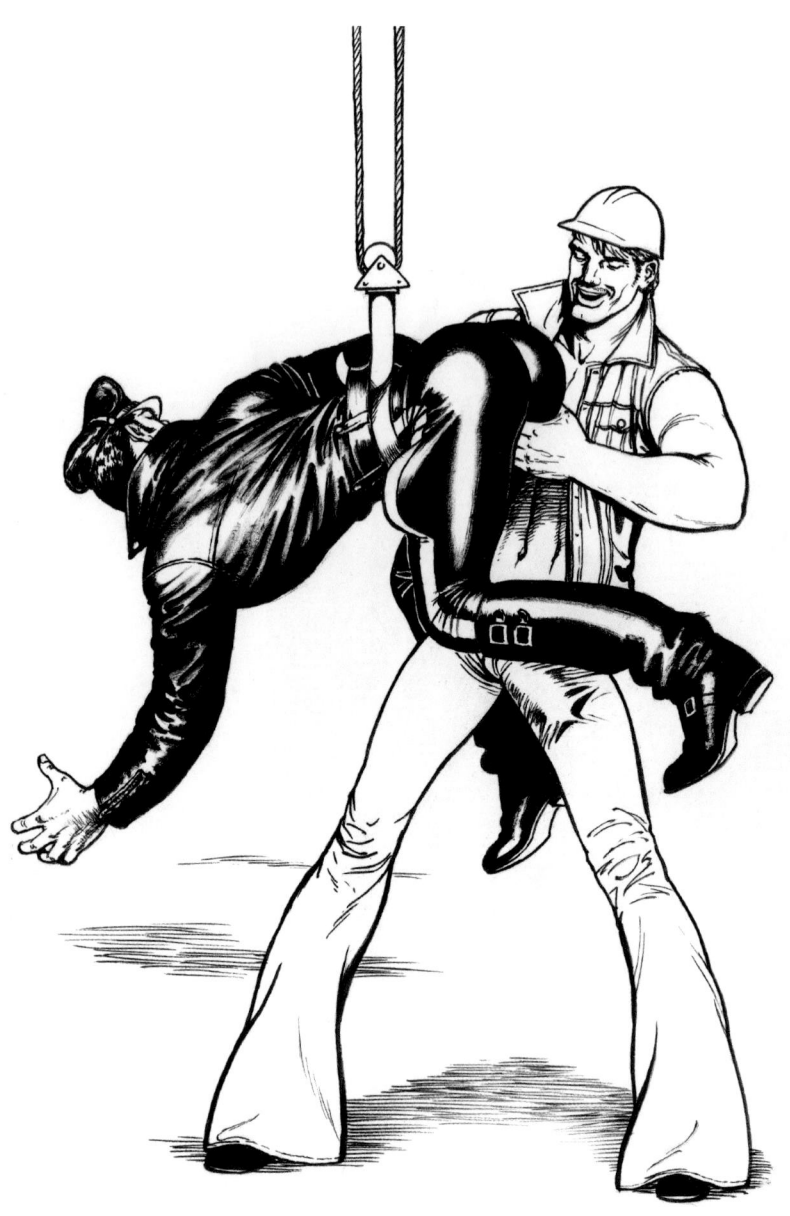

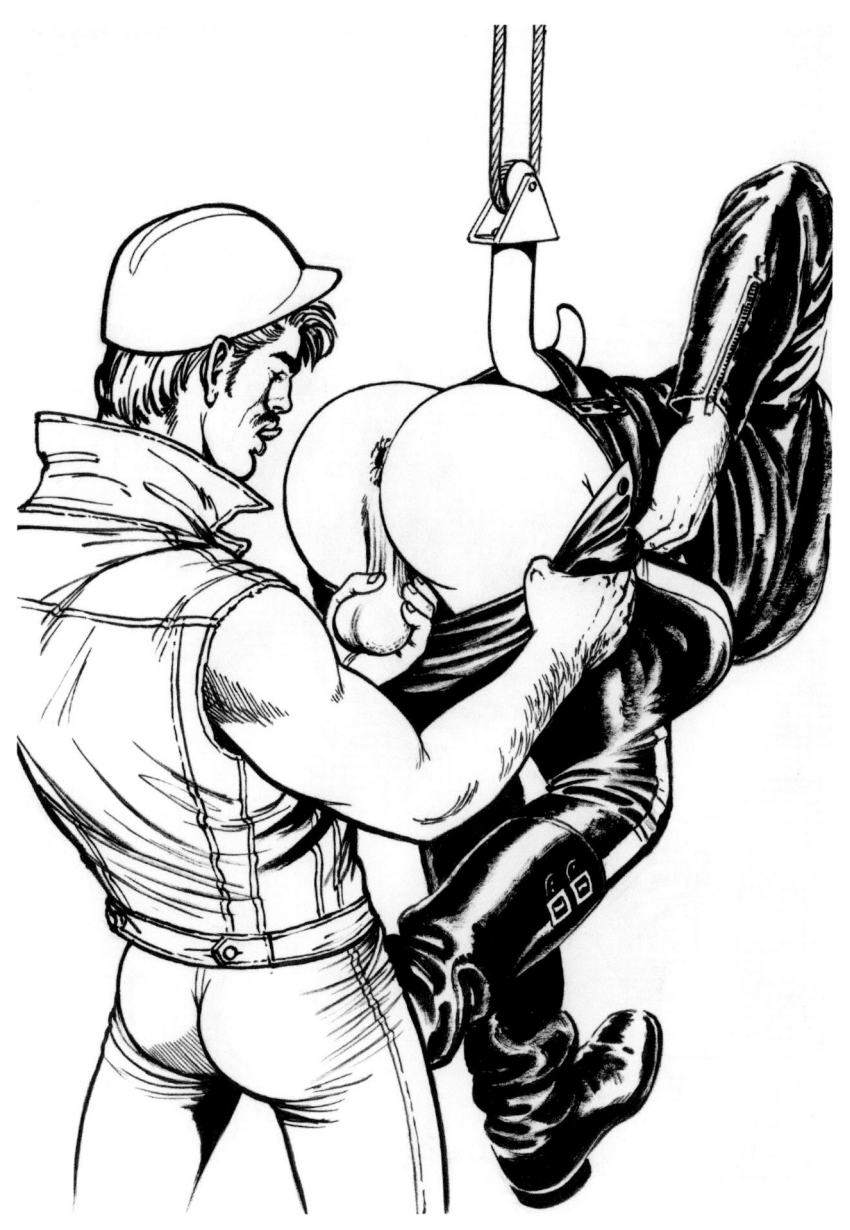

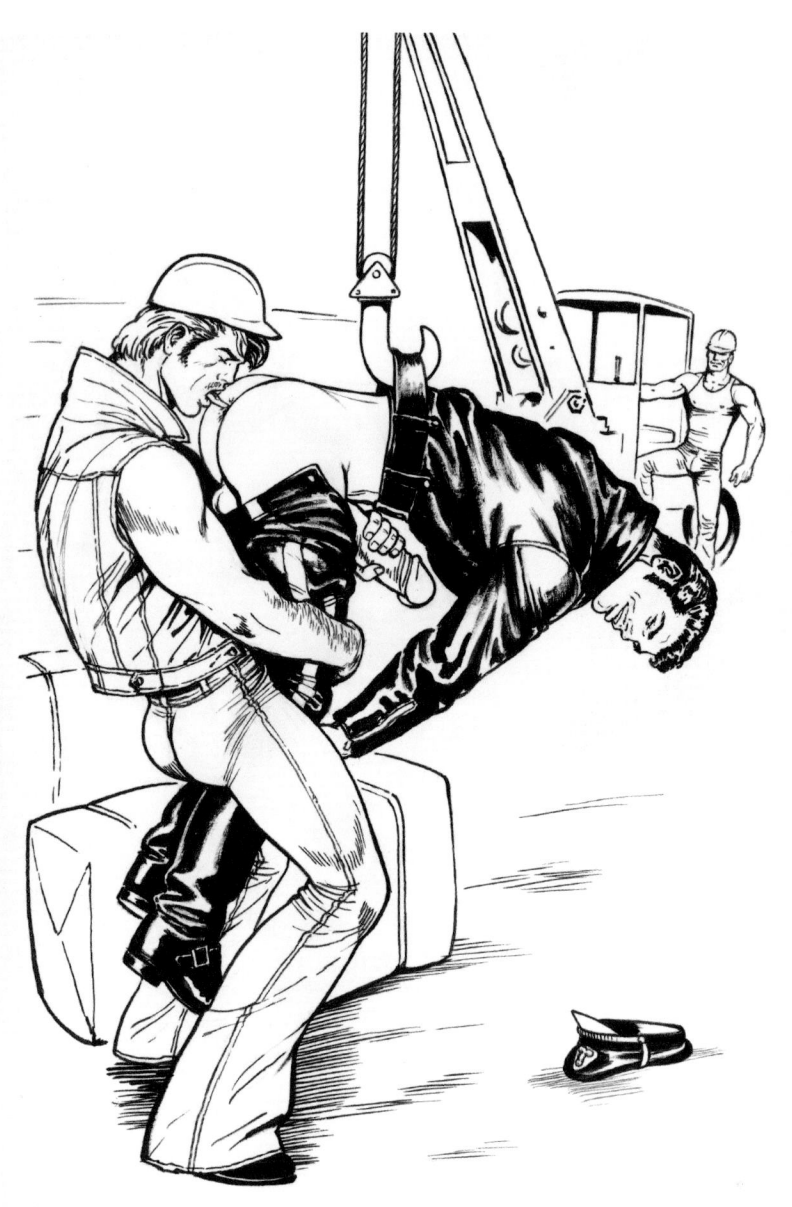

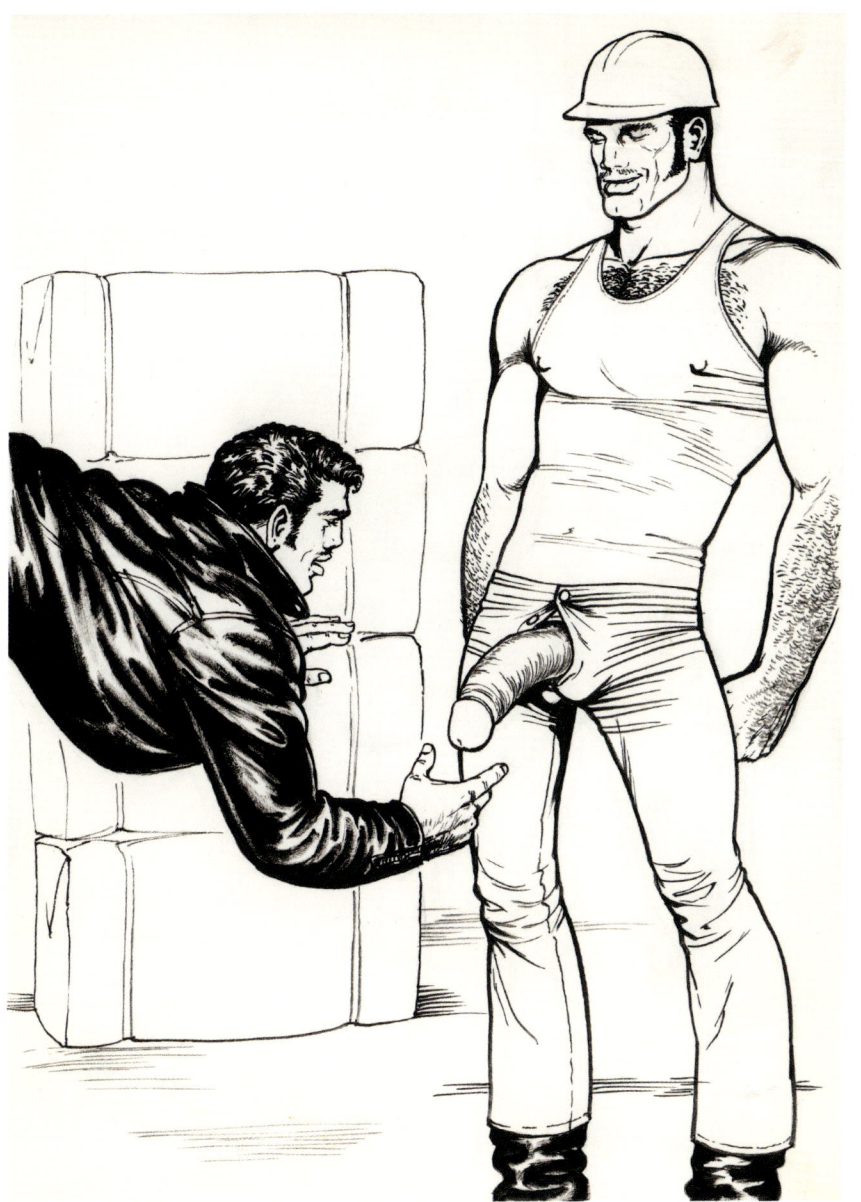

143

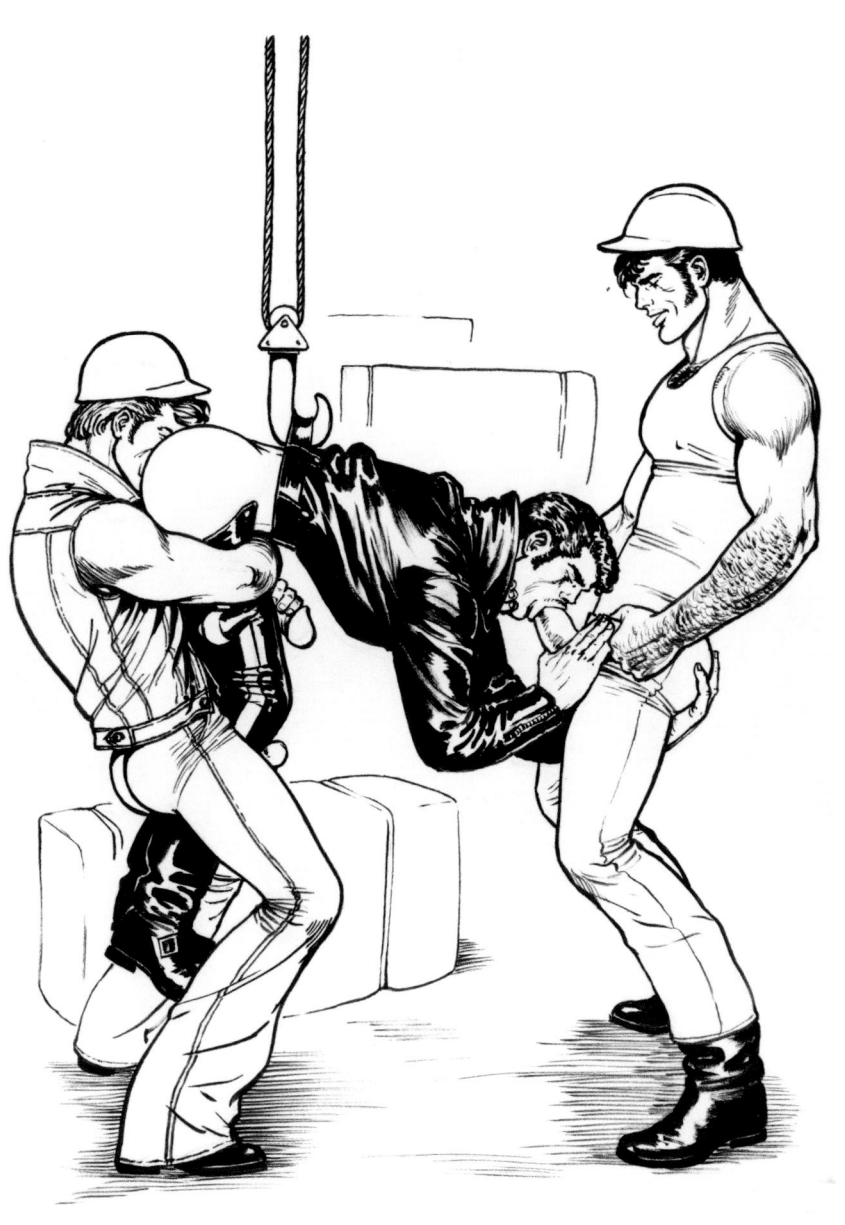

144

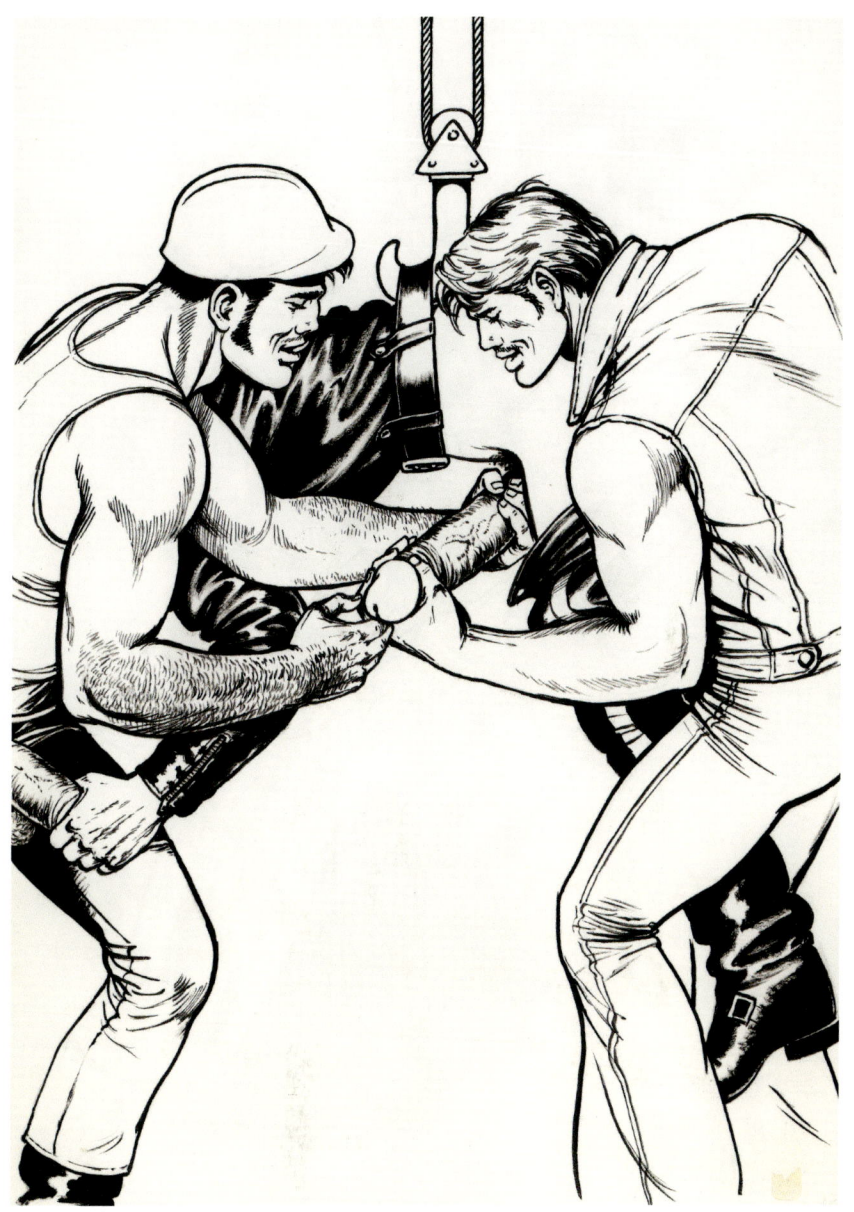

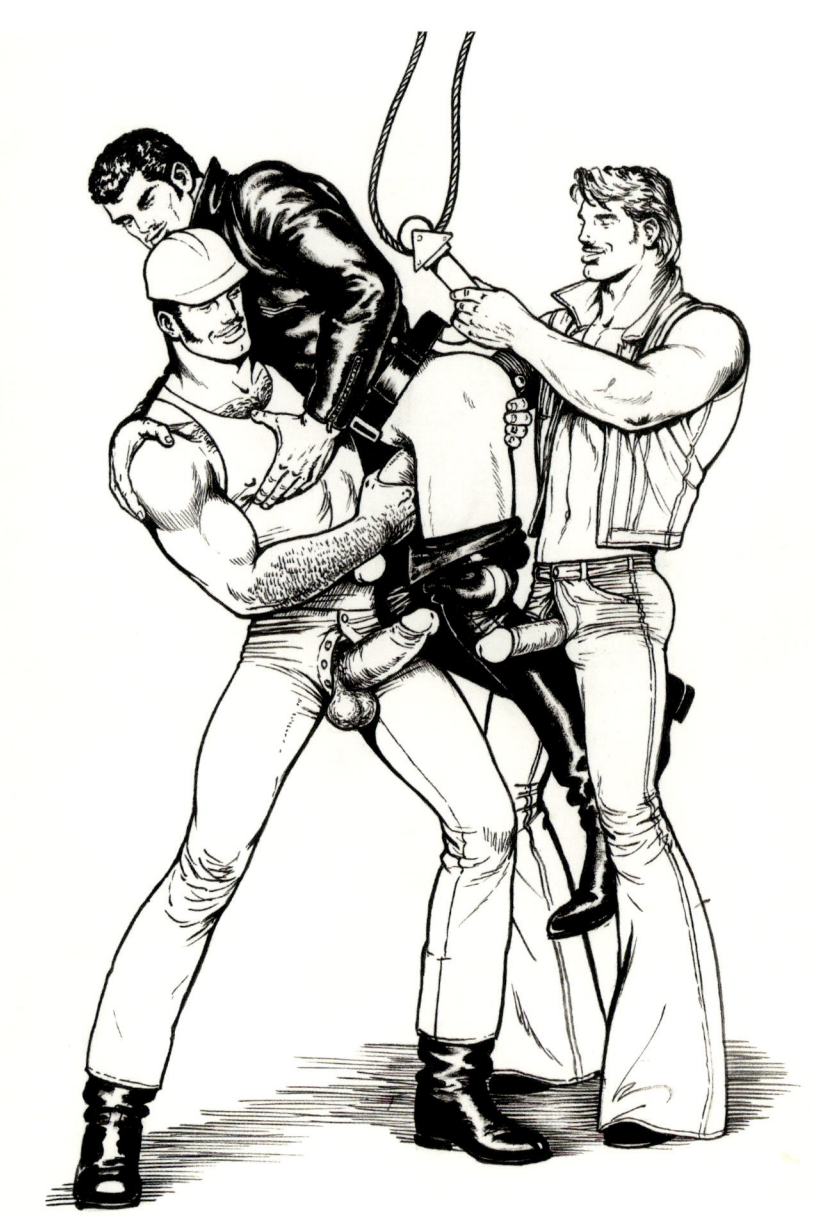

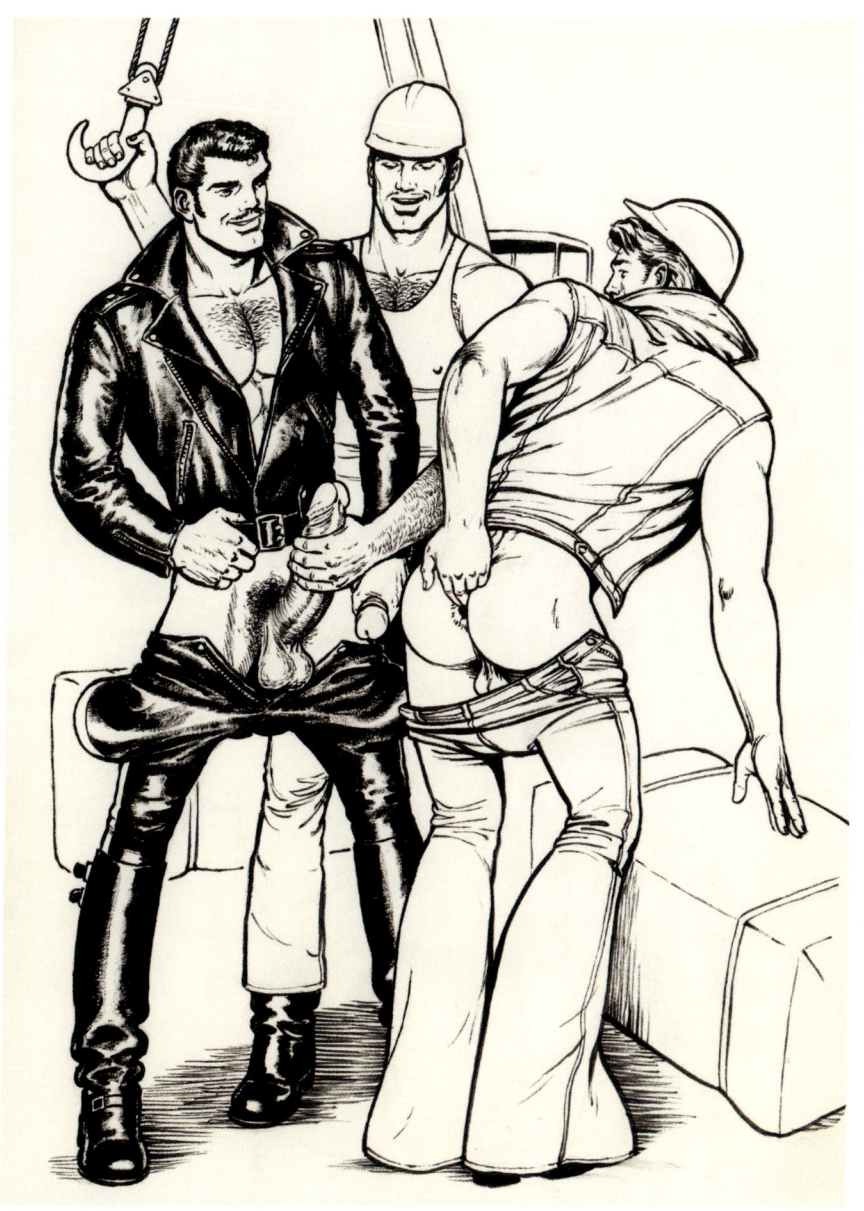

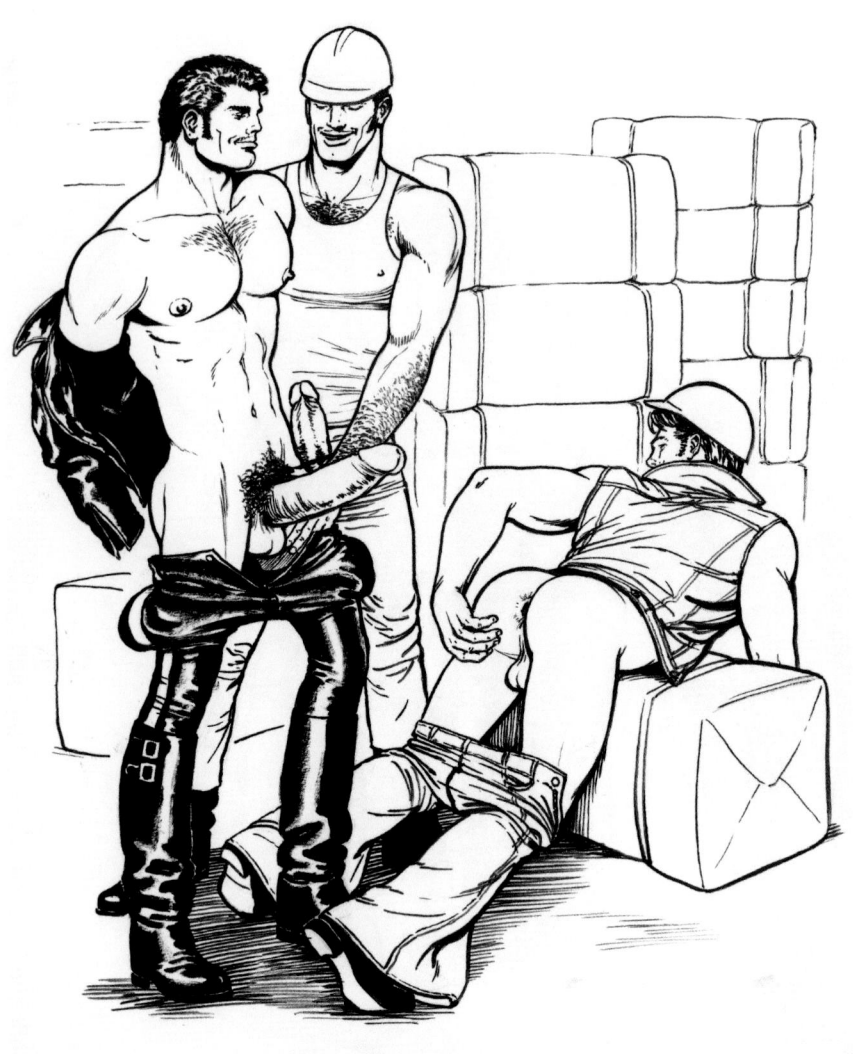

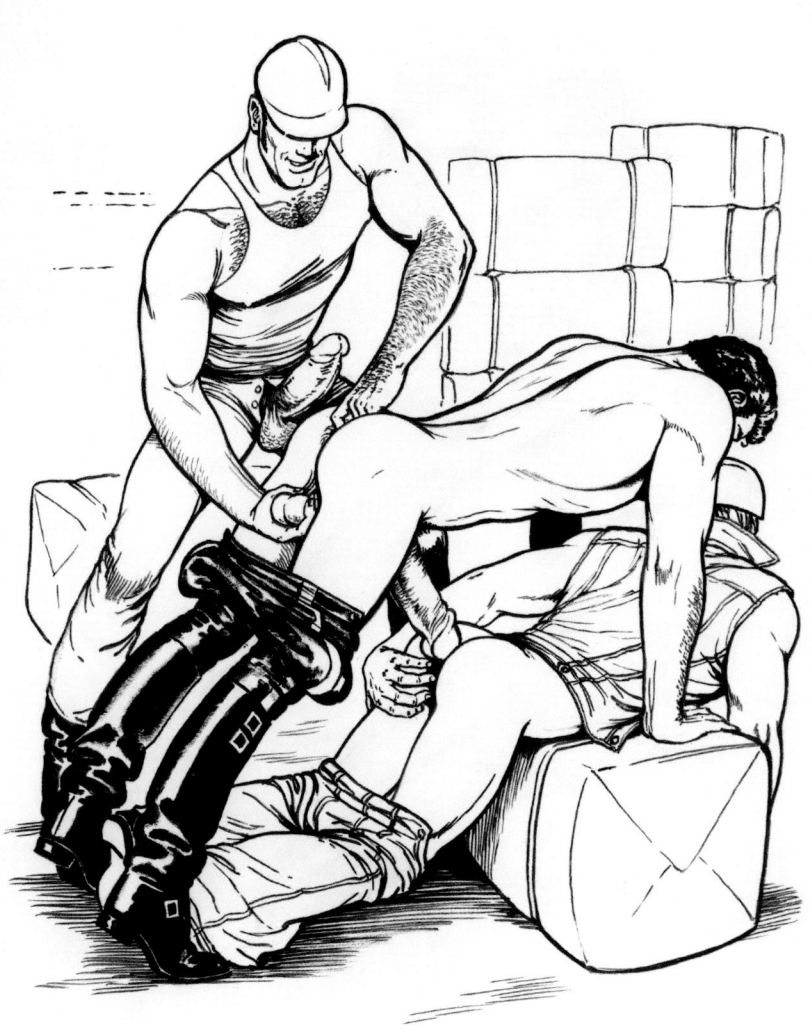

149

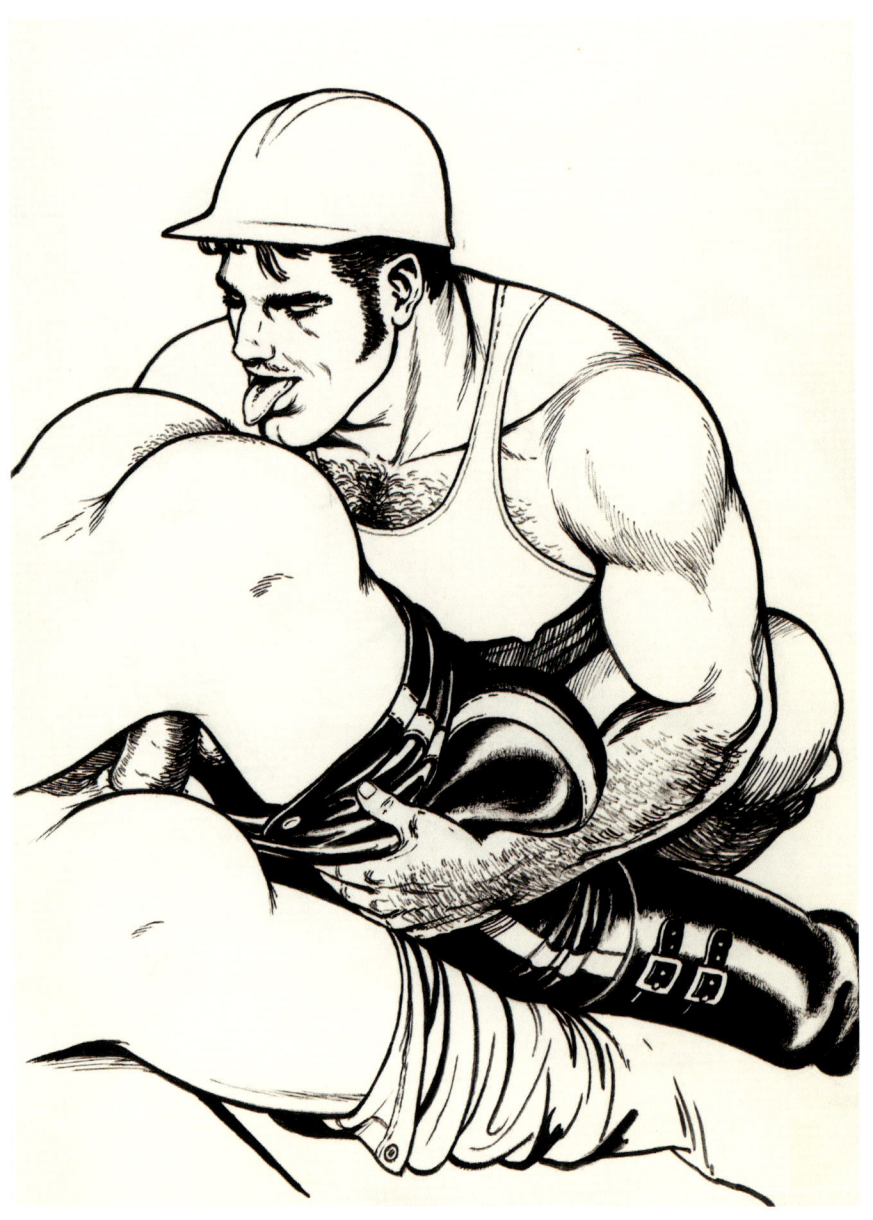

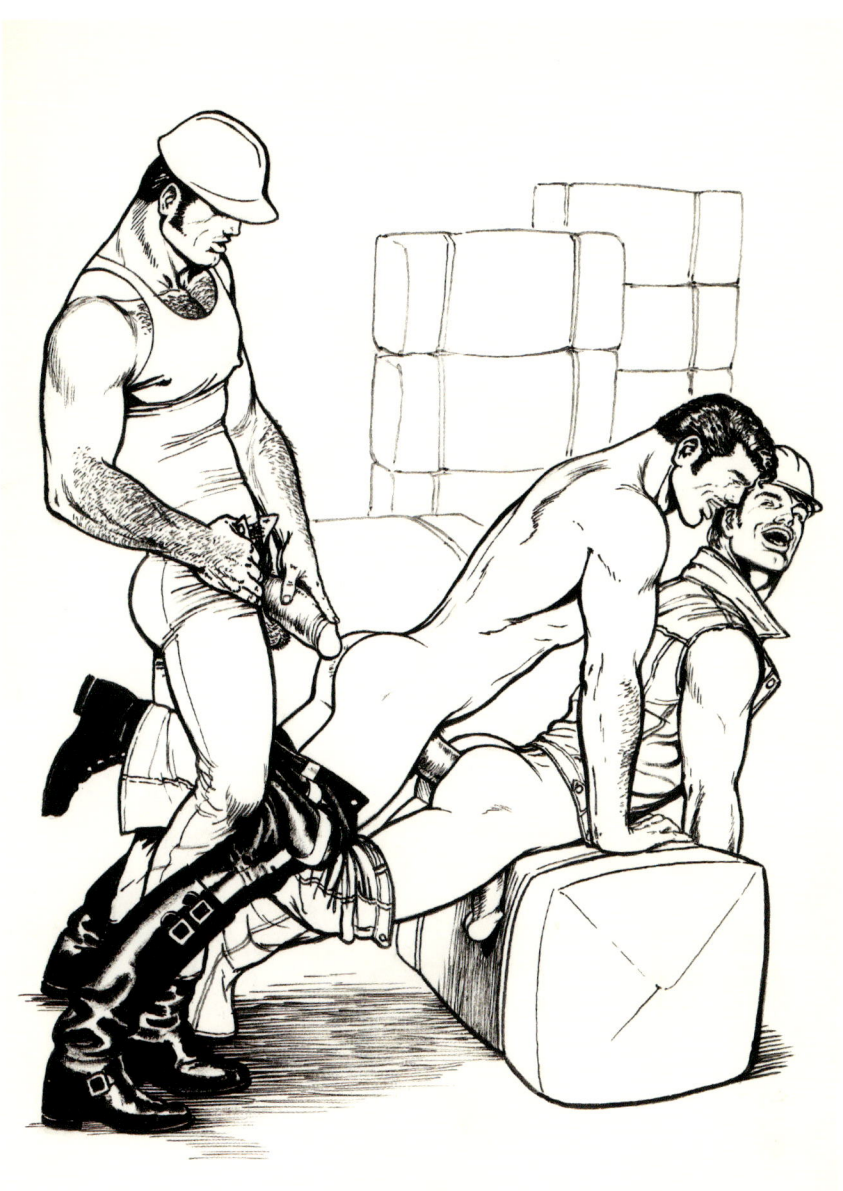

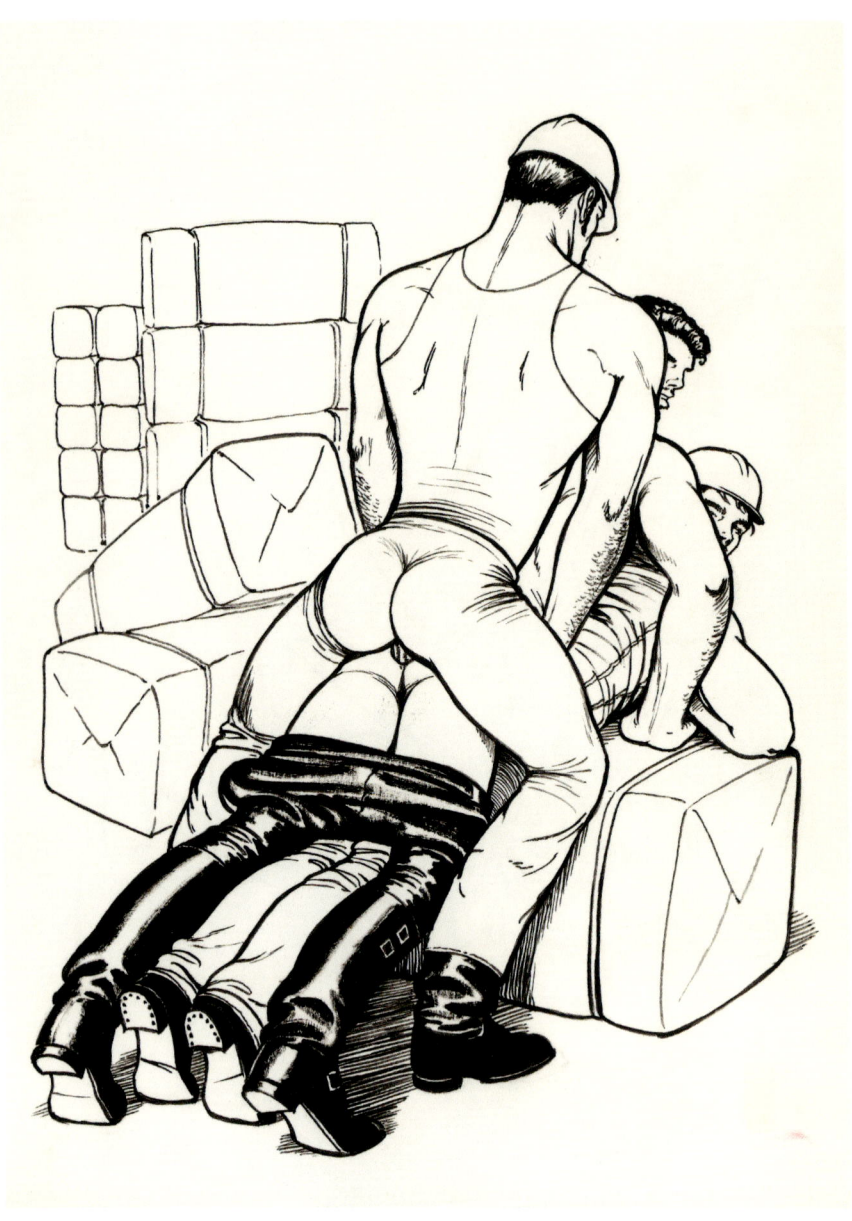

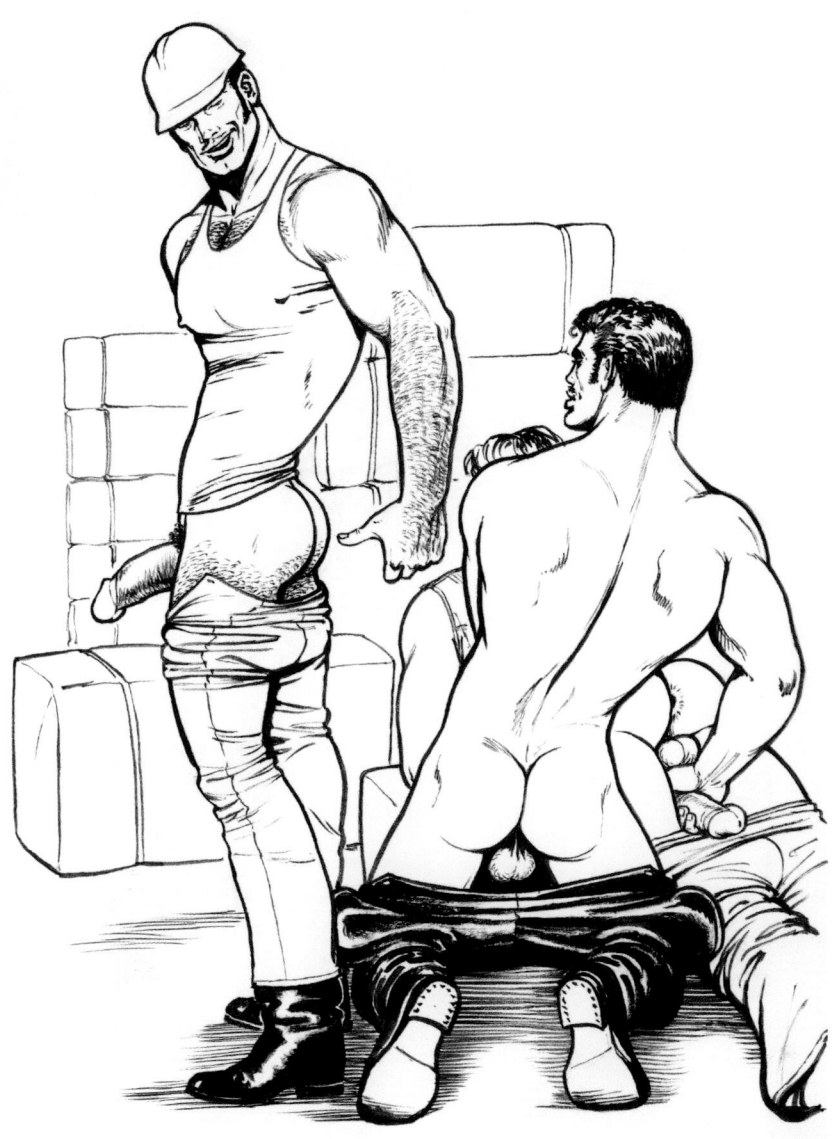

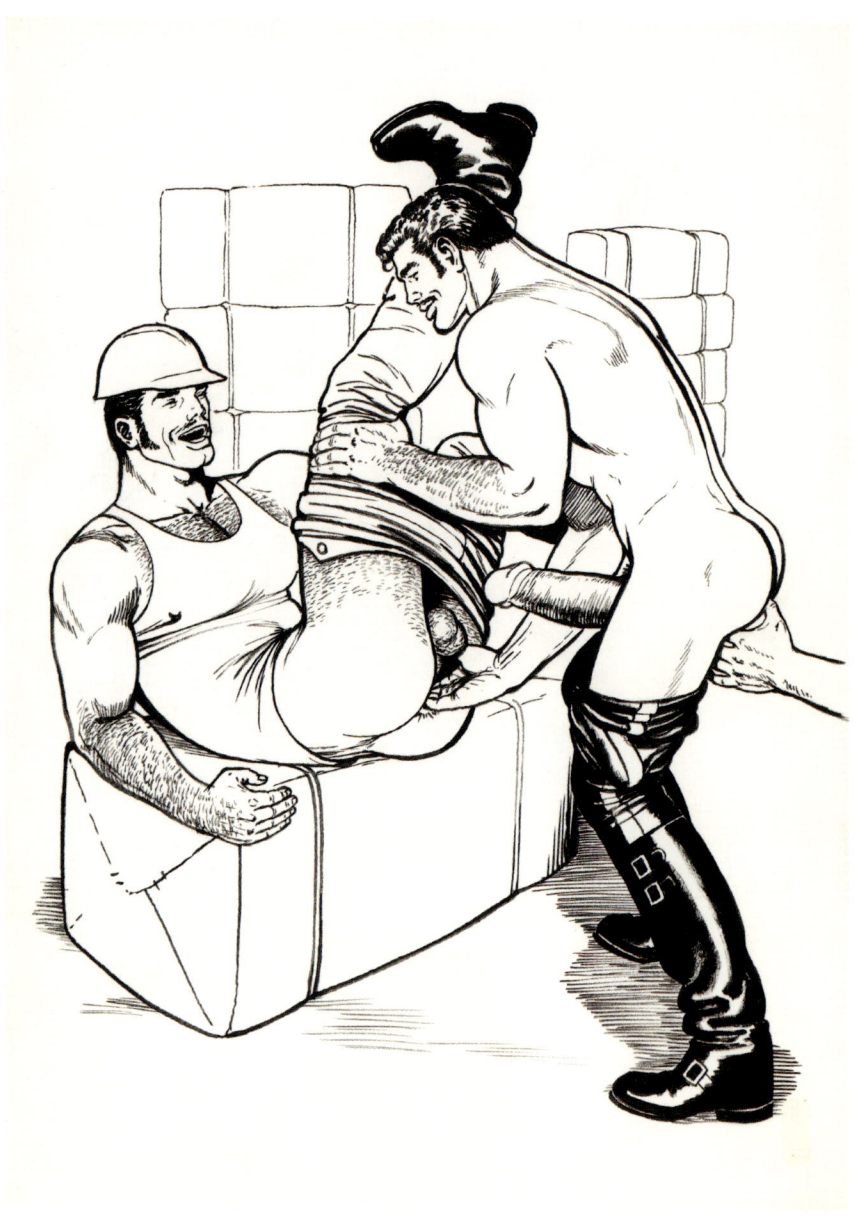

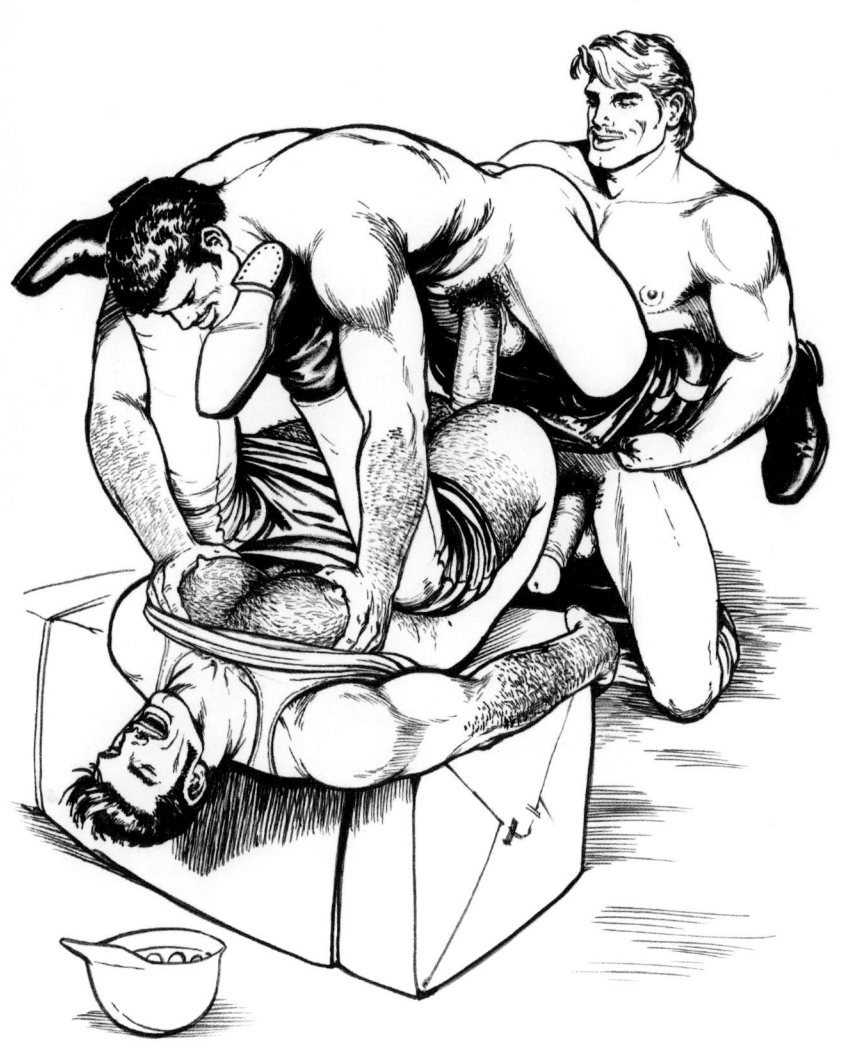

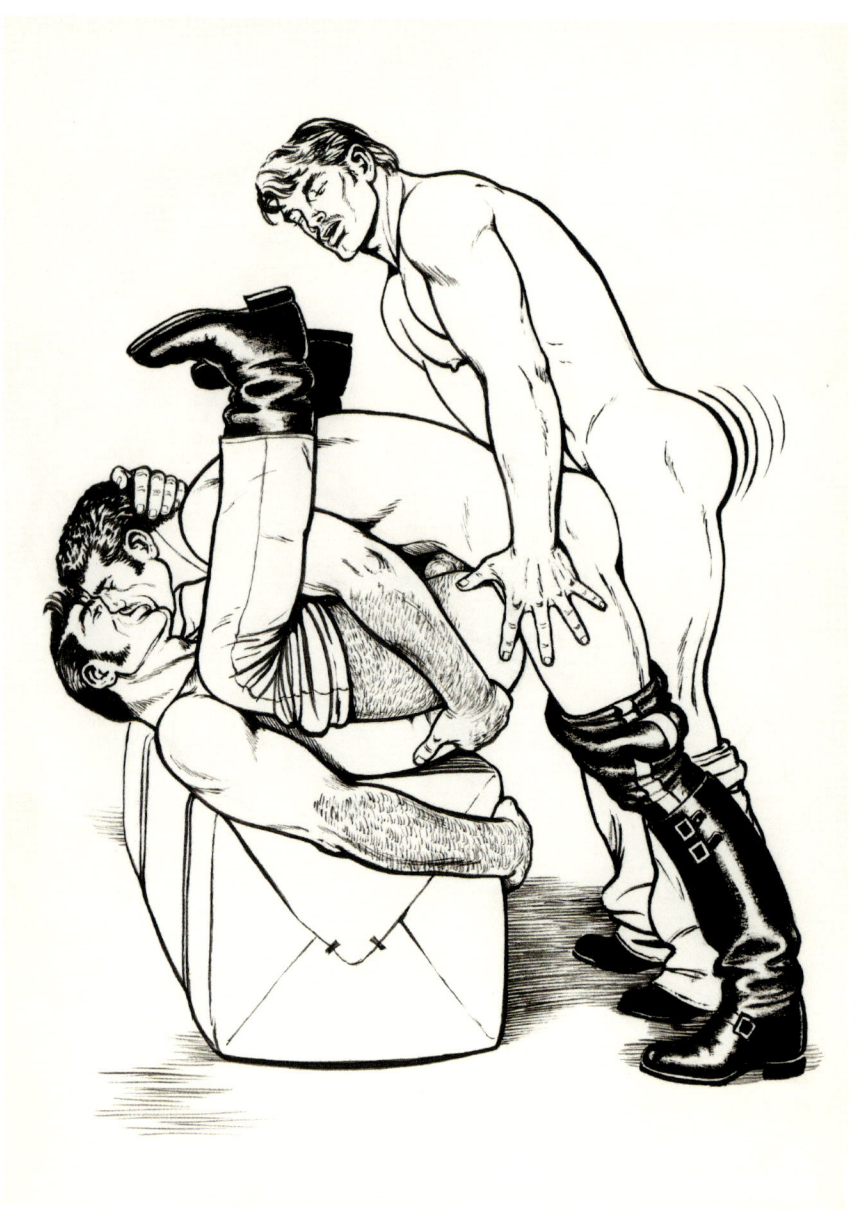

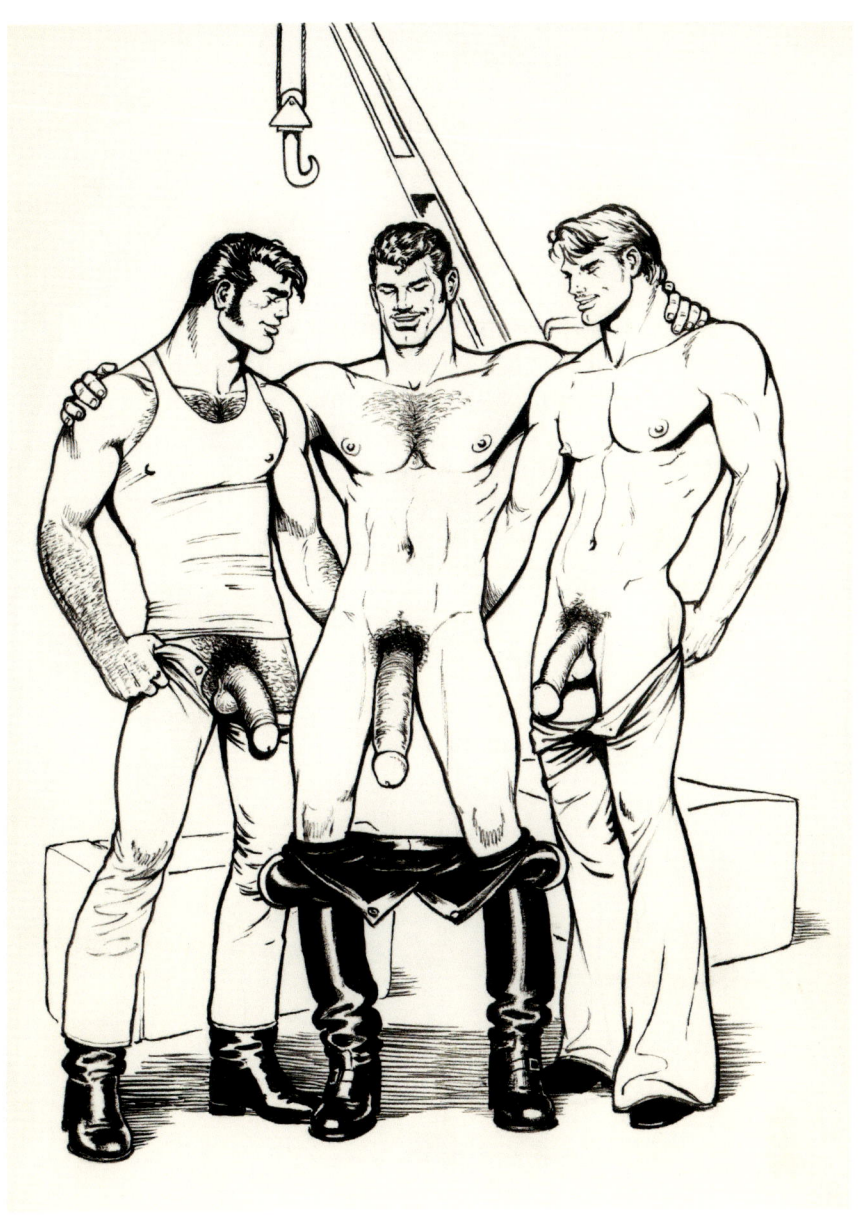

*"Homosexuals growing up in the age
of Tom were no longer pansies and poofs,
or a third sex that was neither man nor
woman, nor were they mentally ill perverts
eroding the moral fiber of society."*
—DURK DEHNER

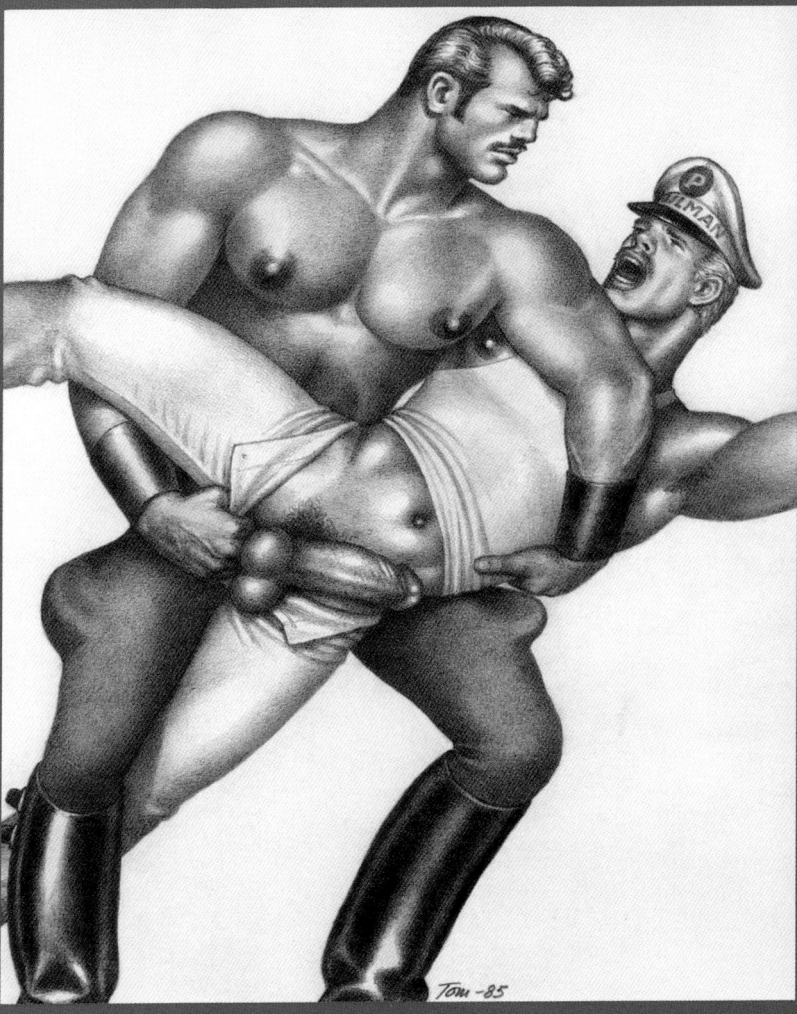

KAKE
POSTAL RAPE   25

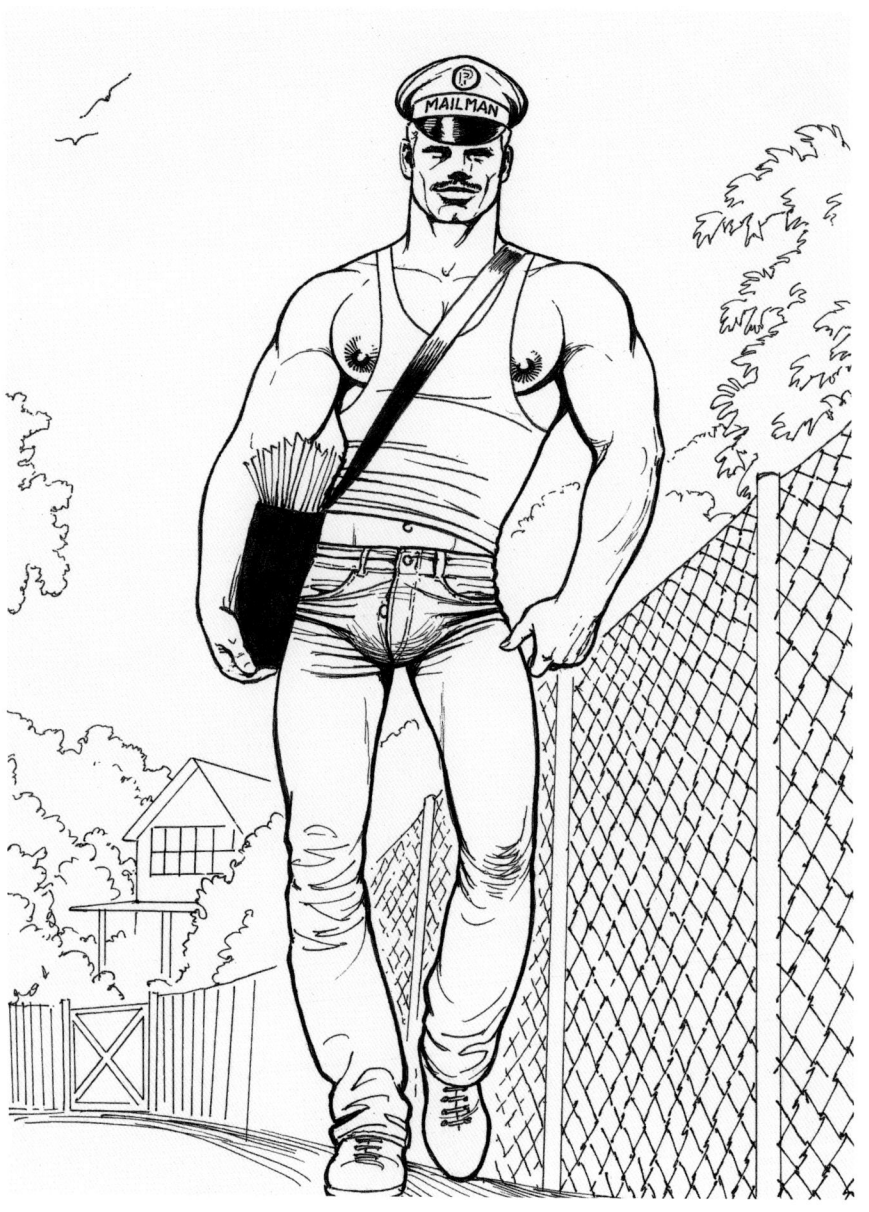

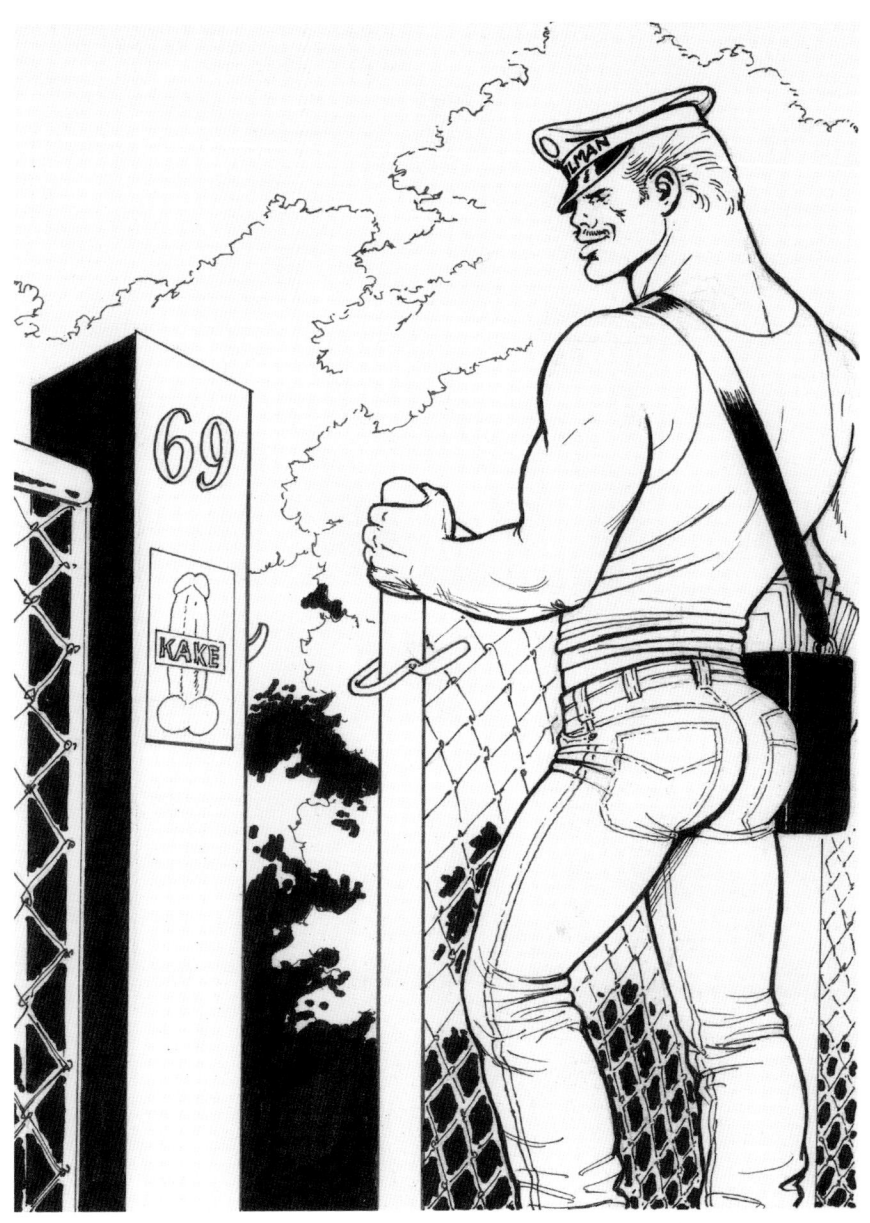

PAGES 160–189 1984, *Kake Postal Rape*, pen and ink on paper

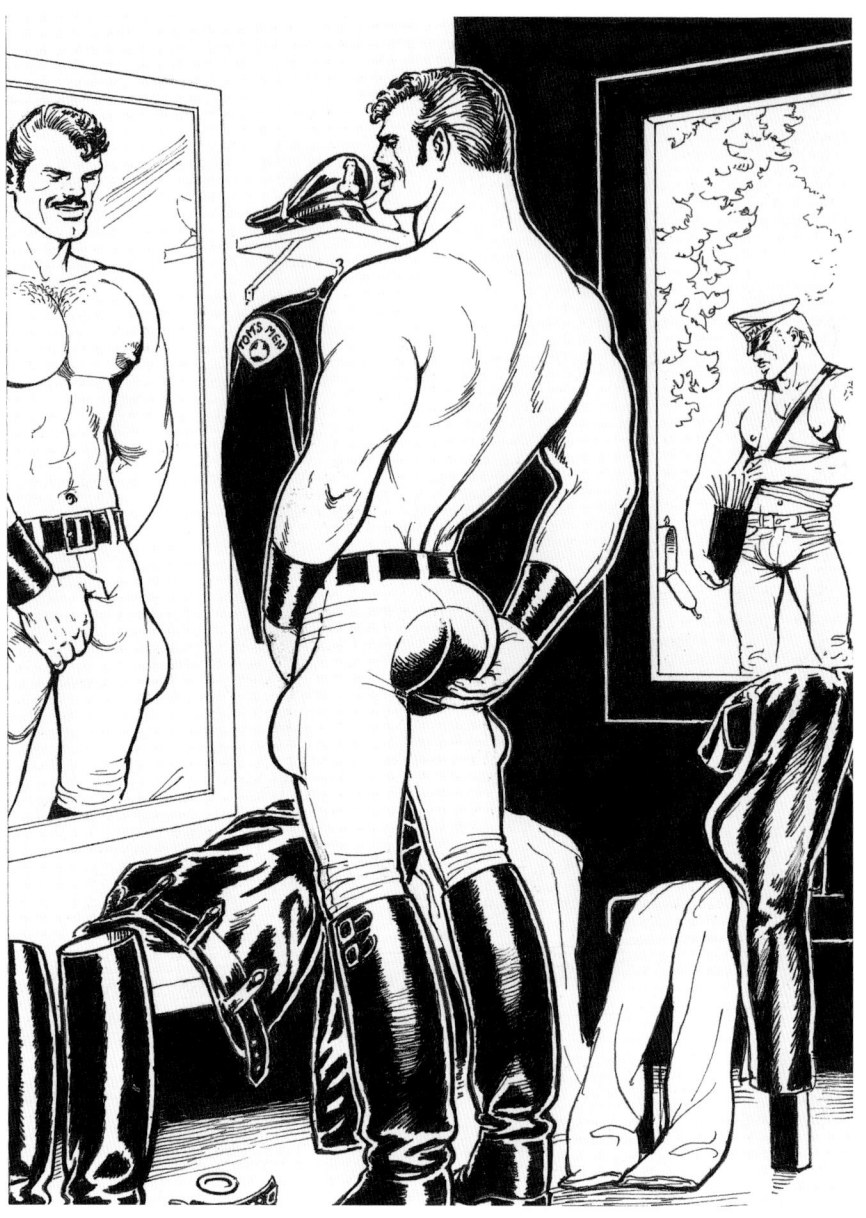

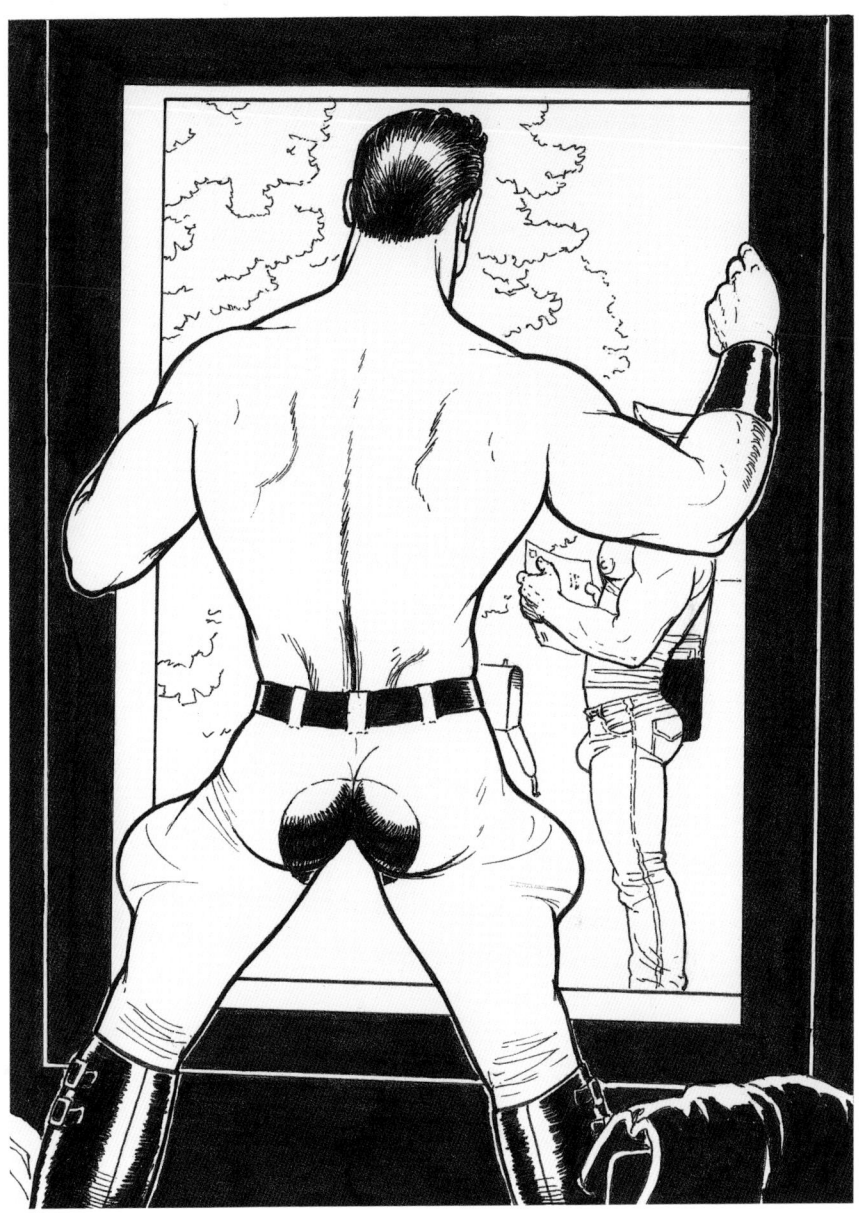

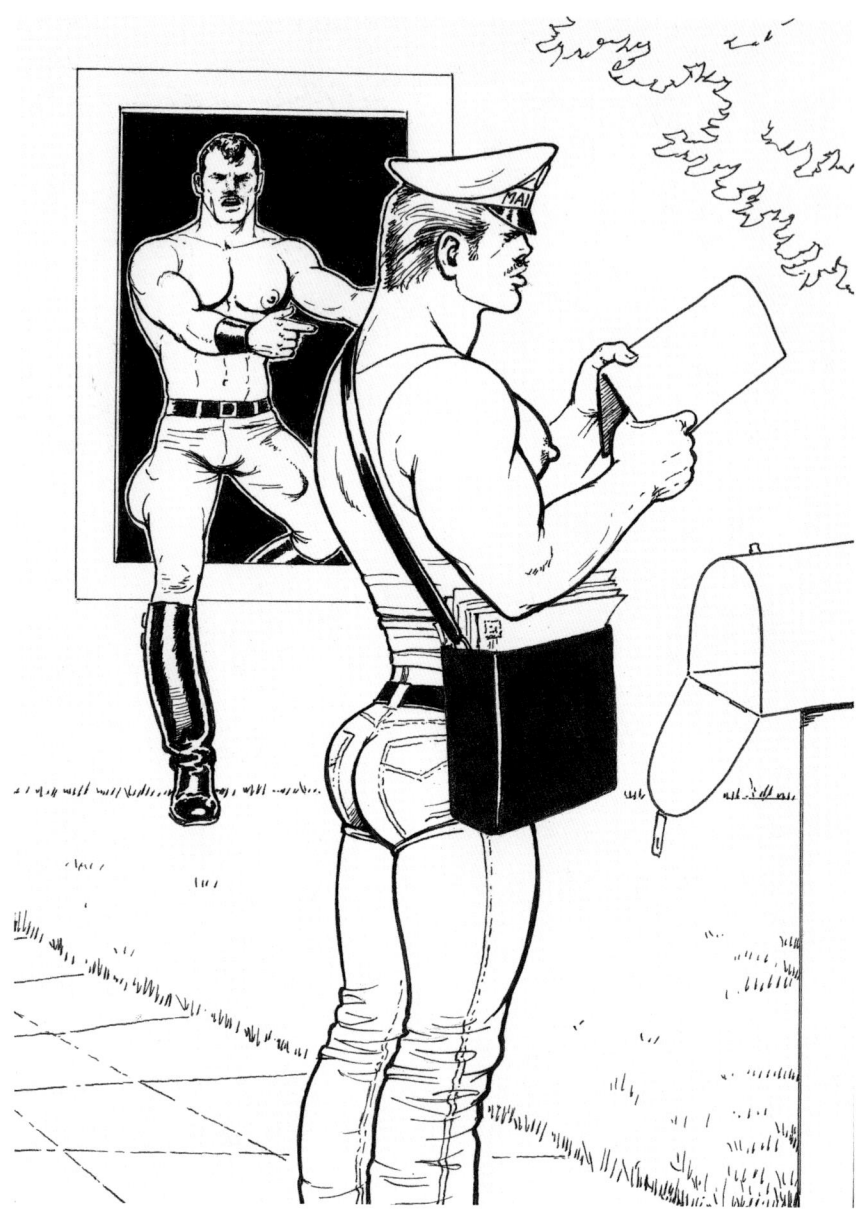

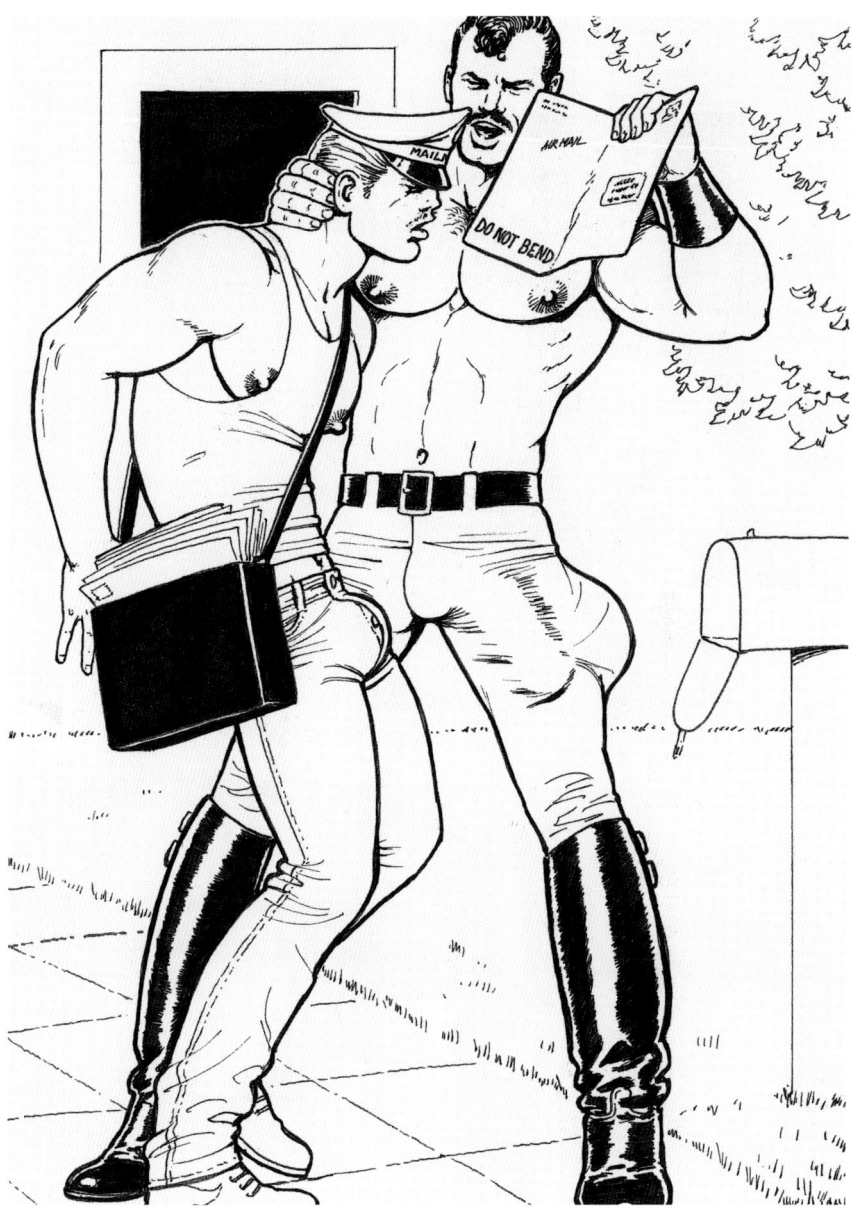

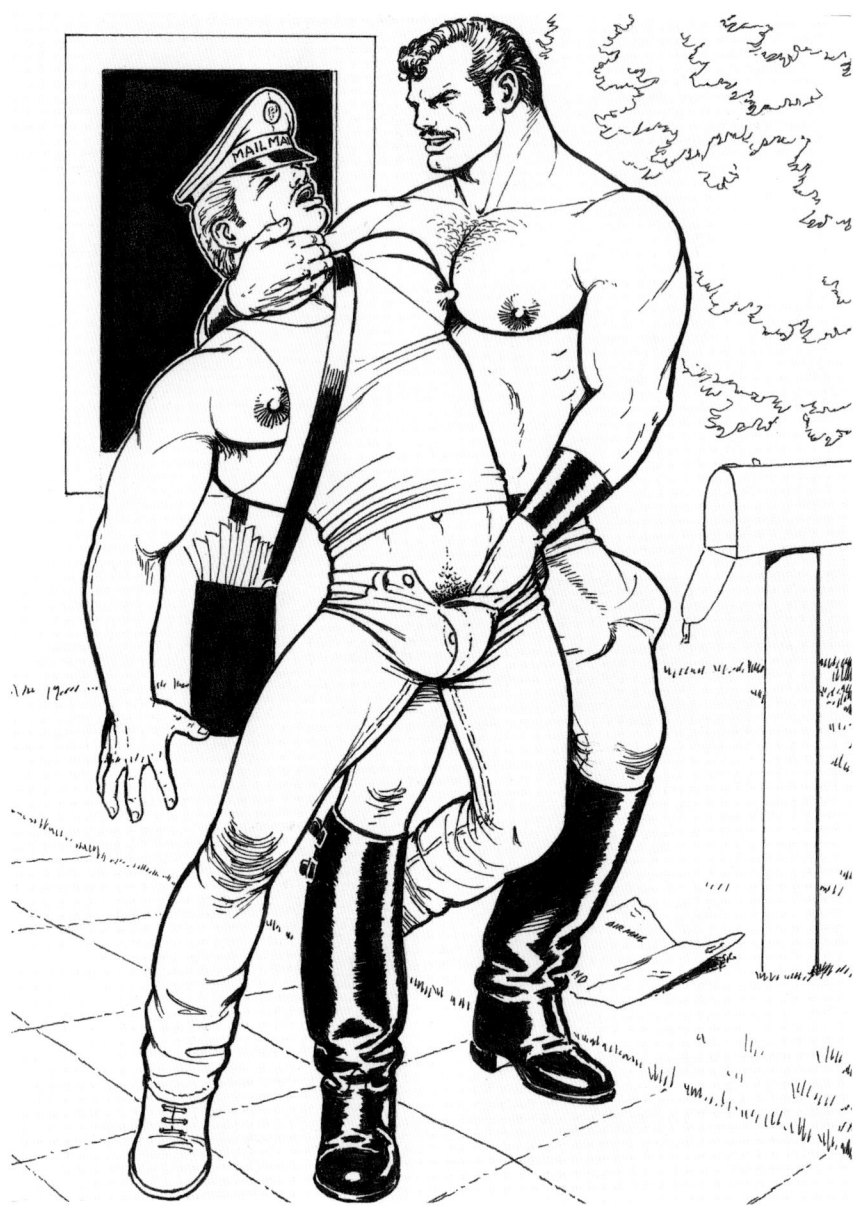

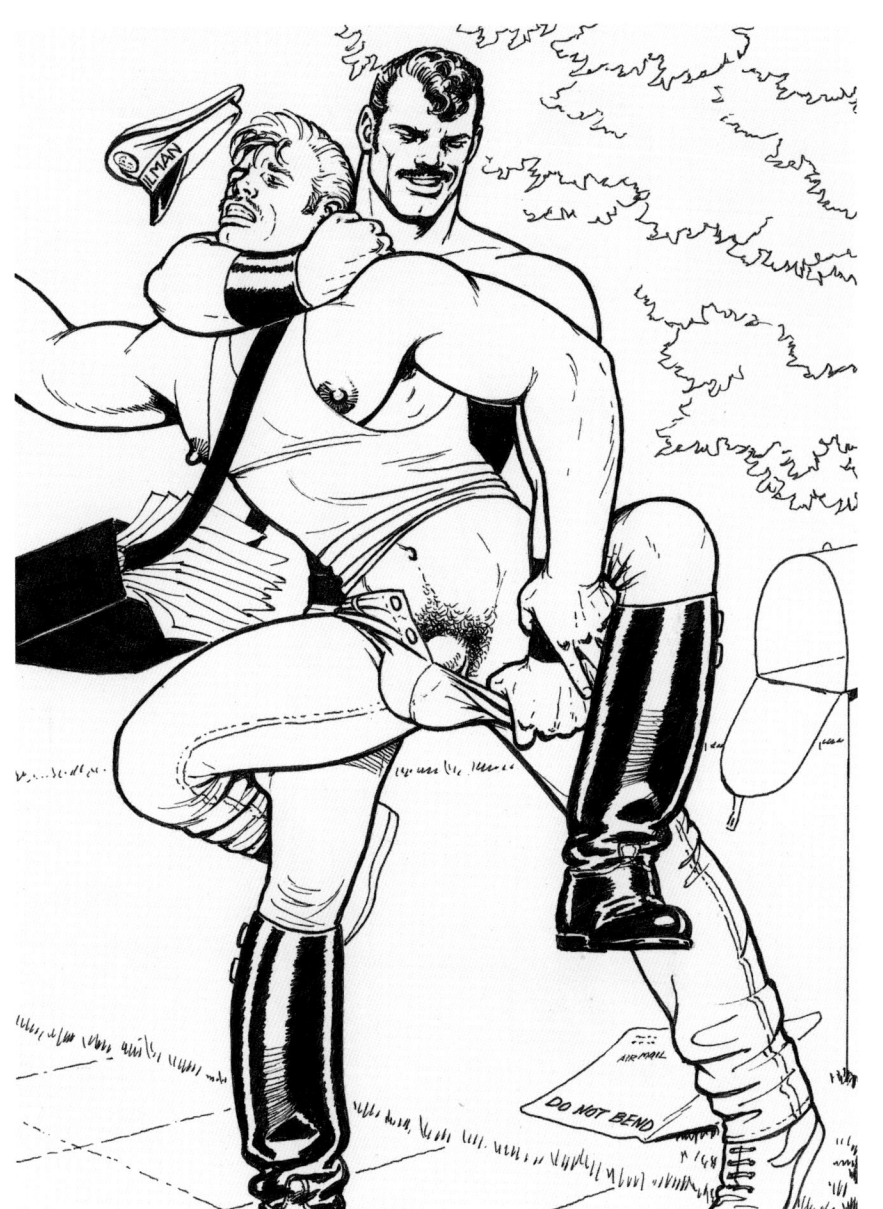

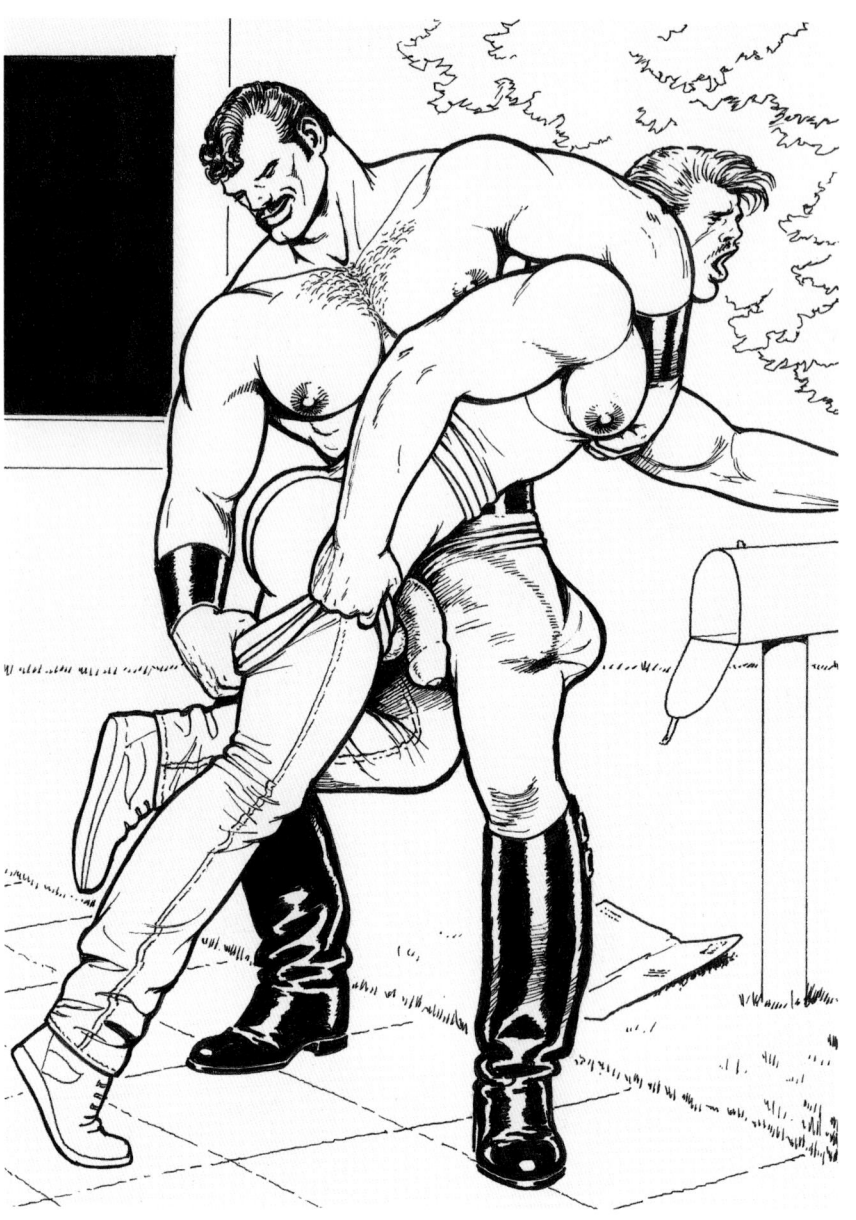

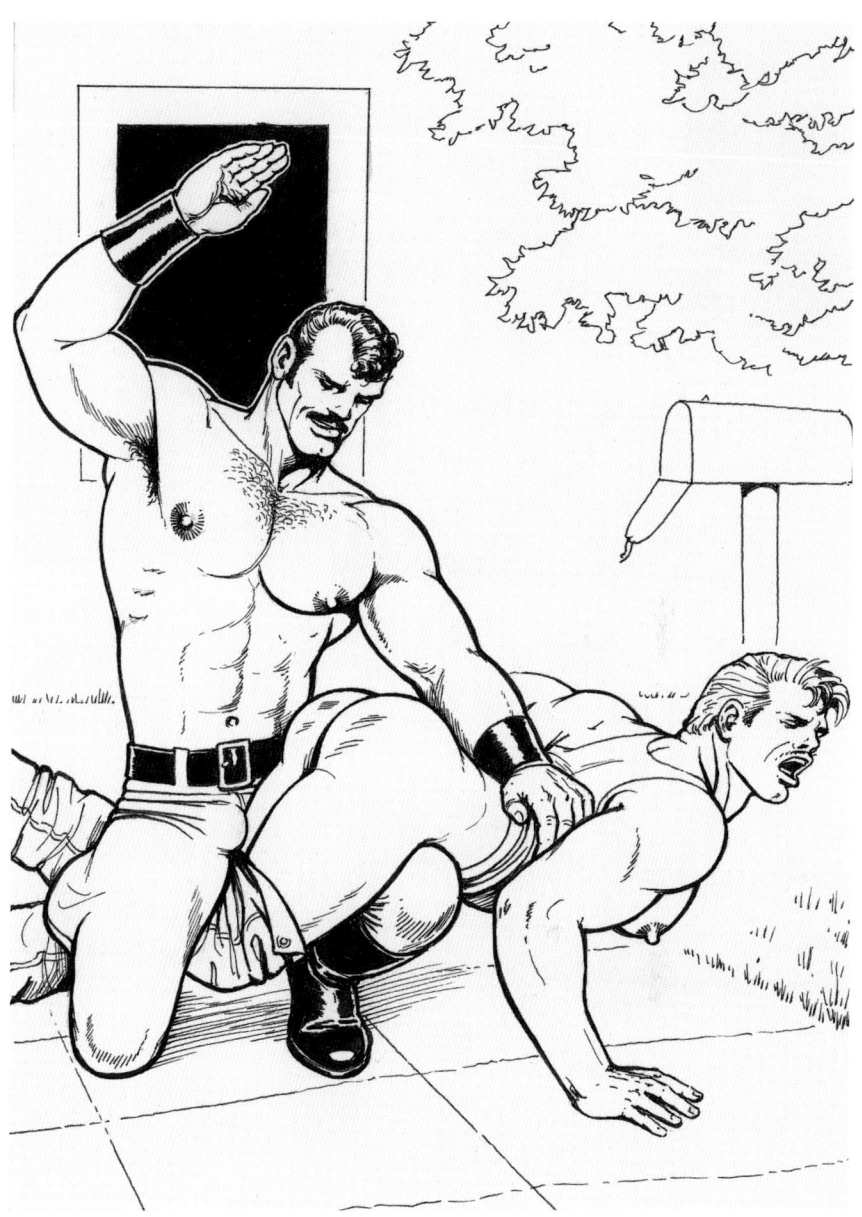

169

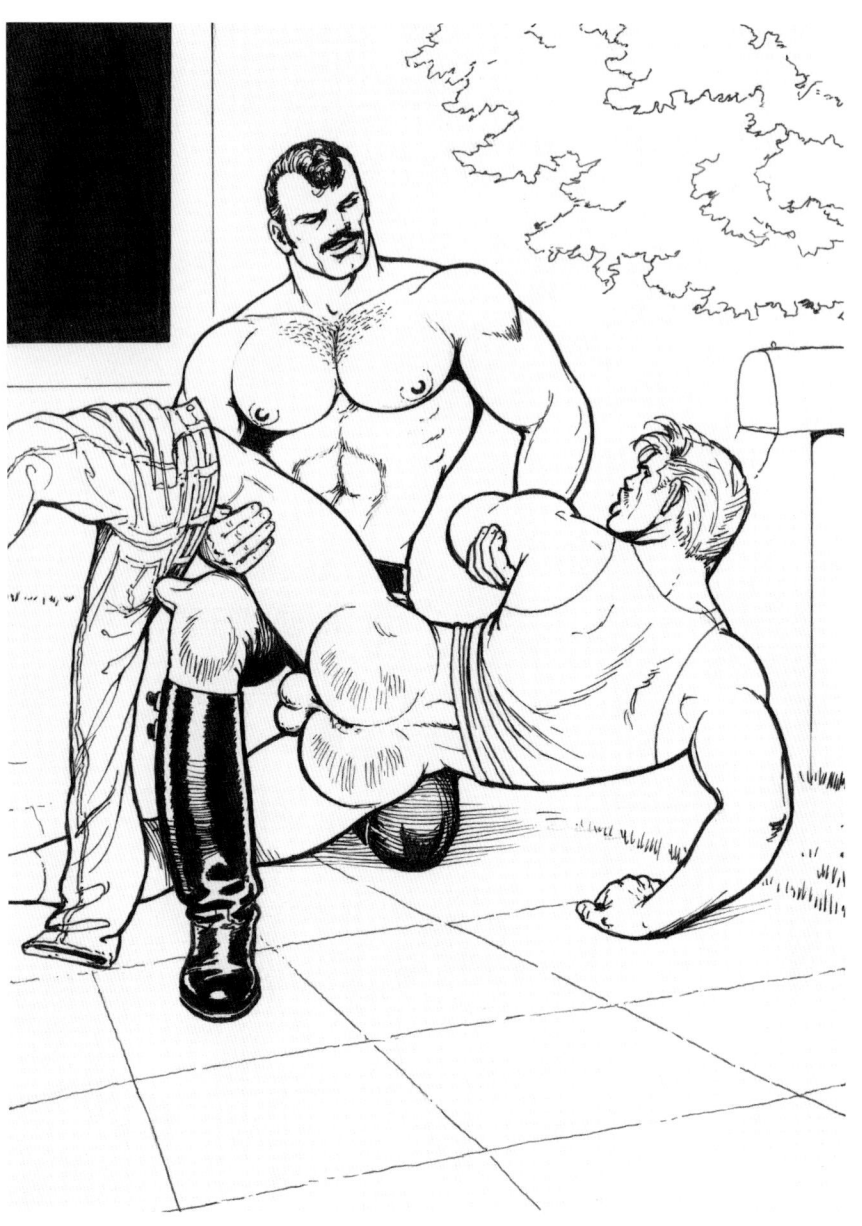

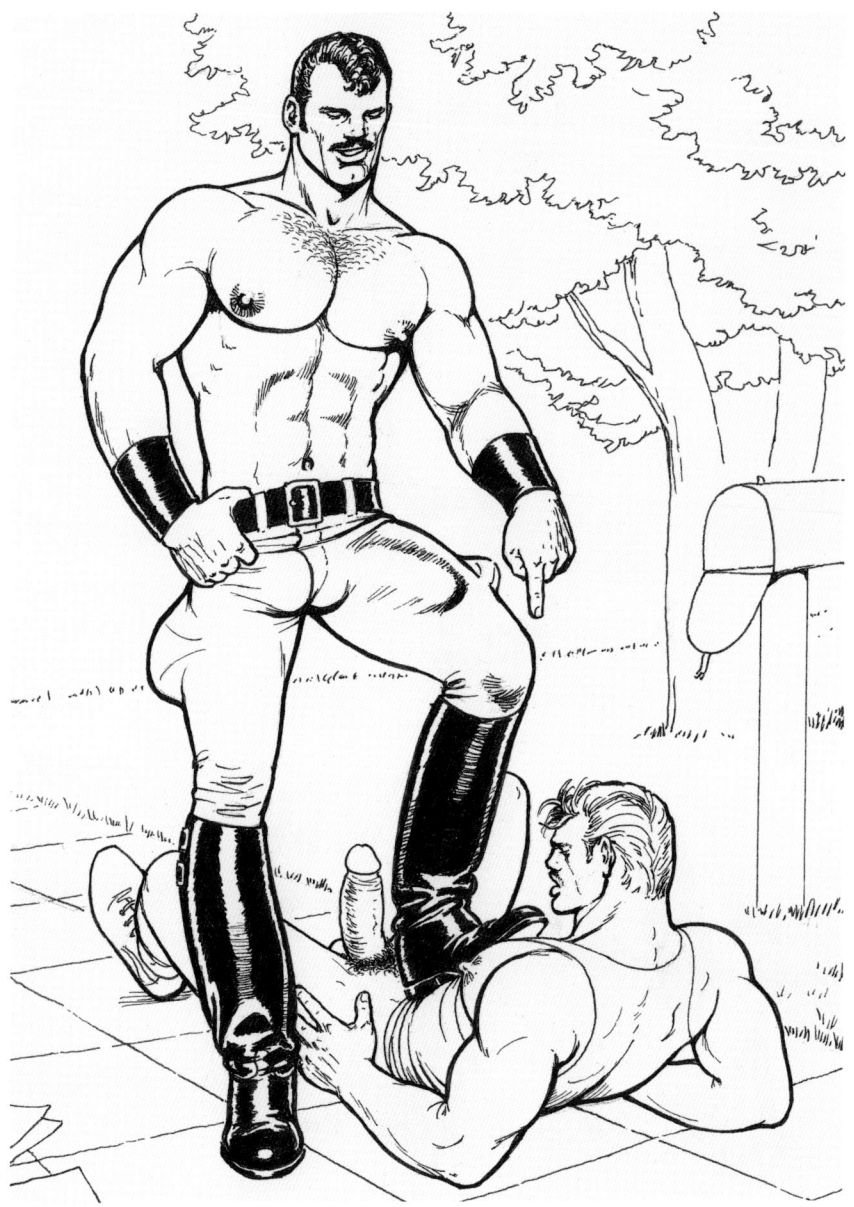

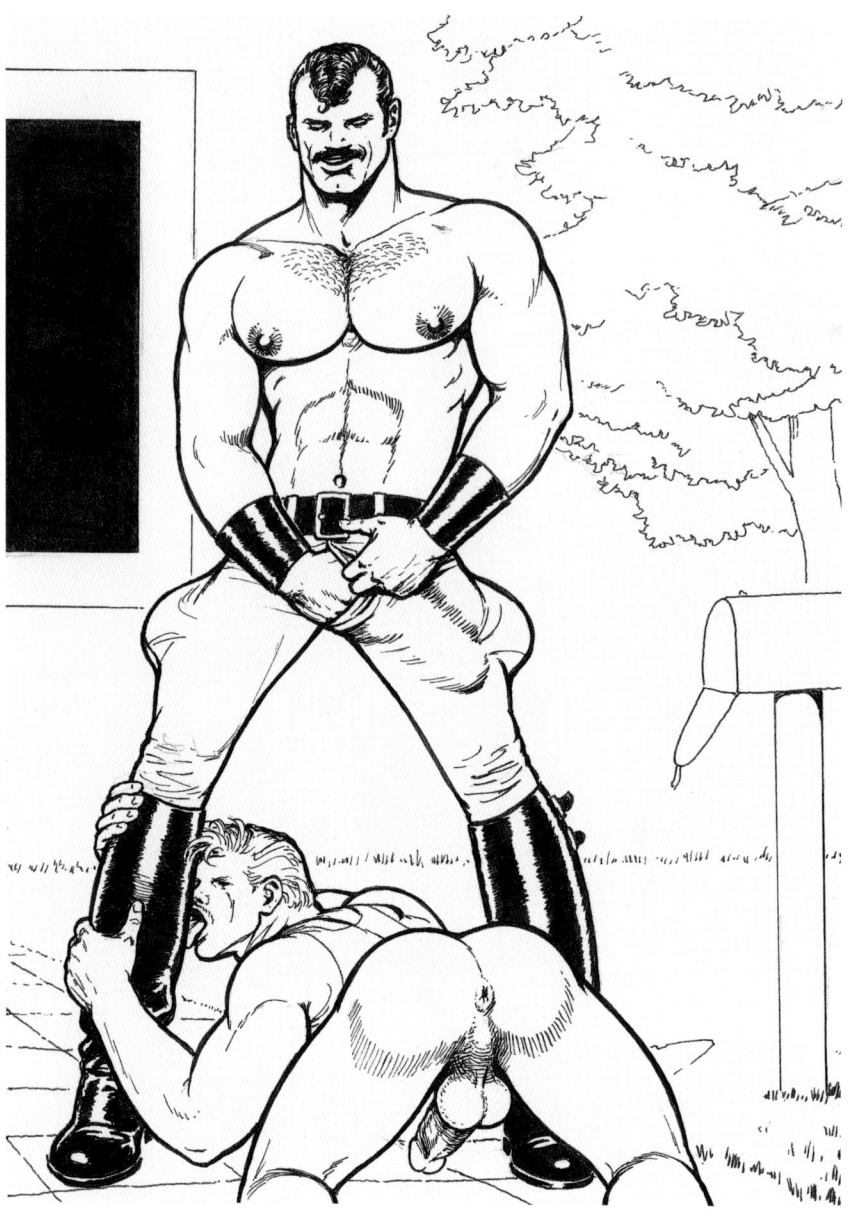

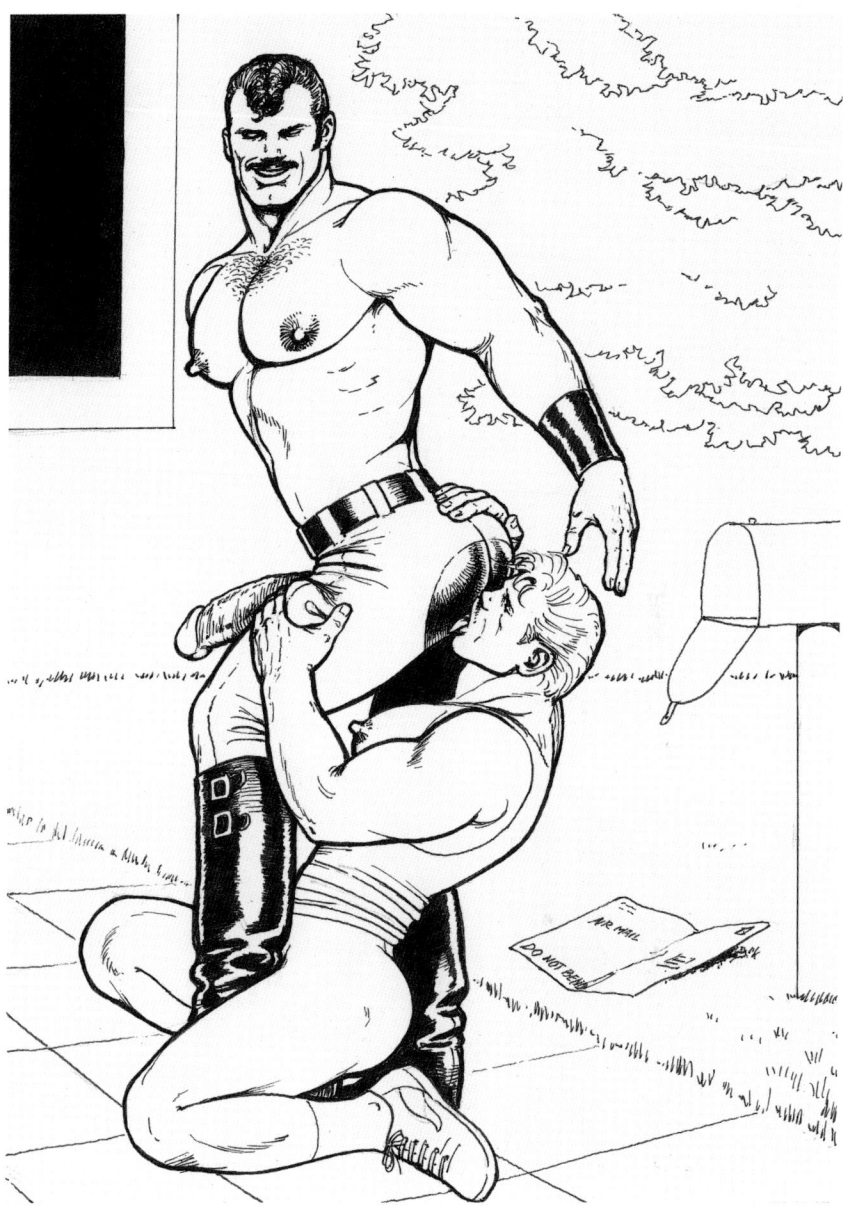

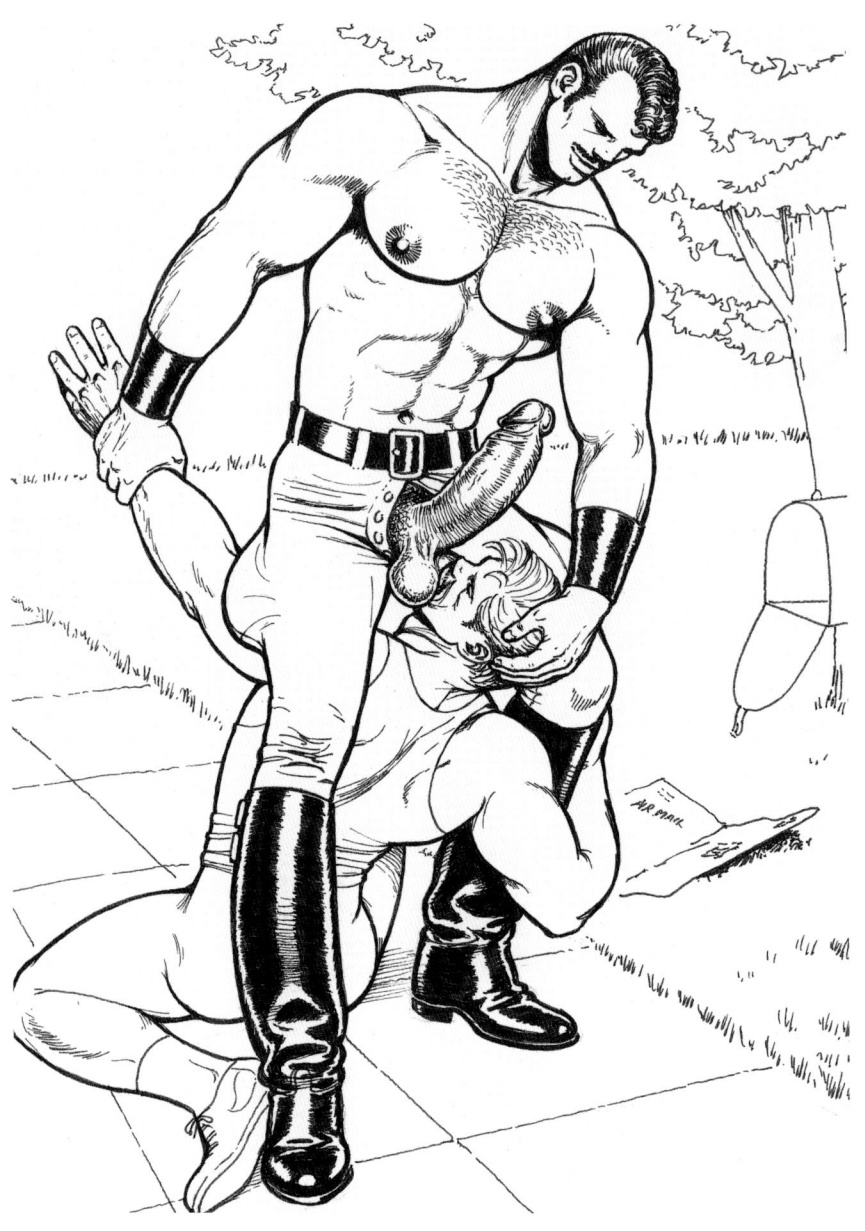

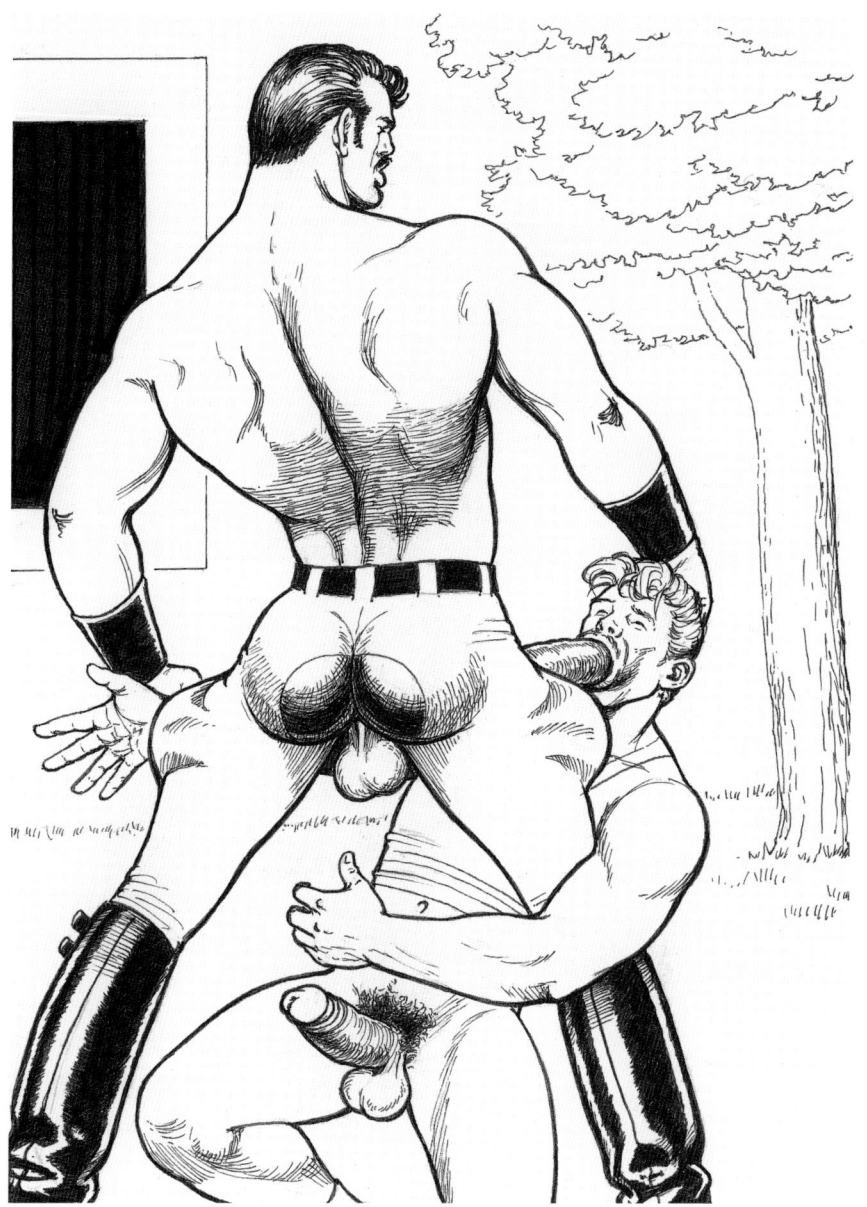

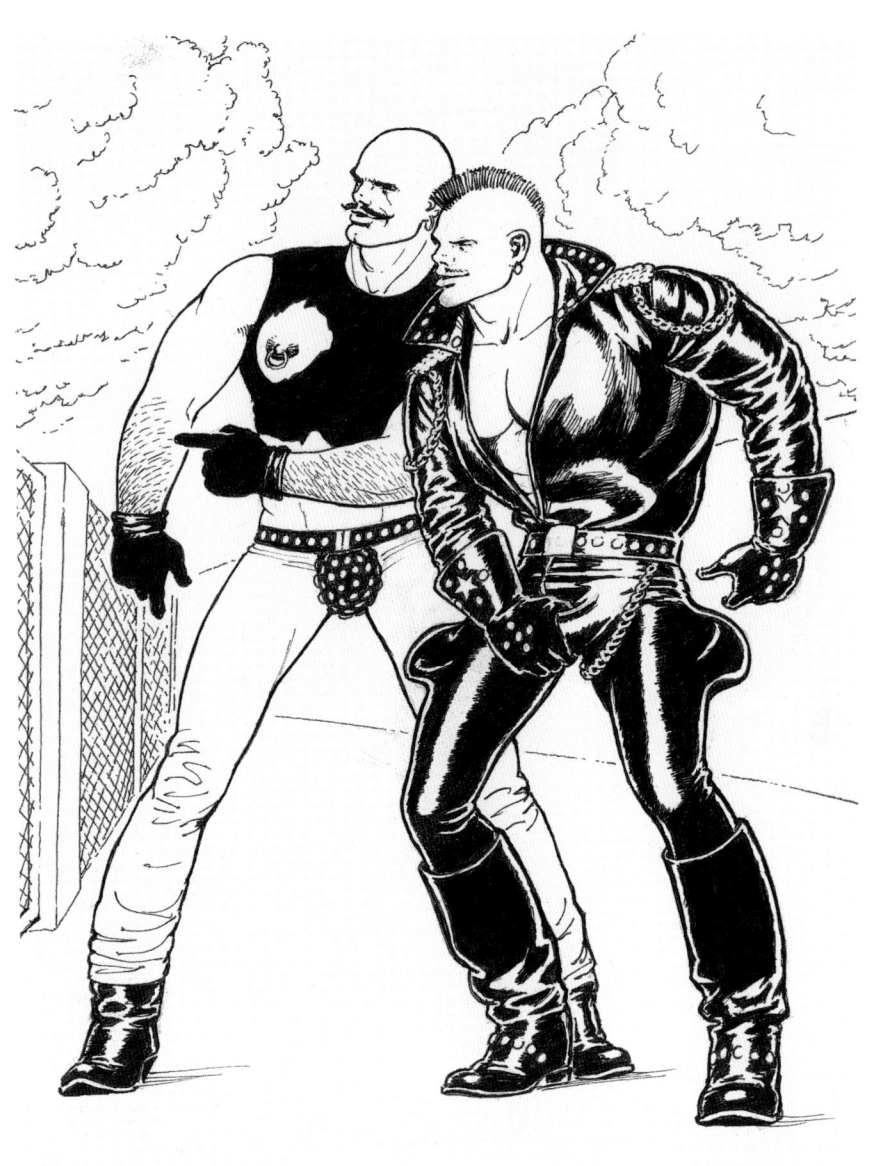

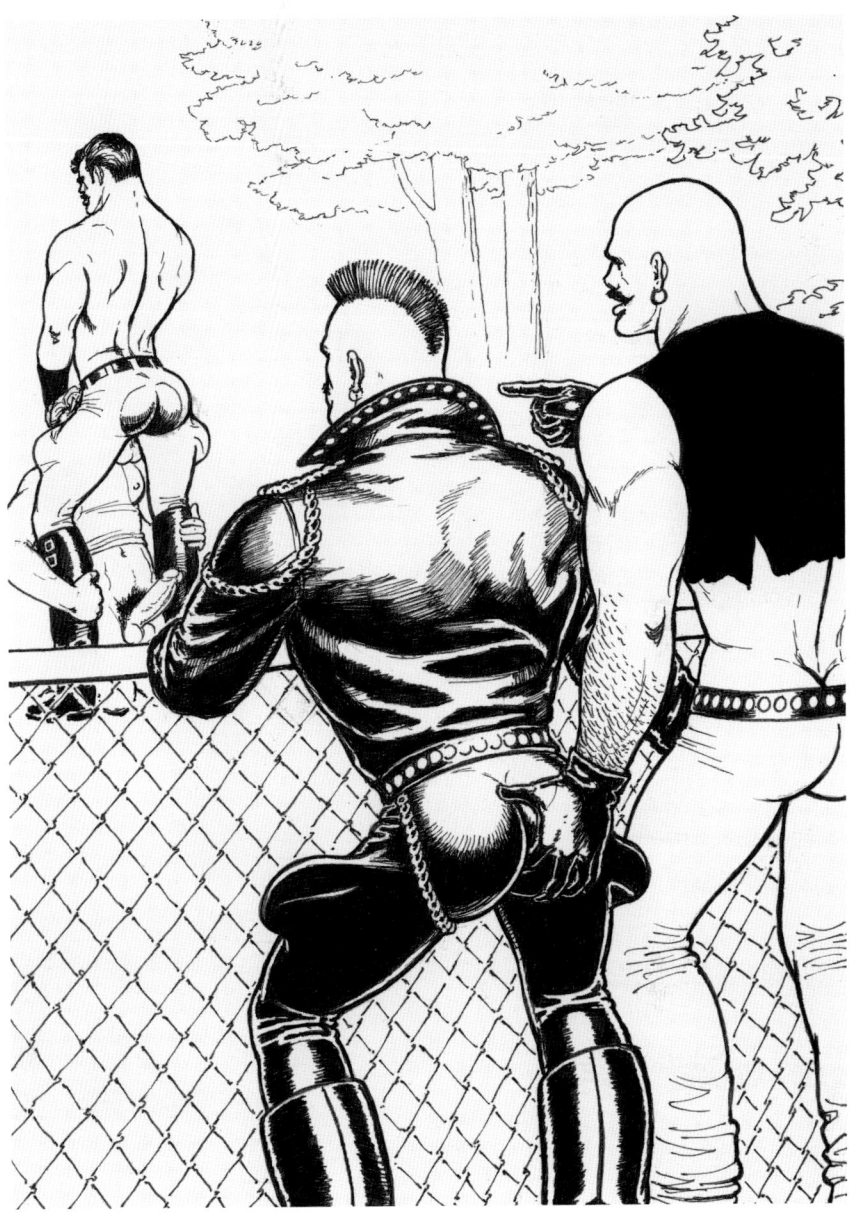

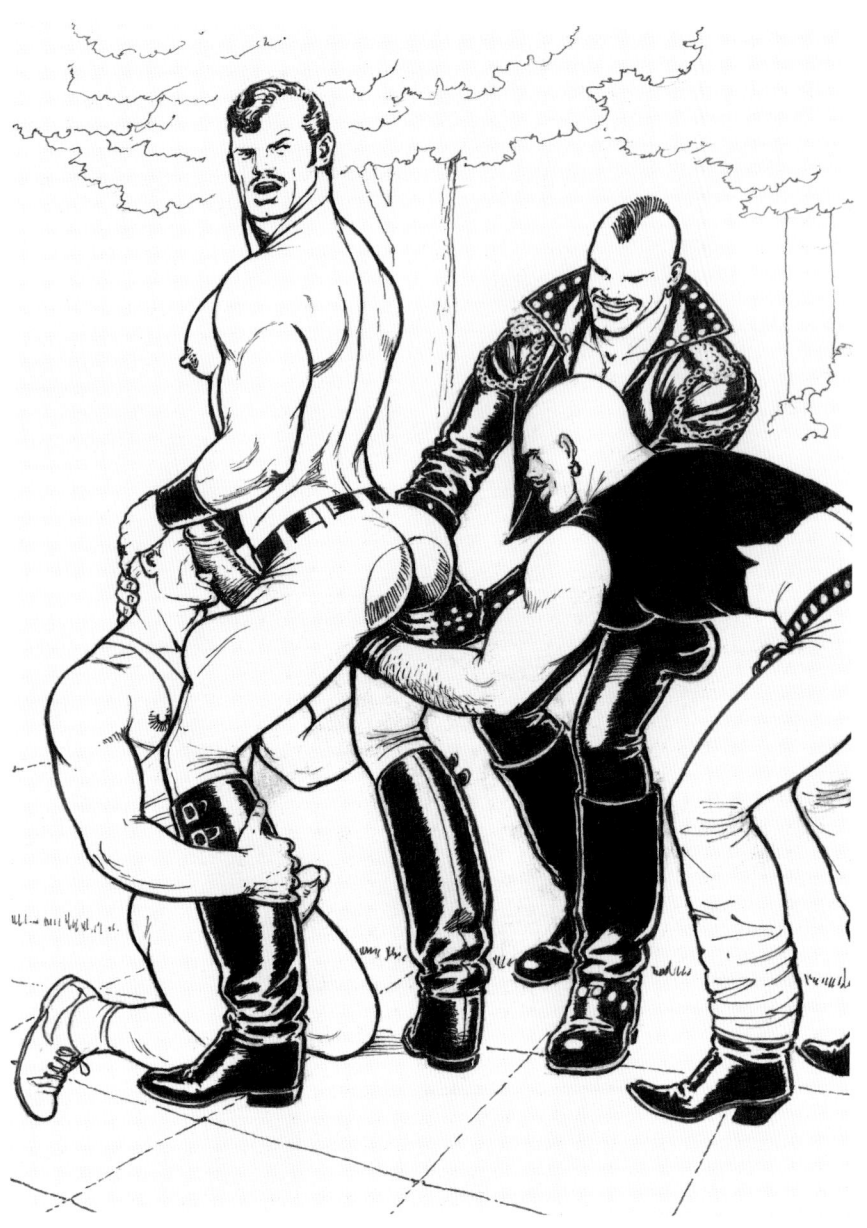

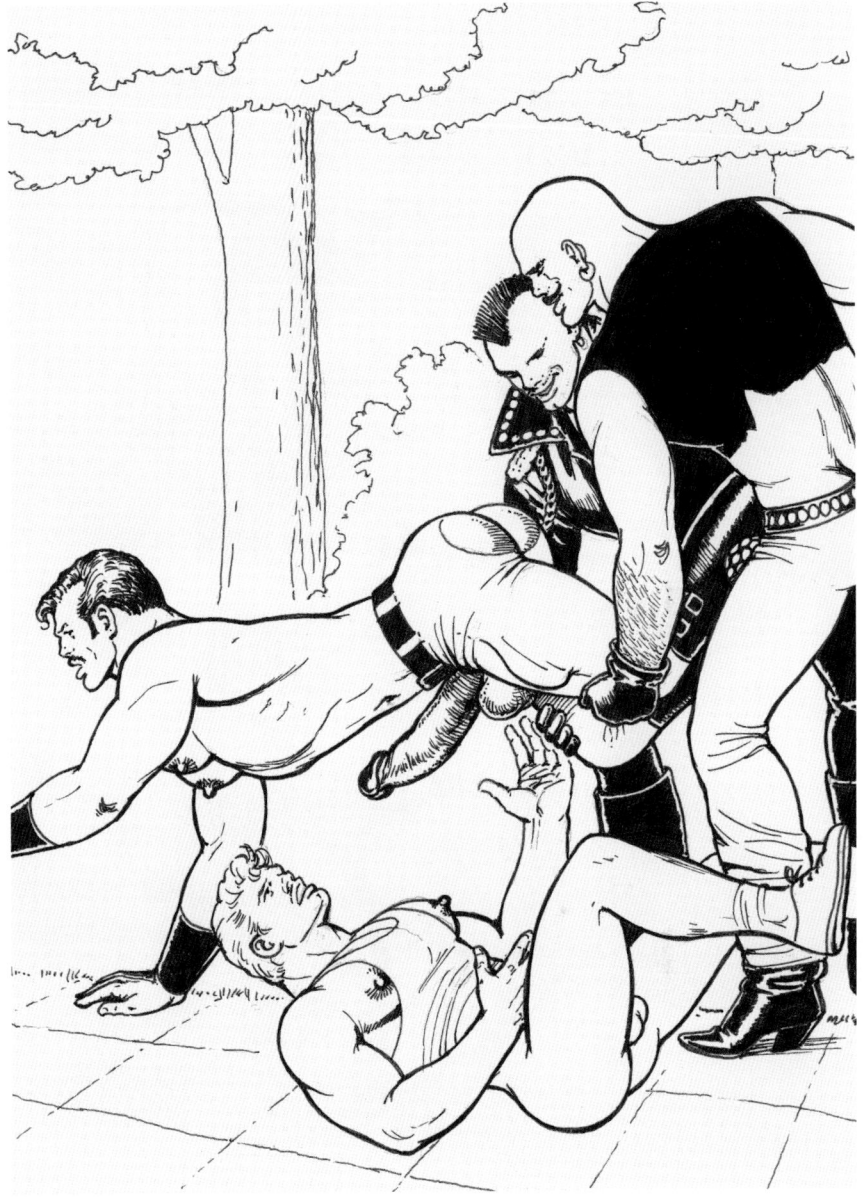

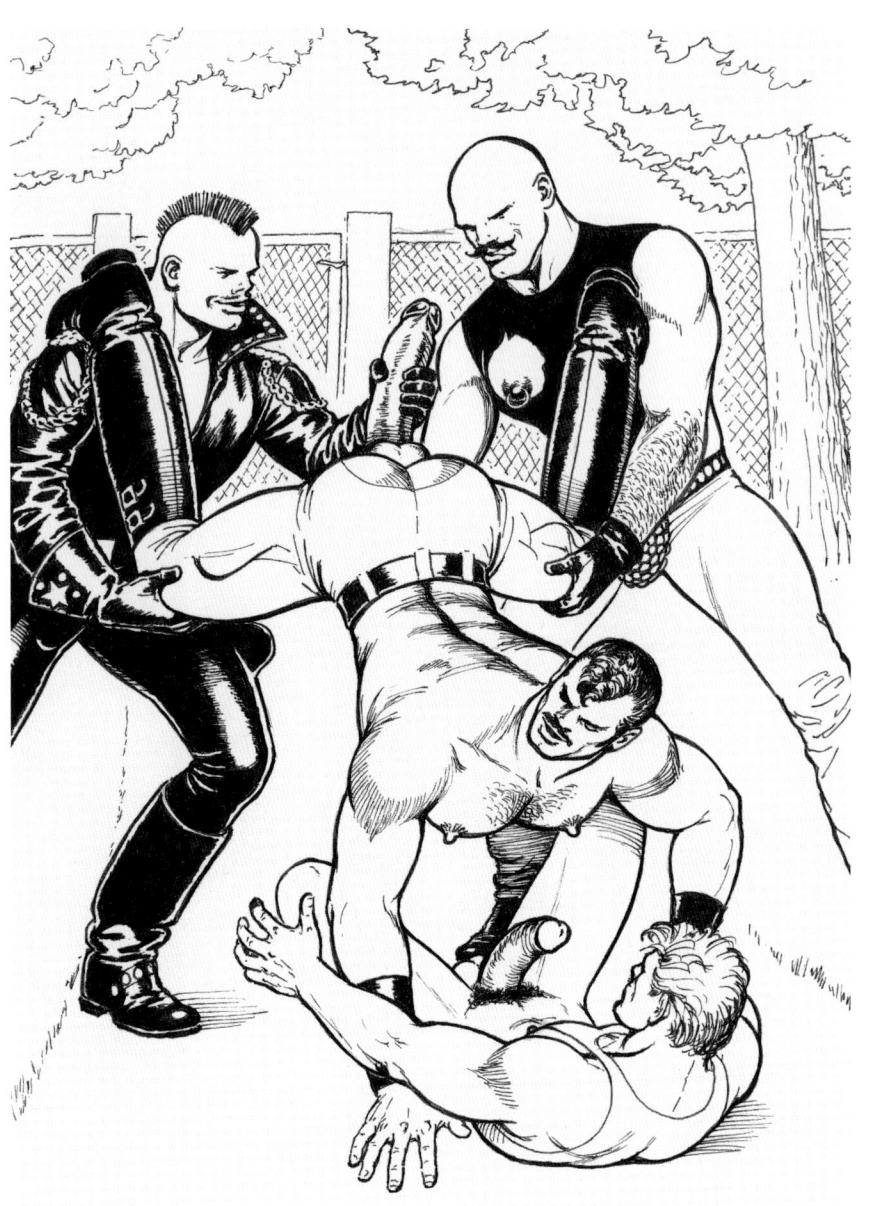

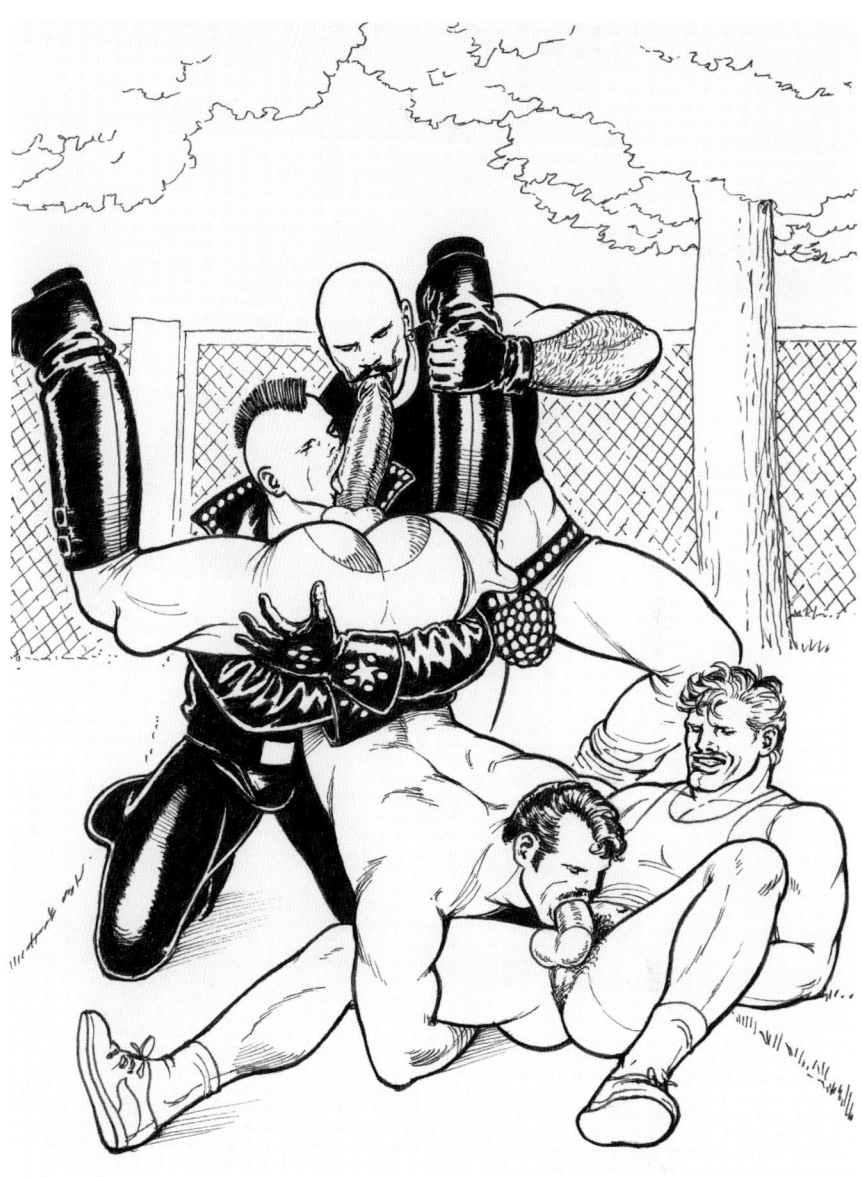

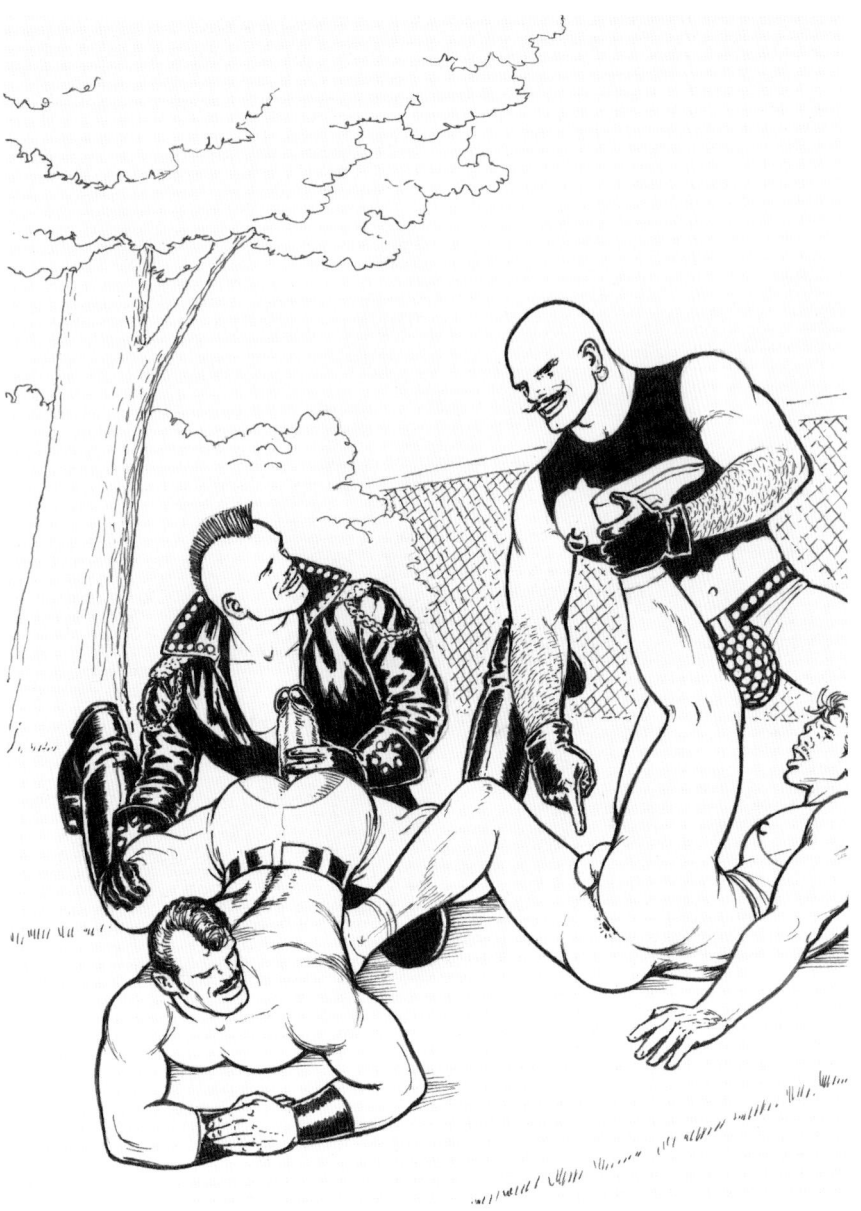

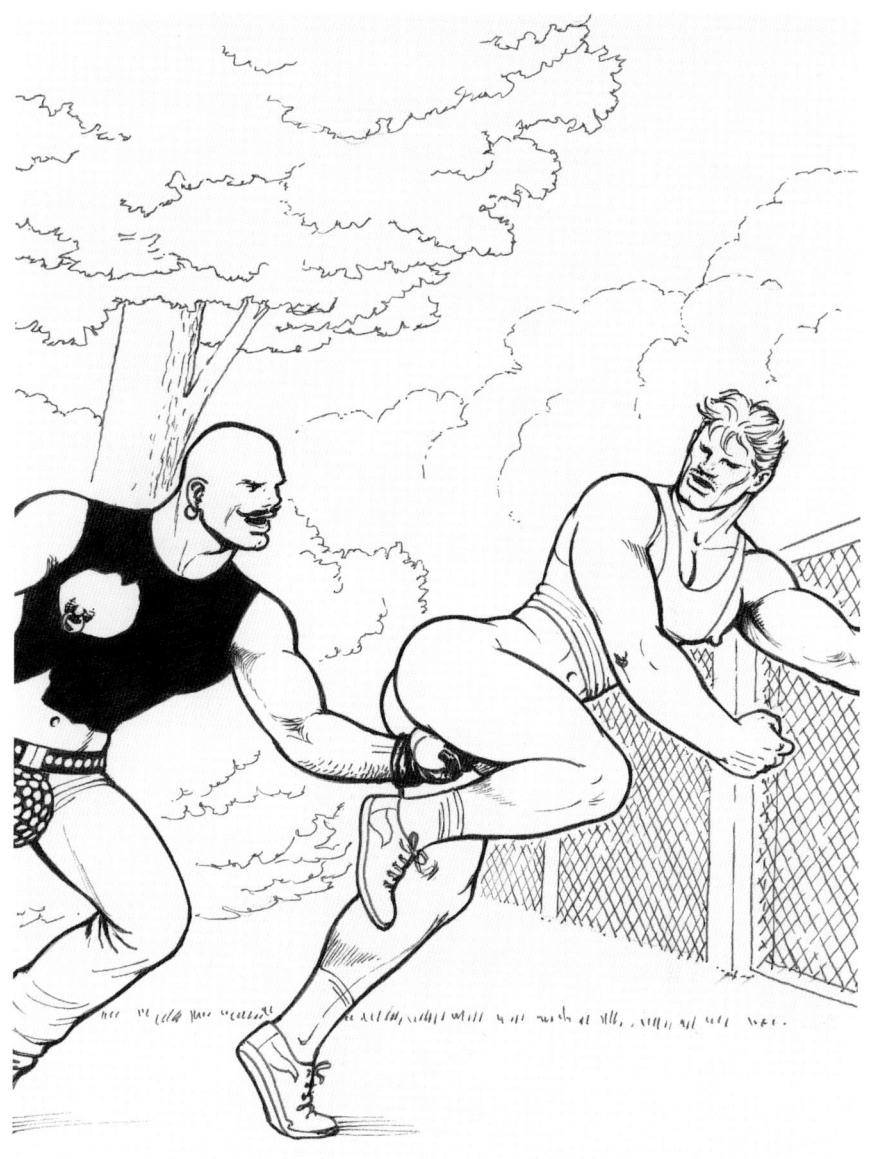

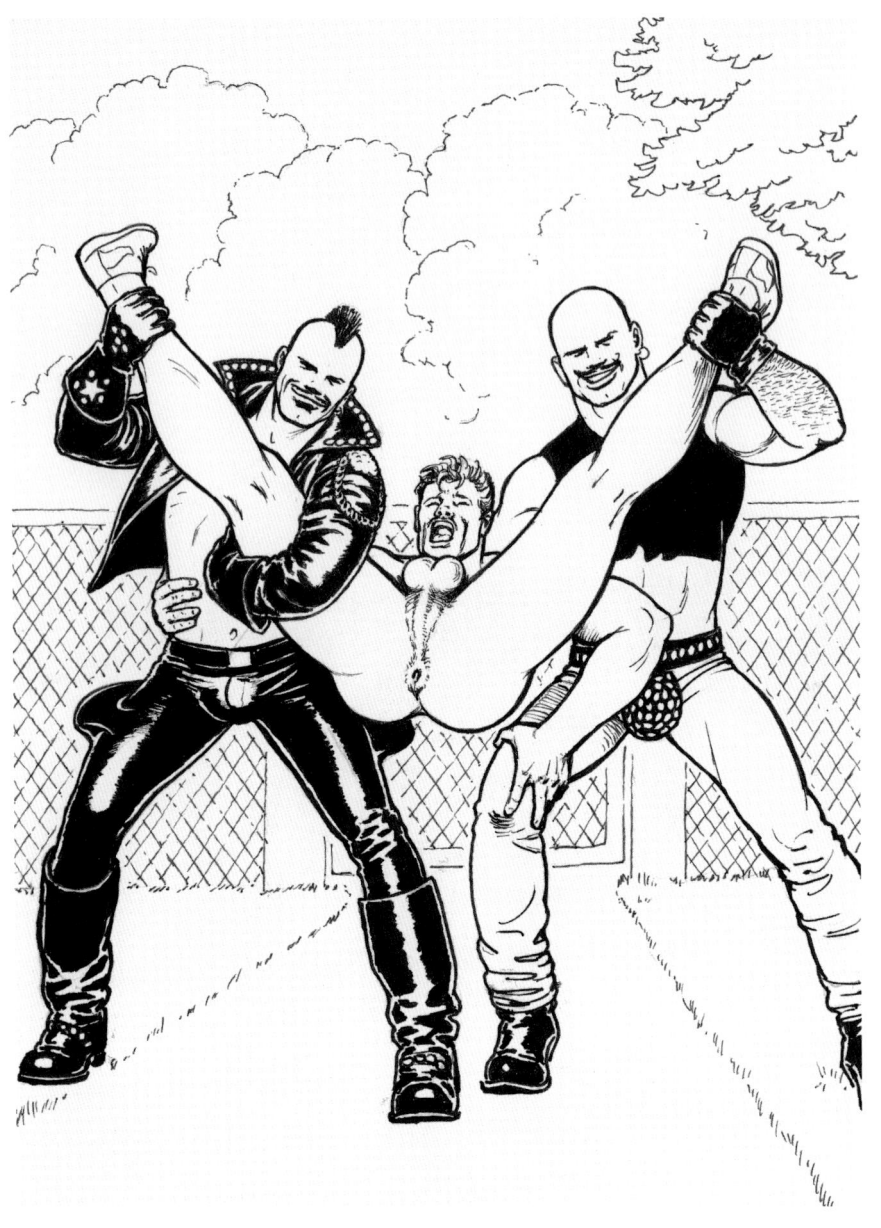

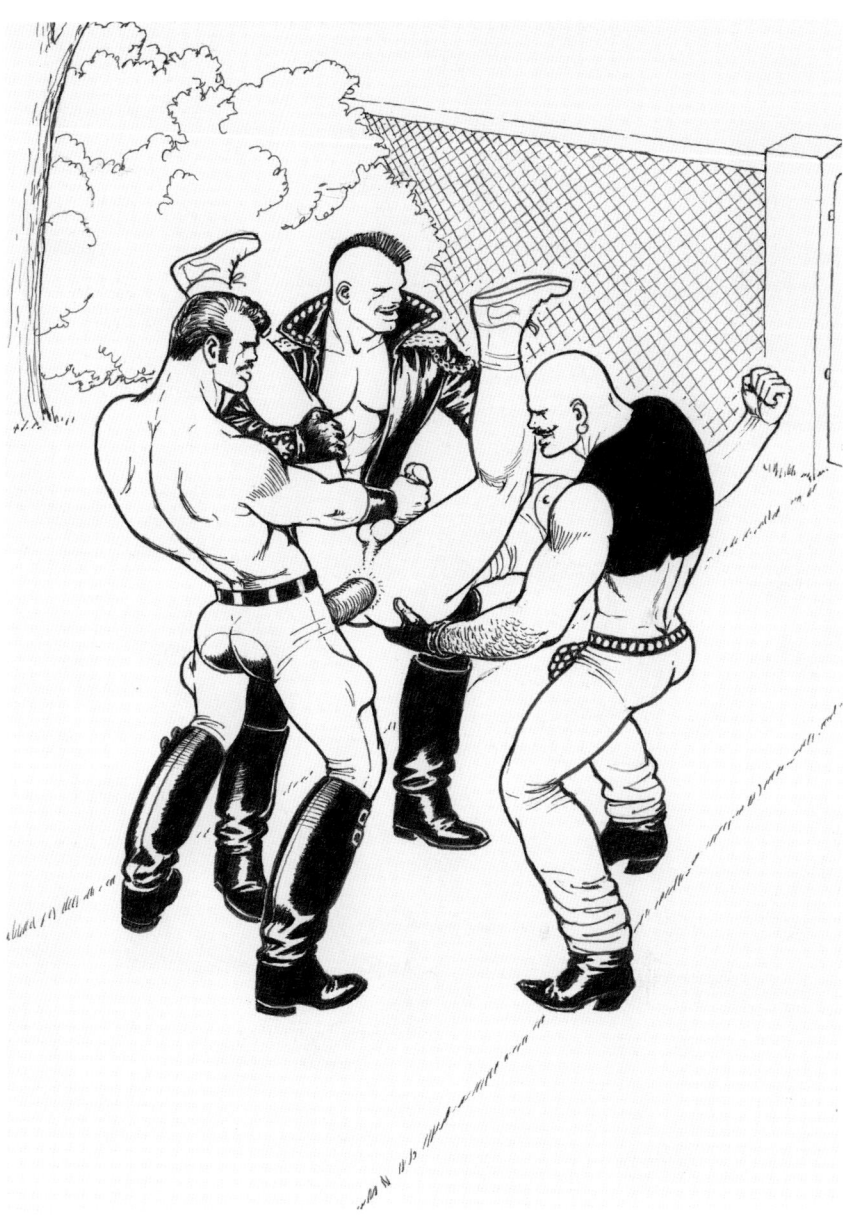

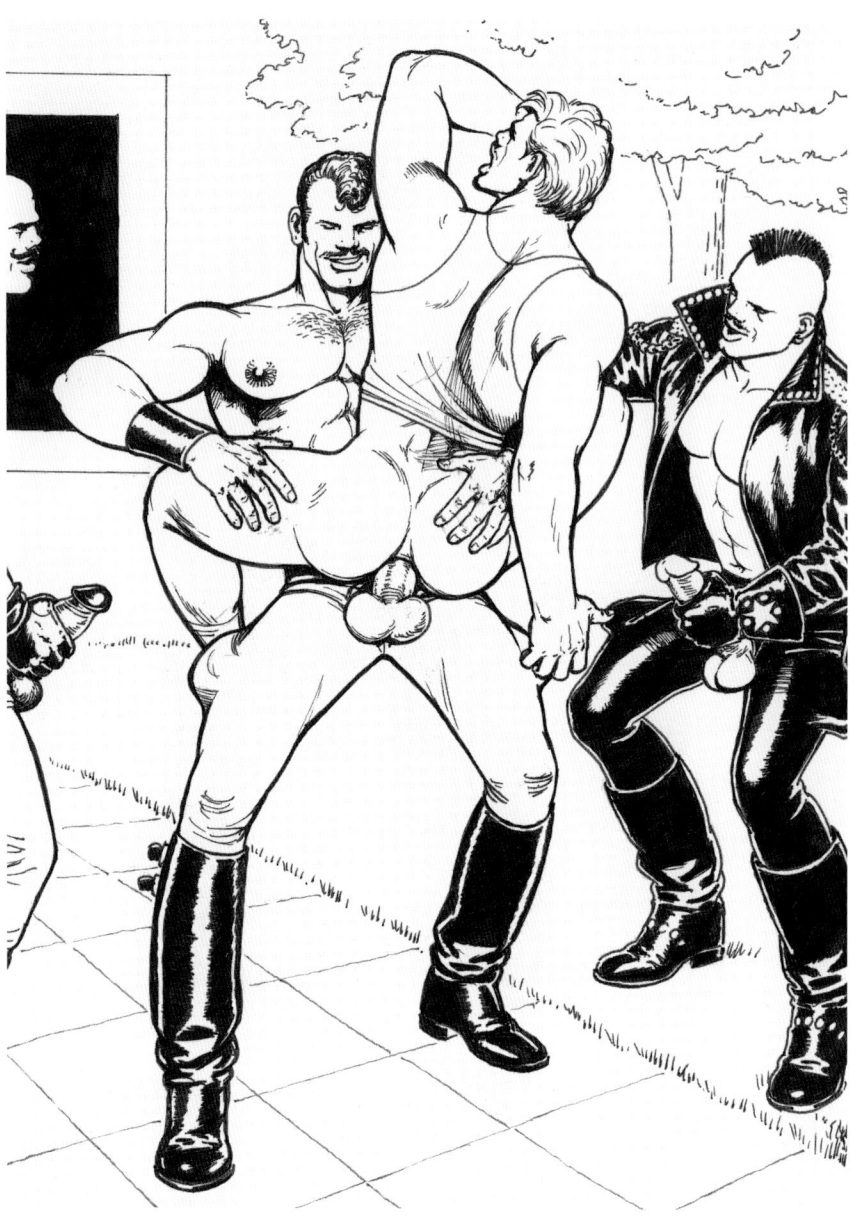

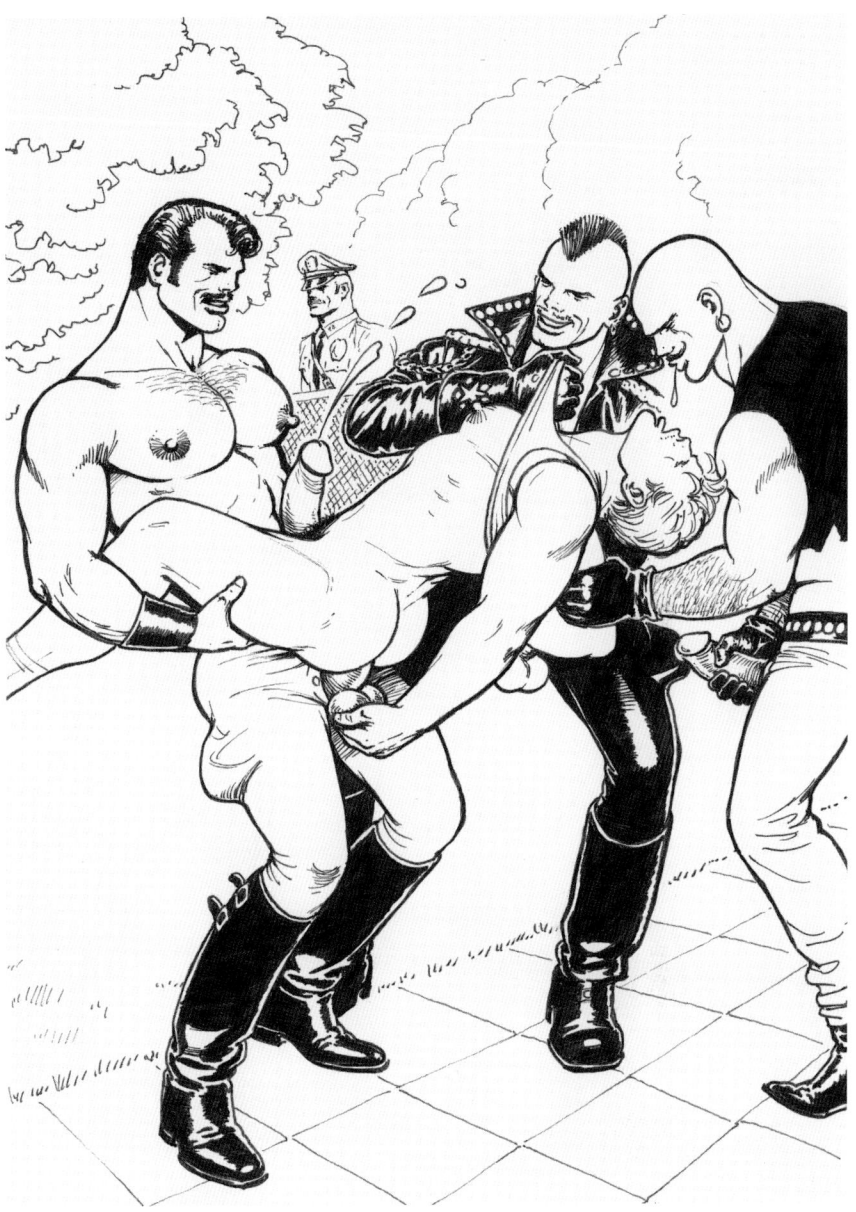

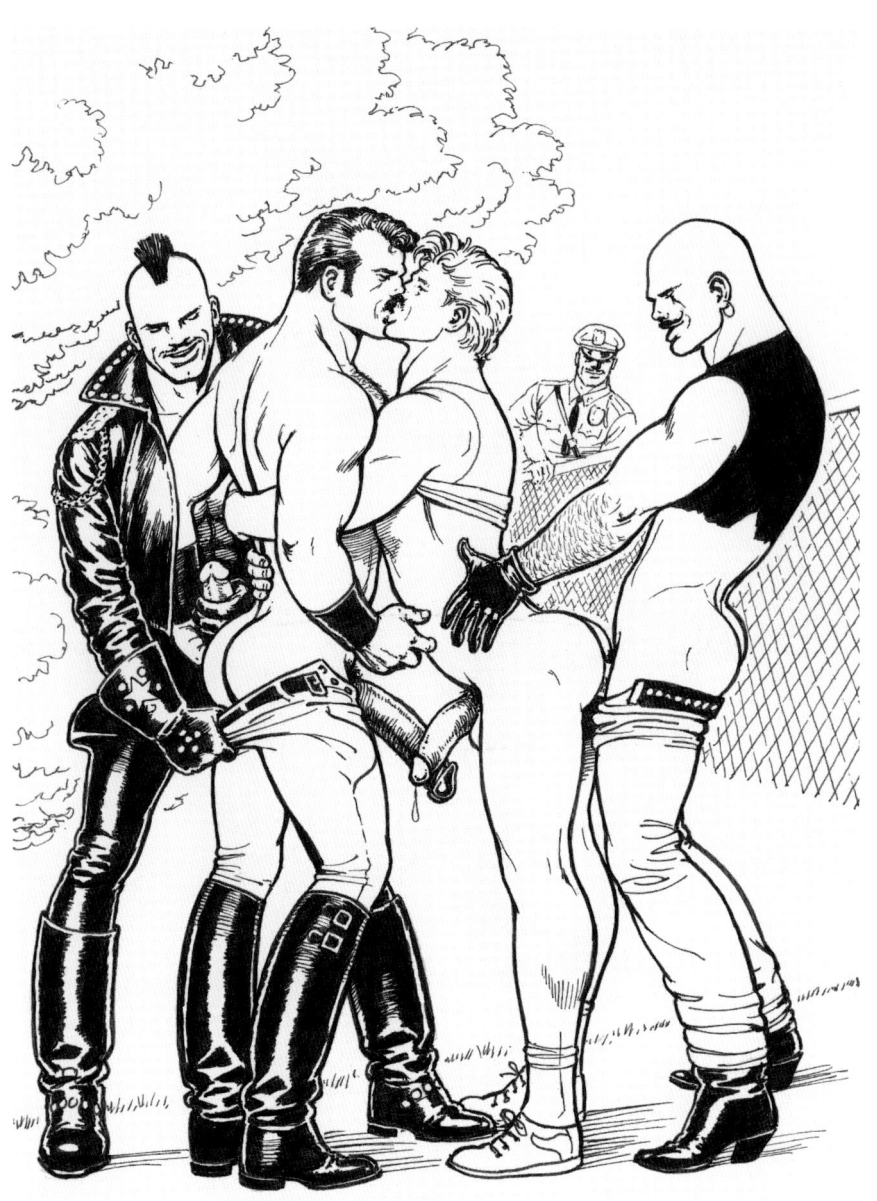

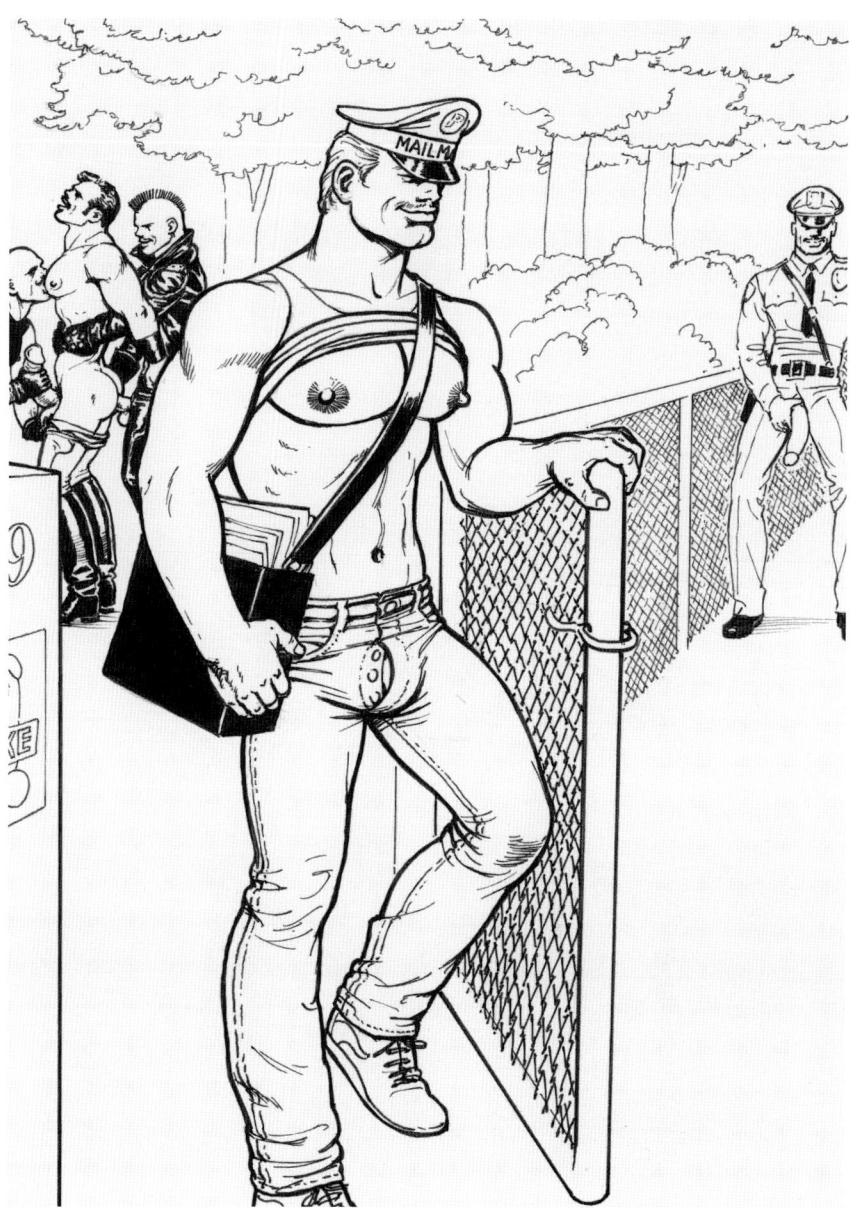

ACKNOWLEDGMENTS

All images are from the Tom of Finland Foundation collection, with the following exceptions: Page 134: Permanent collection The Art Institute of Chicago. Pages 26 and 56: Dennis Bell collection. Pages 80/81: EroticArtCollection.com. Page 7: Dian Hanson collection. Pages 18, 20, and 30: Volker Morlock collection.
Colorization of the cover image by Nemuel DePaula.

PROTECTING, PRESERVING, AND PROMOTING EROTIC ART

Tom of Finland Foundation was conceived by the artist Touko Laaksonen and his business partner Durk Dehner in 1984 as a nonprofit art institution to house and preserve the collective works of the artist. It has evolved into a support facility and library serving all artists working in the visual field of human sexuality.

Today the Foundation has over 500,000 visual records and over 3,000 original works of art by Tom of Finland and hundreds of other artists from around the globe.

The Foundation is only able to continue its work of protecting, preserving, and promoting erotic art through the public's generous support, including donations and membership in Tom of Finland Foundation.

We invite you to visit us on the web at *www.tomoffinlandfoundation.org*

When in Southern California you may book a tour of TOM House.
Please click "VISIT" on our website for more information.

Write us at Tom of Finland Foundation,
P.O. BOX 26658, Los Angeles, CA 90026
Phone: (001) 213 250-1685
Email: *administration@tomoffinlandfoundation.org*

TOM BY TASCHEN

1992   *Tom of Finland*
1998   *Tom of Finland: The Art of Pleasure*
2005   *Tom of Finland: The Comic Collection*
2008   *Tom of Finland: The Complete Kake Comics*
2009   *Tom of Finland XXL*
2011   *Tom of Finland: The Comics*
2012   *Tom of Finland: Bikers*
2014   *Tom of Finland: The Complete Kake Comics* (reissue)
2016   *Tom of Finland XXL* (reissue)
2016   *The Little Book of Tom: Blue Collar*
2016   *The Little Book of Tom: Cops & Robbers*
2016   *The Little Book of Tom: Military Men*
2022   *The Little Book of Tom: Bikers*
2022   *The Little Book of Tom: Blue Collar* (reissue)
2022   *The Little Book of Tom: Cops & Robbers* (reissue)
2022   *The Little Book of Tom: Military Men* (reissue)

© 2022 TASCHEN GMBH

Hohenzollernring 53, 50672 Köln
www.taschen.com

Editor: Dian Hanson
German translation: Edgbert Baqué
French translation: Philippe Safavi

Printed in Slovakia
ISBN 978-3-8365-8865-2

EACH AND EVERY TASCHEN BOOK PLANTS A SEED!

TASCHEN is a carbon neutral publisher. Each year, we offset our annual carbon emissions with carbon credits at the Instituto Terra, a reforestation program in Minas Gerais, Brazil, founded by Lélia and Sebastião Salgado. To find out more about this ecological partnership, please check: www.taschen.com/zerocarbon
Inspiration: unlimited. Carbon footprint: zero.

To stay informed about TASCHEN and our upcoming titles, please subscribe to our free magazine at *www.taschen.com/magazine*, follow us on Instagram and Facebook, or e-mail your questions to *contact@taschen.com*.

FRONT COVER 1986, graphite on paper
PAGE 1 1968, graphite on paper
PAGE 2 1975, gouache on paper for the comic book *Sex in the Shed*
PAGE 192 1965, graphite on paper
BACK COVER 1980, graphite on paper

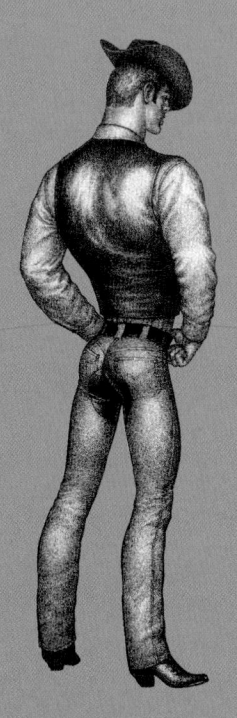